MILITARY ORIGINS

MILITARY ORIGINS

by

Major Lawrence L. Gordon

Edited by Lieutenant-Colonel J. B. R. Nicholson, retired
Editor of *Tradition*

A. S. BARNES & CO.
NEW YORK & SOUTH BRUNSWICK

First American edition 1971
A. S. Barnes and Co., Inc.
Cranbury, N.J. 08512

© 1971 Kaye & Ward Limited

Library of Congress Catalog Card Number: 71 137846

ISBN 0 498 07813 2

Printed in Great Britain by
Willmer Brothers Limited, Birkenhead

CONTENTS

Chapter   *Page*

Acknowledgements   vi

List of Line Drawings   vii

List of Plates   viii

Preface   9

1   Royal Bodyguards   11

2   Heraldry   22

3   Early English Armies   44

4   Cavalry   62

5   Artillery   69

6   Engineers   84

7   Medical Services   90

8   Personal Firearms   101

9   Military Music   121

10 Military Finance   133

11 Aeronautics   149

12 Miscellany   169

Index   251

Acknowledgements

We have to acknowledge our indebtedness to Messrs Belmont-Maitland publishers, Ltd, 188, Picadilly, London, W.1. publishers of *Tradition* Magazine for the loan of all the colour and half-tone blocks, and for many line blocks in the text, and also to Messrs Norman Military Publications for permission to use the illustrations by the late C. C. P. Lawson from his *History of the Uniforms of the British Army.*

LIST OF LINE DRAWINGS

	Page
Yeomen of the Guard at the Field of the Cloth of Gold	13
A twelfth century knight showing the simple flat-iron type of shield with heraldic device	24
Standards of the Household Cavalry	41
A Man-at-Arms c 1450	57
A Bowman c 1340	59
A pikeman of Cromwell's New Model Army	61
A Horse Grenadier, c 1687	65
Dragoons c 1680	66
Lifeguard, c 1900	67
Artillery of the time of Marlborough	81
Royal Fusiliers, c 1700	82
Engineer officers of the time of Marlborough. The figure on the left wears the special armour worn when tunnelling or mining	87
Kettledrums and trumpeter of the Lifeguards c 1700	126
Band of the Foot Guards c 1750	128
Drum Major of a Line Infantry Regiment at the time of Waterloo	132
A cuirass	198
Left, Wing worn by officers of Grenadiers, Light Infantry and Fusiliers up to the Crimean War. Right, Epaulette worn over a wing by Field Officers of Light Infantry and Fusiliers from c 1816 to 1830	203
An officer's gorget	209
A Horse Grenadier c 1750	212
An officer's charger of a Hussar Regiment of the time of Waterloo showing the shabraque or saddle cloth and leopard skin covering	238
Austro-Hungarian Army shakos, 1. Hussar, 1770, 2. Grenz-Infantry 1796, 3. Hussar, 1798–1806, 4. Regular Infantry, 1806	240

LIST OF PLATES

COLOUR PLATES

Between pages 48–49

Plate 1. A fully accoutred mediaeval knight, Arms of d'Abernon. Model by Charles Stadden. Courtesy Norman Newton, Ltd.

Plate 2. Richard Neville, the Kingmaker. Model by Charles Stadden. Courtesy Norman Newton, Ltd.

Between pages 64–65

Plate 3. An officer of the 7th Hussars, 1808.

Plate 4. Officers of Hussars, Horse Guards, Life Guards and Footguards, 1828. Courtesy of the Marquis of Cambridge.

Between pages 112–113

Plate 5. Changing Guard. The 6th Dragoon Guards, 1832. Dubois Drahonet.

Plate 6. Madras Light Cavalry c 1835, Officer, Indian Officer and Trooper.

Between pages 128–129

Plate 7. The 17th Lancers in 1839. Courtesy of the Marquis of Cambridge.

Plate 8. An Officer of the 7th (Queen's Own) Hussars, c 1835.

BLACK AND WHITE PLATES

Between pages 208–209

Plate A Officer's Grenadier cap, Suffolk Militia, c 1750. Courtesy S. R. Butler, Esq, Wallis & Wallis, Lowes, Sussex.

Plate B A General Officer of Hussars, c 1830.

Between pages 224–225

Plate C Full Dress and Undress Sabretaches, Royal Artillery, c 1890, Dress Sabretache, 2nd West Yorkshire Yeomanry Cavalry, c 1890.

Plate D Hussar Busbies c 1900. The centre one is an officer's.

The contents of the following pages constitute my endeavour to put between two covers the answers to questions I was asked as an army coach before and, as a chief instructor at an Officers Cadet Training Unit, during part of the last war.

In addition to these experiences, the number and variety of questions that I have been asked as a result of my writings on medals has shown that there does not appear to be any one book in which one can find the answers to most of the more usual questions. In a correspondence that runs into many thousands of letters, I would be correct in saying that 90 per cent of the questions not concerned with medals start off 'When was the first . . . ?'; not only the first British but the first ever. Sometimes the research necessary to find anything at all about the subject has taken me weeks and many many miles of travelling.

Though a large audience may be interested in military matters generally, the book has been divided into sections. Some will be particularly interested in uniforms and buttons, some in old weapons, some military music, and so on. For one person to attempt to write a comprehensive book covering all the sub-divisions of military history would be both stupid and impossible. It would require a large team. I have, therefore, only included what seemed to be the more popular questions and grouped them as far as possible into separate chapters, thus obtaining a continuous account that includes the required answers. For many of the items this was impossible so they have a chapter on their own.

In compiling a book of this nature, one lays oneself wide open to the accusation of being eclectic and of dealing too much with one subject and too little with another. I do not see how this can be avoided for it is too much to expect every item to interest everybody.

I hope that this book will answer some of the questions that must have arisen in the minds of those already interested in, and those prepared to be interested in, military matters.

L. L. Gordon

Gnosall,
Stafford.

Royal Bodyguards

Serjeants-at-Arms

The name of sergens or servientes was, in the reign of Philip Augustus, given to gentlemen who served in the armies of France, but were below the rank of knights. They, like knights, furnished their own horses and weapons.

Philip formed a body of troops some 150 to 200 strong to act as his personal bodyguard during his campaign in the East against the Assassins, who were the followers of the mohammedan Hassan-ben-Sabad and who settled in Persia in 1090. It was this fellow who gave instructions that all the youngsters should be taught the fine points of murder so that they could destroy those whom their chief disliked. It is, of course, from them that we get our word assassin.

Philip was at one time in alliance with Richard Coeur de Lion during the Third Crusade. When Richard became king, after the death of his father Henry II, he formed a body of serjeants-at-arms in complete armour to guard the royal tent. The original strength of this guard was twenty-four, but the number was subsequently increased until the size of it aroused the anger of Parliament because, instead of a bodyguard, they became royal tax gatherers. The crisis came in 1470 when a rebellion broke out in Lincolnshire, lead by Sir Robert Wells. The rebels were defeated in a battle which went by the strange title of 'Lose Coat Field', fought at Empingham, in Rutlandshire.

As a matter of fact it was one of Richard II's tax collectors, maybe one of his serjeants-at-arms, who insulted Wat Tyler's daughter, an act which was one of the causes that led to the Peasants' Rebellion, 1381. The feelings between the king and his subjects deteriorated from bad to worse prior to his dethronement in 1399. One of the things he did before he was imprisoned by Parliament was to agree that the number of his serjeants-at-arms should not exceed thirty.

The Yeomen of the Guard constitute the first permanent corps in the English army and appears in the Army List.

Two of the serjeants, by royal permission, attend the two Houses of Parliament. The office of the serjeant-at-arms in the House of Commons is to keep the doors of the House, and to arrest offenders against the privileges of the Commons as the Speaker may direct.

The heads of some departments in the Royal Household have the prefix serjeant, as the serjeant-surgeon, etc, but this denotes a rank rather than a member of a bodyguard.

Royal Bodyguard of the Yeoman of the Guard

In our early history a yeoman was ranked as the leader of the class immediately below that of gentleman. They are specially mentioned in a statute of Richard II in which they, in common with all persons under the rank of esquire, were forbidden to wear any lord's livery unless they formed part of his household which, in my opinion, is another way of saying that they were liveried servants and not soldiers.

The Yeomen of the Guard, a body of foot guards to the sovereign, are said by some historians to owe their origin to the Yeomen of the Crown who guarded the person of Edward III. The corps as it exists today was instituted by Henry VII on 30th October, 1485, the day of his coronation.

Henry received, if I may use a military expression, his promotion on the field as he was crowned by Lord Stanley on Bosworth Field immediately after the conclusion of the battle (22nd August 1485) with the crown that had fallen off the head of Richard III. The rightful heir to the throne was Edward of Clarence, Earl of Warwick, whom Henry put in the Tower of London. Henry's succession was, therefore, not universally popular, so to guard his person he raised a body of yeomen, fifty strong. The excuse that he gave to Parliament for this act was that he considered that a sovereign should be accompanied by pageantry wherever he went, and especially at the time of his coronation.

Having formed the bodyguard he then created the rank of Captain of the Yeomen of the Guard to command them.

Henry VIII increased their number considerably and, so as not to affect the susceptibilities of Parliament, he called all those over the strength of an hundred super-numeraries.

Yeomen of the Guard at the Field of the Cloth of Gold.

The greatest strength to which they ever attained was six hundred during the reign of Henry VIII. At the time of the Restoration in 1660, they were reduced to an hundred, which is their strength at present.

The Captain of the Yeoman of the Guard must be a peer, who resigns his office on a change of government; the Lieutenant is a retired colonel or lieutenant-colonel; the Ensign and Clerk of Cheques must have been lieutenant-colonels or majors; and, retired army captains hold the appointments of Exons, of whom ther are four. The Privates are ex-regular soldiers not below the rank of sergeant.

In addition to the Yeomen there are the Warders or, to give them their full title, Yeomen Warders of Her Majesty's Tower, composed of forty ex-regular non-commissioned officers commanded by the Lieutenant of the Tower.

Though the attendance on the Sovereign by the Yeomen of the Guard is now mostly ceremonial, it is well to recall that it was a Yeoman who saved the life of George III when attacked by that attempted female regicide Margaret Nicholson; and that they were especially ordered to guard St James's Palace, in 1848, at the time of the Chartist Rising.

No mention of Yeoman of the Guard would be complete unless it made reference to their jocular appellation of beef-eaters. There is a story concerning the visit of Henry VIII to a monastry – some say on a hunting expedition – dressed in the uniform of one of his Yeomen during which he is supposed to have polished off a particularly large helping of beef. This story sounds just a bit too pat for me to believe. I think that the term is derived from the French *bufferier*, which denoted one who waited at table.

I suggest, with no concrete evidence to go by, that certain Yeomen were detailed to serve and wait on certain ceremonial occasions whilst others attended to the sideboards, or buffets. On referring to an old French dictionary I find that a buffet is described as a cupboard, and also a side-board furnished for the service of the table. The concluding sentence reads, *Buffet se dit aussi des officiers ou valets qui servent au buffet.*

The government of the Tower of London is vested in the Constable, an officer of the highest rank. The Duke of Wellington was a Constable of the Tower.

All who are interested in English history should visit the Tower as it is from institutions such as this that the nation draws its sap. The Tower and British history are inseparable, as is the Tower from its Warders.

The Honourable Corps of Gentlemen-at-Arms

This title is probably derived from the early bodyguards of the

French kings who employed mounted men only, known as *Gens-d'Armes*. The name was subsequently changed to that of *Gardes-du-Corps* when its composition was altered from entirely mounted men to both mounted and dismounted.*

Louis IX of France (1226–70) formed a company of gentlemen, which he limited to 250 strong and called *Gentilshommes d'Armes* as well as his Scots Guards as it was composed almost entirely of young Scottish nobles. Charles VII added the prefix 'Royal' in 1441 and the bodyguards of the French kings remained till the formation of the Republic.

Our present corps owes its origin to that splendour-loving monarch Henry VIII who, in 1509, appointed 'a retynue daily of certaine Speres called men-of-arms, to be chosen of gentlemen that be comen and extracte of Noble Blood'. This retinue was called the King's Pensioners and Speares.

The apparel of these gentlemen was of the most expensive damask, embroidered in gold and silver costing, so one authority says, five pounds a yard, which must have been a fabulous sum for material to cost in those days.

Soon after the formation of this corps – in 1520, to be exact – Henry went over to Calais to meet Francis of France and the scene when they met was so magnificent that it became known as the Field of the Cloth of Gold. Little did Henry care that many of his nobles pawned practically their all so as to bedeck themselves with gorgeous apparel which they could not afford. Henry, that monarch of pomp and perfidy, made a great fuss of Francis and called him his dear brother and, with a deceit worthy of a Hitler or Stalin, immediately after the meeting concluded an alliance with Francis's rival Charles.

The corps was disbanded soon after this magnificent spectacle but was reformed in 1526 with the new name of 'Band of Gentlemen Pensioners'. They were now a dismounted corps armed, so a contemporary illustration depicts, with battle-axes They went overseas and were present at the surrender of Boulogne on 14th September, 1544.

They paraded in all their finery at a review held in St James's

* The words *Gens-d'Arme* and *Gendarmerie* coming to denote what we understand by police.

Field to mark the accession of Henry's young son, by Jane Seymour, Edward VI.

The projected marriage of the next sovereign, Mary, with her cousin Philip II, caused a great deal of dissatisfaction throughout the country and led to the rising known as Wyatt's Rebellion, during which the Gentlemen were on duty guarding the royal apartments in Whitehall. Mary appealed to the people and promised not to marry Philip without the consent of Parliament. After a desperate fight between the rebels and the Queen's supporters, which took place between Knightsbridge and Charing-Cross, Sir Thomas Wyatt surrendered at the Lud Gate entrance to the City. Parliament gave consent to the marriage on the condition that Philip was not crowned. The Gentlemen Pensioners attended the Queen at the wedding feast.

The Gentlemen blotted their copy-books very badly during the reign of James I as the Duke of Northumberland, their Captain, had something to do with the Gunpowder Plot; while Thomas Percy, one of their members, rented a house next to Parliament House, through the nine feet thick walls of which the plotters proposed to make a hole. As a matter of fact, Guy Fawkes, assuming the name of Johnson, posed as one of Thomas Percy's servants. However, as everyone knows, the plot was revealed and the conspirators fled. Catesby and Percy were killed at Holbeach House, Dunchurch, where a meeting of Catholic gentry were posing as a hunting party; whereas Fawkes and some others were hanged, drawn and quartered in various parts of London.

The bodyguard redeemed this sorry story at the Battle of Edgehill, the first of the Civil War, when a gentleman by the name of Matthews saved the life of the Prince of Wales, who was about to be killed by one of Essex's troopers.

After the execution of Charles I, the Gentlemen Pensioners were disbanded, though it is worth noting that Cromwell formed a personal bodyguard of one hundred and forty specially chosen gentlemen.

The corps was reformed by Charles II and its number limited to forty gentlemen, excluding officers, as it is today.

John Chamberlayne, writing in about 1700, gives an account of the Gentlemen Pensioners in the part of his father's work,

Magnae Britanniae, which he completed. He said that it was the duty of the Gentlemen Pensioners to be in attendance in the presence-chamber carrying their poleaxes. They were to escort the King from his Chapel to the Privy Chamber and to attend the sovereign on all ceremonial occasions and to share the duties of guarding the king's person with the Yeomen of the Guard.

The next milestone in their history occurred in 1745 when London was in a state of panic due to the Jacobite Rising. The royal jewels were placed on board a warship moored in the Thames so as to be taken to sea if the situation became too serious. The Gentlemen-at-Arms were called out at full strength and were formally recognized as forming part of the armed forces.

Their present title, The Honourable Corps of Gentlemen-at-Arms was bestowed on them by William IV in 1834, and in 1861 the purchase of membership was abolished.

The Corps has the distinction of being Her Majesty's nearest Guard and Principal Military Corps of the Household. It attends the Sovereign's person on all Royal State Occasions, and what are termed Royal Progresses. This means that they supply the personal guard to Her Majesty when she opens Parliament, visits the Guildhall or St Paul's Cathedral, holds levees, and the ceremony of installing Knights of the Garter.

The Yeomen of the Guard are on duty in, but not beyond, the Guard Room. The Gentlemen-at-Arms attend in the Throne Room and Presence Chamber at all functions held at the Palace.

Another distinction may have been noted on the occasion of lyings-in-State at which the Gentlemen stand watch on the platform whereas the Yeoman stand below.

Appointment to the Corps is strictly regulated. Officers must be under fifty on appointment. Only those who have seen active service are eligible for membership.

The Corps is commanded by a Captain whose appointment is political – that is to say that his appointment is made by the Sovereign on the recommendation of the Prime Minister, and he retires on change of government. On his appointment he receives from the Sovereign a Gold Stick of Office which he returns on retirement or resignation.

The next senior officer is the Lieutenant who is promoted from the Gentlemen. He, too, has a Stick of Office.

The next is the Standard Bearer who, like the Lieutenant, receives his appointment by promotion and a silver-headed Stick of Office.

The next is the Clerk of the Cheque whom I think I might describe as the combined adjutant and paymaster for all matters except the actual pay of the members. He, too, receives a Silver Stick on appointment.

The next officer has the unusual title of Harbinger, formerly known as Sub-Officer. His Badge of Office is an Ivory Stick.

One of the Gentlemen holds the position of Secretary, but is not an officer of the Corps on account of holding that office.

The Standard of the Corps is most interesting and, as far as my knowledge of the subject goes, unique.

The chief, that is the portion nearest the staff, is occupied by the Cross of St George; then the Royal Cypher surmounted by the Heraldic (or Imperial) Crown; next a portcullis surmounted by (adorned, charged, decorated, or ensigned with are other terms meaning the same thing) a Tudor Crown. There are a pair of bends sinister (which I can best describe to the uninitiated as being similar to the lines used to cross a cheque, when sinister, as in this case, they run from top left to bottom right as regards direction, but they are not diagonals) on each side of the portcullis. Between the pair on the left is the word 'GENTLE-MEN'; between those on the right the words 'AT ARMS' both written with the bottom of the lettering towards the staff. Finally, the two Honours 'GUINGATTE 1513' and 'BOULOGNE 1544'.

The Standard itself is slightly swallow-tailed, crimson, and outlined in gold, which is the colouring of the blazonry.

Where, in my view, the Standard is so interesting is that it depicts two crowns and that the blazonry is not strictly legible in any one position. The position next to the staff is known as the chief so that one normally expects all lettering to read out-wards – not inwards. What I mean is this. If the staff of this Standard is held horizontally and the material allowed to fall, the wording, all upside down, reads from left to right, 'GENTLEMEN ARMS AT'. Hold the Standard vertically above the staff and the wording becomes 'AT ARMS GENTLE-MEN'.

The Honour 'Guinegatte 1513' is by far the oldest of any and refers to the Battle of the Spurs fought on 16th August during one of Henry VIII's prowls round France in an endeavour to gain military glory. The battle is given that name by legend which says that the French used their spurs more than their swords. I am sorry to have to debunk this belief but I feel that the fact that the village of Spours being adjacent to the scene of the fight is the cause of the name. The Honour 'Boulogne 1544' commemorates its surrender to Henry VIII on 14th September.

The axe and staff are together about seven feet long. I have been told that they are of Elizabethan period, but I confess that I took that statement with a very large grain of salt as they do not strike me as much like those I understood to be in use at that time. I would say, with my limited knowledge of axes, that the design was produced for the use of the Corps, for it appears to me to be more artistic than utilitarian. If I am correct in this surmise then I would say that it would be impossible to give their date of manufacture without seeing the original order and receipt.

Note: The weapon appears to be a decorative form of pole-axe – a weapon in great demand in the fifteenth century for jousting on foot.

The Royal Company of Archers, The Queen's Bodyguard of Scotland

There is a a traditional story that this corps originated in the reign of James I of Scotland who appointed a commission to enforce and supervise the practice of archery in all the counties of Scotland. As a result of various competitions, the best marksmen were selected to form a personal bodyguard to the king in battle and on all ceremonial occasions.

The corps as it exists today was formed in 1676 by the Marquis of Athol, in which year it received its charter from the

Privy Council of Scotland. It received the title of 'His Majesty's Company of Archers', and was granted a sum of money for the purchase of a piece of plate which was to be competed for annually. No permanent king's prize was, however, established till 1788 when George III presented a plate which the winners were to hold for a year. With this plate also went a cash prize.

The Royal Company, being opposed to the cause then espoused, were almost suppressed during the Revolution of 1688, but on the accession of Queen Anne, and in 1703, they were revived and received a royal charter confirming all their previous rights and privileges in return for which they were to pay to her and her successors a pair of barbed arrows every Whitsunday.

When George IV visited Scotland in 1822, the Company claimed and obtained the right to be his personal bodyguard – a right they have retained in the case of subsequent visits of the reigning sovereign.

In 1833 William IV presented them with two colours to replace the banners which they had possessed since 1714 and 1732.

The affairs of the Company, which now numbers some five hundred members, are managed by a council of seven. The members, elected annually, have the power of electing or rejecting candidates for admission, and of appointing the officers, the senior of whom is the captain-general.

In addition to granting the Company the right to act as his bodyguard, George IV authorized the addition of 'The King's Bodyguard for Scotland' to the title and presented a gold stick to the captain-general and, by so doing, constituted the Company as part of the Royal Household. He also approved of a full dress uniform to be worn at all court functions in addition to what is termed the field dress. The court dress was originally gold and scarlet, but in 1831 it was changed to the present one consisting of a green coat with green velvet facings embroidered with gold arrows and thistles. Over the tunics, which have gold epaulettes, the officers wear a gold sash in place of that of crimson worn by the file. The green trousers have gold lacing; the headgear is a bonnet with an eagle feather for the archers, two for the officers except the captain, who has three. All ranks wear a sword.

The Captain-General has, as already stated, a gold stick which gives him precedence immediately behind the Gold Stick of England on all occasions of pageantry. The Lieutenants-General have silver sticks, and the seven members of the council those of ebony.

I have seen it written that the uniform of the Company is tartan. This is incorrect. In 1715 the tartan of the Royal Highlanders (The Black Watch) was adopted, but it was discontinued in 1829 when the uniform described was introduced.

I should like to conclude this brief summary of the Company by referring back to my first paragraph in which I mentioned the efforts of James I of Scotland, who reigned from 1406–1437, to promote archery. James I of England reigned from 1603–1625, and it was during his reign – in 1603 to be exact – that the oldest competition now held in the Company was originated. It is known as the Musselburgh Silver Arrow which was given by the magistrates of that town to be competed for annually at a range of 180 yards. The competition, now confined to members of the Company, was then open to all comers. I think that it is possible that the two Jameses have been confused by those who try to date the origin of the Company in connection with its oldest competition.

The silver arrow is a common form of prize among toxophilites and early examples are to be found in the Archers' Hall, the headquarters of the Royal Toxophilite Society, and I think I am correct in saying that a silver arrow is shot for at Meridan, in Warwickshire, by the Woodmen of Arden as well as a silver horn bugle at a range of 180 yards.

Heraldry

Heraldry in its widest sense includes the knowledge to explain all the different terms dealing with coats of arms, crests, badges, and other heraldic devices; also the skill to arrange royal occasions whether indoors or processional.

It is a very big subject indeed and I propose to divide it into two parts. The first I will call the animate side of heraldry; the other the inanimate. I will try and concentrate on the first as much as possible though it will be necessary to cross the dividing line at times to describe what it is that the heralds wear, etc.

The question I am often asked is, 'What is the origin of heraldry?' Before I can answer I have to ask my questioner to describe what he means by the word because, according to his reply, so I can place a date. It might come as a surprise to the reader to know that the difference in the date that I give might vary by something like two thousand years! Let us see why.

If you were to ask a few people what is meant by a coat of arms, or a crest, you will find that 'They are the marks, or badges, which certain families used on their silverware, carriages, notepaper, etc: they are occasionally to be seen at the entrances to large estates on the gate-pillars, or in the ironwork of the gates themselves'.

I think that you must agree that this is a very reasonable answer which, stripped of all technicalities, would satisfy most people, but we are going to deal with origins, so must be a bit more explicit.

You will note that I made our friend introduce the word 'marks' in such a way as to infer that they and badges were the same things which, from the point of view of origins, are separated by hundreds of years.

Marks, then known as marks of honour, were carried by the Romans and the Phrygians, whose country was overrun by the Cimmerians somewhere about 700 BC. The mark of honour of the Romans was an eagle; the Phrygians, a sow; the saxons, a horse; the original French mark was a lion which Clovis, king of the Salic Franks, changed to the fleur-de-lis after the battle of Alemanni in 496. It remained the emblem of France till 1789 when, as one of the many changes that resulted from the French Revolution, the cockerel was adopted as the Republican emblem.

The original marks were in the nature of national standards which were carried into battle to act as rallying points, and visible signs – call them what you will – that denoted friend from foe.

I consider that these marks were the forerunners of heraldry, because all coats and crests are really only the distinguishing marks of various families; whereas marks represented nations, crests denote families.

The origin of heraldry is obscure so that it would be dangerous to try and be too dogmatic about it.

Most authors seem pretty certain that it originated during the twelfth century but are very vague in their reasons for saying so.

If we are agreed that heraldry is very closely connected with badges of recognition, then it would be difficult for us to think of a time when such were more necessary. During the period of heavily armoured knights, the only way of recognizing an individual was by the heraldry on his shield or person in the same way that the contents of a tin can be recognized by the label thereon. Thus a trained herald could tell at a glance who was present on any particular occasion.

The second, third, fourth, and fifth crusades took place during this century. The third was probably the most international of them all. King Frederick (Barbarossa) of Germany, Philip II of France, and our Richard I were all there at one time or another between 1189–1192 so, not forgetting the enemy, there must have been a grand confusion as to which side anyone was on.

Prior to his departure for the crusade, Frederick had had

*A twelfth century knight showing the simple flat-iron type of shield
with heraldic device.*

numerous small wars with his nobles and he is credited with having instituted the idea of his followers wearing badges – an idea which he took with him to the crusade. He was drowned in 1189 so it would seem that Philip, who left the field at half time and went home, or Richard, after being released on ramson, carried on with the idea of sensible and easily distinguishable recognition signs.

Though there are records to show that badges were introduced in the twelfth century it was not till the next that they became hereditary.

The earliest roll of arms in existence was compiled during the Reign of Henry III (1216–72); the earliest heraldic document is that of Edward I (1272–1307).

The Roll of Caerlaveroch, a poem in Norman French, gives the names and the armorial bearings of barons and knights who served with 'The Hammer of the Scots' (Edward I) at the seige of the castle of that name in 1300 and, as one writer of the time of Henry V states, 'Heraldry is therein first presented to us as a science'. There can be little doubt that the many tournaments, at which each knight tried to outdo the other in splendour, played no small part in the increase in the use of armorial bearings.

By 1483 the use of heraldry had become slightly out of hand as, so far, no records had been kept as to which armorial bearings had been adopted by whom so that in this year, the first of his reign, Richard III granted a charter dated 2nd March to a corporation to be known as the Herald's College, or College of Arms. In addition to the charter he also gave the corporation a house called Colde Arbour, in the parish of All Hallows, London.

That avaricious monarch Henry VII employed two fiscal agents, Sir Edmund Dudley (probably one of the youngest-ever privy councillors at twenty-three) and Richard Empson to raise money by fair means and foul. One of the latter was the passing of the Act of Redemption under which the king with the slightest pretext could claim ownership of property. One property so claimed was Cold Arbour which, in spite of repeated protests during that reign and the next, was never returned. Though Henry VIII agreed that these two men would take up less room when beheaded, he regretted that he could not return any of the money or property which his father had stolen. His son, however, Edward VI, in 1550, by a charter dated 4th June returned to the college all its old privileges; and Mary, by a charter of 18th July, 1554, re-incorporated the college and gave it the use of Derby House, near St. Paul's Churchyard. This building was burnt down in the Great Fire of London, in 1666, but the books and records were saved and removed to the Palace of Westminster where the heralds held their chapters till the college had been rebuilt.

The corporation, under the Earl Marshal consists of four Kings-of-Arms, viz: Garter, Principal King-of-Arms; Norry provincial King-at-Arms over all parts of England north of the Trent; Clarenceux King-at-Arms over all parts of England south of the Trent; and Bath King-at-Arms. There are six heralds known as Somerset, Windsor, Chester, Richmond, Lancaster, and York. There are also four pursuivants with the strange-sounding titles of Rouge Dragon, Portcullis, Blue Mantle, and Rouge Croix.

In Scotland there is only one King-at-Arms known as Lyon; and in Ireland one, called Ulster.

To these regular appointments there have been added at various times, by order of the sovereign through the Earl Marshal, certain heralds or pursuivants extraordinary. The son of the Clarenceux King-at-Arms at the time of the funeral of William IV, Mr Albert Woods, was made Fitzalan Pursuivant Extraordinary, to give one example.

We must now retrace our steps and deal first with Commissions of Visitation, to retain continuity of the story as regards the College of Arms; and then back to the middle ages to find out something about the origin of heralds.

It is obvious that when heraldry was at its height there had to be some check to see that the coats were registered and that there were some records to ensure that there was no – at any rate not too much – duplication. For this purpose the College of Heralds sent round, the first at the instigation of Henry IV, commissions about every twenty-five years which summoned all those with coats of arms to attend. These commissions were presided over by the provincial King-at-Arms who recorded what he found.

The idea was eminently sound but, strange to say, they appear to have been given up sometime about 1688.

Anyone now made a peer may devise a most flamboyant coat and register it with the college, though the fashion of crests being displaycd on notepaper, and many other places as of old is now, so it seems, considered snobbery.

As long as imitation remains the sincerest form of flattery, so will those who spent most of their early life agitating a down-with-the-rich policy hasten to devise a coat of arms as soon as they get the chance. It was amusing during my visits to certain places abroad to sit down to a table laid with crested silver and on, I hope, discreet enquiry as to whose it was to be told that they had no idea as it was sent over by one of the sleuths (of whom there are now even more than ever) supplying foreigners with heirlooms. In some countries newly-obtained wealth is making a ludicrous attempt to buy tradition and, para-doxically, the greater the wealth the cheaper it looks.

Now for a few words about heralds who, one might say, have caused all this trouble!

A herald, in the middle ages, was an officer whose duty it was to carry challenges, or messages, from one sovereign, or baron, to another, and to supervise the arrangements for jousts and tournaments. After each combat he was to record the bear-ing of the winner and loser and then report whether a certain contestant should be promoted, or reduced. He was also respon-sible for the arrangements of all state ceremonies whether court functions or processions and dealt with all matters relative to coat-armour. After every battle, he was supposed to go round and count the dead on both sides, so that either in peace or war he seems to have been quite a busy fellow.

The first mention of a herald in England is contained in one of the pell-rolls of Edward III dated 1339, though the office must have existed before then.

There are, as already described, three grades of heralds. Their early history, and ceremony of inauguration, is very well described by Gerald Upton in his *De Militari Officio*, written during the reign of Henry V. This work was translated by

Juliana Barnes, otherwise Berners or Barners, in 1486 under the title of *The 'Boke'* (or Book) *of St Albans*. The account given therein concerning heralds is too good to be altered so I propose to give an extract:

It is necessary that all estates should have couriers as their messengers for the expedition of their business, whose office it is to pass and repass on foot, being clad in their prince's colours 'parted upright'.

'Parted upright' meant half of one colour and half of another with the arms of their sovereigns painted on the boxes in which they carried their despatches, and which were fixed to their girdle on the left side. It was not permitted to them to bear the arms of their lord in any other manner. They were knights in their offices, but not nobles, and were called Knights-Caligate of Arms, because they wore startuppes (a sort of gaiter) to the middle leg.

When they had conducted themselves properly in this situation for seven years, they were made chevaliers of arms, and rode on horseback to deliver their sovereign's messages, clad in one colour, their garments being only guarded or trimmed with the colour of their sovereign, and bearing their boxes aforesaid, with the arms painted on them, on the left shoulder and not elsewhere.

From these runners and riders the three orders of heralds were supplied, the chevalier of arms, having served another seven years, being created a pursuivant in the following manner:

The herald of the province, to whom he was to be pursuivant, wearing his coat of arms, took the candidate by his left hand, holding in his right a cup of silver, filled with wine and water, and leading him to his sovereign, in the presence of many witnesses duly summoned for this purpose, inquired by what name the pursuivant was to be created; and upon the sovereign's answer proclaimed his style accordingly, pouring some of the wine and water upon his bare head. He then invested him with the tabard, or harald's coat, emblazoned with the arms of the sovereign, but so that the sleeves hung upon his breast and back, and the front and hindparts of the tabard over his arms, in which curious fashion he was to wear it till he became a herald.

Here let me interpose that Joseph Strutt, in his *Regal and Ecclesiastical Antiquities*, produced in 1773, gives an illustration of a pursuivant so attired. His picture was taken from one of the many manuscripts of Robert Harley, the first Earl of Oxford. A selection of these rare manuscripts was published under the title of *The Harlean Miscellany* in 1744–6.

Let us now return to our extract with the pursuivant standing with his tabard on sidways.

> *The oath of office was then administered to him, and lastly the sovereign presented him with the silver cup aforesaid.*
>
> *Having once been made pursuivant, he might be created a herald, even the next day, which was done by the principal herald or king of arms leading him in like manner before the sovereign, but bearing a gilt instead of a silver cup, and turning the tabard so that the sleeves hung in their proper places over the arms. A collar of SS was then put about his neck, one S being argent, or silver, the other sable, or black, alternately, and when he was named, the prince himself poured the wine and water on his head, and after the oath was administered gave him the cup as before; whereupon the herald cried, 'A largesse'.*
>
> *The kings of arms were created and solemnly crowned by the sovereigns themselves, and distinguished from the heralds by richer tabards, the embroidery being on velvet instead of satin, gilt collars of SS, and coronets composed of a plain circle of gold surmounted by sixteen strawberry leaves, eight of which are higher than the rest.*

This account is very interesting, quite apart from its clear description of the ceremony of appointing a pursuivant and herald, and that it also gives the early history of despatch cases, usually found with the regimental crest thereon, so often to be seen in pictures of about the time 1800–1900.*

* I believe the military origins to be different—see Sabretache. *Editor.*

The collar of SS of which mention was made is a collar of levery. A collar as an adornment of rank is very old indeed, in fact it was the Roman Titus Manlius who put on the collar of an enormous Gaul giant that he slew and then assumed the name of Torquatus (after the twisted chain worn by his adversary) in 361 BC.

The origin of the SS had puzzled historians for some time. The letters may stand for St Simplicius, the martyr, or 'souveraigne' meaning sovereign. At any rate the collar was adopted by Henry IV during the Wars of the Roses, in the reign of Richard III, it was adopted as the Lancastrian badge. A collar now forms part of the insignia of orders of knighthood.

Heraldry and pageantry have now given way to paypacketry and the more is the pity. The nobles and gentry were accused of grinding the faces of the workers, who have been so busy lately kicking the other ends of their employers that both have lost their shapes and we are now in a world in which everyone is so busy trying to run other peoples' businesses that, as a nation, we have lost our prestige and power. Queen Elizabeth II cannot visit Gibralter, so it seems, without the persmission of Spain. The statesmen and sailors of the first Elizabeth told Spain where to go and helped her on her way and Europe was a much nicer residential district afterwards. These upstarts who have cropped up over Europe are a beastly nuisance and completely gutless when tackled in the correct way – vide Hitler and Mussolini.

The crude splodge which the old Briton daubed on his chest is as much the forerunner of the present elaborate crest as was the first flying machine of the Wrights that of the present multi-engined aeroplane.

Heraldry is displayed on almost every cricket field either in the form of the flags of the competing teams or in the badges on the cricketers' caps. My dictionary defines a blazer as one who spreads abroad or proclaims, so that a blazer blazons the side to which the wearer belongs. It would not come amiss to mention at this stage the use of 'livery colours' in regimental ties and those of educational establishment immortalized under the title (beloved or anathematized according to your political complexion) 'the old school tie'. These are now exported in large numbers and may be worn by anyone with the purchase price, without the fatigue of actually serving in the regiment or attending the school.

In an effort to avoid confusion, I am going to omit the mention of flags because they are really only banners which in their turn are called by various names according to their function. A ship flies (or wears) an ensign; a regiment has colours and so on. As a matter of fact I cannot think of many uses of the word flag by a soldier except in the case of the white flag, or flag of truce. Let us, therefore, concentrate on the terms which form part of military history and take them in alphabetical order.

Banners

The exact derivation of the word is uncertain though it is probable that it had some connection with 'Ban', which was the old name for a rallying point.

The size of a banner has nothing whatever to do with its precedence which is judged solely by its colour and the devices on it. For instance, the White Ensign is senior to the Red, though the latter may be twice the size of the former. The knights of old were very fond of display, but a banner which was too large could not open in the breeze so that there automatically arose a size which was not too large to serve its purpose and did not fall around the staff instead of floating out for all to see.

The ancients did not carry banners but standards which were called eagles from the gold or silver representations of that bird which were mounted on long poles. The eagle was used to denote the symbol of empire by the Persians in the time of Cyrus the Great, in 529 BC and this idea was copied by the Romans who also carried standards bearing representations of the wolf, the horse, the minotaur, and the boar. Xenophon, in his Anabasis, describes the Persian standard of Cyrus the Young at the Battle of Cunaxa (410 BC) as being a golden eagle raised on a spear. These Persian and Roman standards served precisely the same purpose as the material banners in that they marked the location of the commander, and also the rallying places for those who become lost in, or after, a battle.

The first mention of banners in English history was made by the author-monk The Venerable Bede (673–735) who described the meeting between Augustine and his followers with Ethelbert, King of Kent. Augustine, he says, approached the king with his followers bearing banners on which were silver crosses and the picture of Jesus Christ.

We see, therefore, that the earliest recorded carrying of banners had a religious significance, as it still does in Catholic countries.

The English monastries had their own banners which were brought out for particular occasions and on the anniversary of the patron saint of the particular monastry. They were sometimes allowed to be taken out and displayed in the field. There was the banner of St Wilfred at Ripon; at Beverley, that of St John. Both were displayed in the field at Northallerton in the reign of Stephen. The old rolls show that Edward I paid one of the priests of Beverley the sum of $8\frac{1}{2}$d a day for carrying the banner of St John in his army, and penny a day while taking it back to his monastry!

There is a very good description of the banner of St Cuthbert, of Durham, given in a book published in 1672 entitled *The Antient Rites and Monuments of the Monastical and Cathedral Church of Durham* an extract from which is, I think, worth quoting in detail.

The prior caused a goodly and sumptuous banner to be made, with pipes of silver to be put on the staff, being five yards long, with a device to take off and on the pipes at pleasure, and to be kept in a chest at the refactory, when they were taken down, which banner was shewed and carried in the said abbey on festival and principal days. On the height of the overmost pipes was a fair pretty cross of silver, and a wand of silver, having a fine wrought knot of silver at either end, that went underneath the banner-cloth, whereunto the banner-cloth was fastened and tied; which wand was of the thickness of a man's finger, and at either end of the said wand there was a fine silver bell. The wand was fastened by the middle of the banner-staff hard under the cross. The banner-cloth was a yard broad and five quarters deep; and the nether part of it was indented in five parts and fringed, and made fast all about with red silk and gold; and, also, the said banner-cloth was made of red velvet, on both sides most

c

sumptuously embroidered and wrought with flowers of green silk and gold; and in the midst of the said banner-cloth was the said holy relique and corporax cloth (this was the cloth with which St Cutherbert in his lifetime had used to cover the chalice when he said mass) inclosed and placed therein: which corporax cloth was covered with white velvet, half a yard square every way, having a red cross of velvet on both sides over the same holy relique, most artificially and cunningly compiled and framed, being finely fringed about the skirts and edges with a fringe of red silk and gold, and three little fine silver bells fastened to the skirts of the sand banner-cloth, like unto sacring bells; and being so sumptuously finished and absolutely perfected, was dedicated to holy St Cuthbert, to the intent and purpose that the same should be presented and carried always after to any battle, as occasion should serve; and which was never carried or shewed at any battle, but, by the especial grace of God Almighty, and the mediation of holy St Cuthbert, it brought home the victory.

This particular banner was made in 1346, but it was not the first banner of St Cuthbert for there is mention in the wardrobe accounts of Edward I for the years 1299 and 1300 of a payment of five pounds to William de Gretham, a monk of Durham, for his expenses in carrying the banner of St Cuthbert from 3rd July–24th August, and for returning it to Durham.

The fame of this banner was well-known for it is on record that the Earl of Surry (not Surrey), who commanded an expedition into Scotland during the reign of Henry VIII, stopped at Durham on his way so as to take this banner with him.

Having said so much about this banner, I had better give its final history and say that it was burnt, during the time of the Reformation, by the French wife of Whittingham, then Dean of Durham.

There is frequent mention in stories of chivalry of a banner known as an oriflame, which should be correctly described as *the* oriflame. This was the banner of St Dennis which was borrowed from the abbey of that name near Paris, and carried with the French armies. It was perfectly plain and flame-coloured and unembroidered. The bottom part was divided into three parts, and it was fastened to the staff by a green silk cord. It was carried in the army of Louis de Gros when he defended France against the Emperor Henry V, and again in those of St Louis and Philip de Bel. All this, however, concerns French history and I only mention it to show the importance which banners played before the arrival of firearms, cannons, and mortars which completely reversed the whole idea of trying to make oneself as conspicuous as possible.

There were two reputed saints among the Saxon kings, Edmund the Martyr and Edward the Confessor. Their banners were taken to the wars during the reigns of the Edwards and Henries and probably played no small part in their victories. John Lydgate, a monk of Bury and also poet to the court of Henry IV, has described the banner of St Edmund as having a representation of Eve in the Garden of Eden being tempted by the serpent and, presumably on the other side, three crowns signifying Royalty, Continence, and Martyrdom. The banner of St Edward the Confessor probably bore the cross and martlets which are carved on his tomb in Westminster Abbey. Henry V carried two banners known as the Banner of the Trinity, and Banner of the Virgin.

In the time of the middle ages, war could not be carried on without the help of the Church; and, in fairness to war, one must add that the churches could hardly carry on without war as they derived great benefit from the spoils. It was, however, advisable for the king to display the fact that his campaign had divine blessing so that the saintly banners proclaimed this fact as well as having purely military uses as marking rallying points and headquarters. The religious connection is still maintained in that regimental colours are consecrated before presentation, and in the fact that churches are still the depositaries for old colours. The banners of the Knights of the Garter hang in the Chapel of St George at Windsor, and those of Knights of the Bath in Henry VII's Chapel at Westminster. It was the custom of nations, as well as private persons, to place themselves under the tutelage of a particular saint. St George was, and still is, despite recent papal abolition, the patron saint of England. Who has not read of the old war-cry 'St George for England'? The device was a plain vertical red cross on a white field. Whatever other banners were present, this was the senior; and to this day the red cross forms the most conspicuous feature of our national flag.

The remaining parts of our national banner consist of the crosses of St Andrew and St Patrick. These are what are known as saltier, this means that the arms of the crosses are diagonal extending from opposite corners. The Cross of St Andrew was white on a blue field. Three years after James VI of Scotland became James I for England, on 12th April, 1606, to be exact, he directed that the Cross of St George should be united with that of St Andrew to form the Union Flag, commonly known as the Union Jack. The latter word is considered to be a corruption of the word James, Jacobus, or Jacques. The banner of St Patrick was red upon a white field which was incorporated with the others on Ireland joining the Union. The present Union Jack dates, therefore, from 1st January, 1801.

I have dealt almost exclusively with religious emblems and traced the outline of banners from their inception to our beloved National Flag so we must now retrace our steps and deal with the military aspect of the subject.

The Lions of England were what were known as the personal achievement of the king in the same way as a commander-in-chief flies a small Union Jack on his car. An achievement – or, an achievement of arms to give it its full description – signifies a complete composition. A coat of arms may be composed of any number of blazons but the whole is called an achievement, so that the royal achievement to which I refer signifies that there was only one or more lions on the banner. Such a banner was always carried near the person of Richard I, prior to whose reign they cannot be traced. It is probably that other banners bearing the favourite devices of the king were also carried either for sentimental reasons or show, but this does not alter the fact that the senior of them all was that bearing one or more lions. We know, for instance, that Edward IV had a banner bearing the white rose of York, and that Henry VII presented to the then Church of St Paul three banners immediately after the Battle of Bosworth.

In feudal times, the armies were made up of units brought by the barons, and led by them in person so that they copied the royal idea of carrying banners to mark their whereabouts.

The banners of the barons bore the insignia of their houses and there is little doubt that each tried to outdo the other in the magnificence of their trappings.

Heraldry in those days was, as I have already tried to explain, a sign language. You may call it a form of conceit and use all the vile terms you can think of to describe it but you cannot get away from the fact that it was also a military necessity. The nobles in their armour, especially when their visors were down, looked alike, so how was anyone to know who was whom without some distinguishing mark? Was not the Earl of Gloucester, grandson of Edward I slain in Scotland by mistake at a time when he was not wearing his armourial insignia? It is hard enough now to recognize a particular officer in the field, how much more so would it have been when his face is not only blacked but completely covered?

The need for recognition gradually brought about a multiplicity of banners. There were those of the king, the church, the barons, and a great number of lesser persons who commanded small units and thus came about the arrival of banners to denote the headquarters of armies and others down to the company.

When the feudal system went out, the use of baronial banners went with it, but the practice of marking headquarters remained. Private banners reappeared in the Parliamentary armourial bearings. The usual practice was to display some slogan, or moral sentiment, in lettering from which the horrible habit of parading the streets with slogans has probably arisen.

I need hardly mention that banners from the earliest times of their institution have also stood for ownership. About the first thing an army does when it captures a fortress is to raise its own national banner on the highest point to signify its capture. The converse is, in a sense, also true in that, when a flag is lowered, except at night, it is a signal admitting submission.

Bannieres-Quarres

This denotes that the banners are square and has no other significance.

Colours

This term is used to denote the banners of infantry regiments. They are of two kinds known as 'The Queen's* Colours' and 'Regimental Colours'.

The Colours of the regiments of Foot Guards are reverse to those of the infantry regiments. With them the Queen's Colour is crimson, with or without the cantoned Union Jack, but always charged with (bearing) the Royal Crown and regimental device in the centre. The Regimental Colour of the Foot Guards is the Union Jack. Both are charged with the regimental battle honours.

In the case of Regiments of the Line the Queen's Colour is the Union Jack charged with the regimental numerals and some, or all, of the regimental devices. The Regimental Colour is of the same colour as the regimental facings. It is cantoned with the Union Jack (which in this case means that the Union Jack is in the top corner nearest the staff), and bears the Royal Crown, regimental numerals, crest, motto, and battle honours.

There was originally one colour per company, then three per regiment; now, since 1751, there have been the two just described.

The ceremony of Trooping the Colour, which in its present form originated in 1755, derives its name from the musical troop, or tune, which was played during the ceremony of lodging the colours of safe custody.†

The Royal Regiment of Artillery and rifle regiments have no colours. The former because the guns themselves are the rallying point, whilst the original role of the latter was to act as scouts and advance guards so that the less seen the better they were able to perform their function.

Ensigns

There are three English ensigns known as the white, red, and blue.

---

* When a king reigns — eg George VI, King's Colours'.

† The idea of carrying the Colours along the lines of troops in slow time was to impress them upon the soldiers' memories, that they might always recognize them in battle, and so know their place and rallying point.

The White Ensign, whose use on service is restricted to the Royal Navy, consists of the red cross of St George on a white field cantoned with the Union Jack; the Blue Ensign consists of a dark blue field cantoned with the Union Jack; the Red Ensign is similar but with a red field.

Until 1864 an English fleet was divided into three squadrons known as the white, the red, and the blue after the colour of the ensign that they wore. In the year mentioned Queen Victoria decreed that the White Ensign, together with its broad and narrow pendants, should henceforth be considered as the Ensign of the Royal Navy. Ships of the Royal Yacht Club are also allowed to fly it.

The Blue Ensign may be worn by ships commanded by officers of the Royal Naval Reserve and those in the service of certain public bodies. The Red Ensign may be worn by all other ships belonging to British subjects that are registerd in the Commonwealth.

All ships lower their ensigns in salute to the White Ensign on a man-of-war; and, it is the custom for a ship to lower her's in salute when passing another, though I must admit that in voyages to many parts of the world I have noticed a strange apathy in this connection.

The word 'Ensign' was also at one time to denote the lowest rank of commissioned officer in the infantry – now known as second-Lieutenant. The equivalent cavalry rank was 'Cornet'.

Gonfannons

These are purely religious banners which hang vertically from transverse bars at the top of the staff. They are usually swallow-tailed.

Guidons

These are swallow-tailed banners which were the colours of regiments of Dragoons, Hussars and Lancers, but Hussars and Lancers no longer have them. They are swallow tailed.

Pencils, Pennoncelles or Pennoncilles

These are difficult to distinguish from pennons as there is no ruling as to the maximum length of pennons. Broadly speaking, then, they are long pennons.

Pendants or Pennants

These are long narrow streamers worn by ships commanded by a commodore, and also on the occasion of the commissioning, or paying off, of a warship.

Pennons

Pennons, introduced by Henry III, were small pointed banners fixed immediately below the lance head and constituted the personal ensigns of the knights carrying them. They were charged with the armourial devices of their owners in such a way that they were correctly displayed when the lance was in a position of charging, ie horizontal. A pennon-shaped banner with the devices in the normal position, ie when the staff is vertical, is a form of standard.

Standards

The early standard was far too large to be carried – in fact it was not intended to be. The standard consisted of a scaffold from which was flown the banner of the sovereign and one or more saints. The whole was mounted on a cart drawn by oxen. The priests held their services around the standard which was guarded night and day by a number of knights specially detailed by the sovereign.

Historians will recall the invasion of England by the Scots under David Bruce and how he was defeated by the barons and yeomen at Northallerton on 22nd August, 1138. This battle was also known as the Battle of the Standards because the Archbishop of York came on to the field at a time when the English were having the worst of the engagement, with a standard bearing the consecrated banners of St Peter of York, St John of Beverley, and St Wilfred of Ripon. I have already referred to the oriflame, which belonged to the Abbey of St Dennis, which was taken on the field of Agincourt by the French in 1415.

Standards, as regards cloth insignias, were introduced during the reign of Edward III when they were very much longer than today – that is longer in relation to their width. They bore the device, or crest, of their owners but never his coat of arms.

Standards in present military parlance are the colours of

Standards of the Household Cavalry.

regiments of Household Cavalry and Dragoon Guards and are rectangular.

Regiments of Lancers and Hussars have neither standards no guidons with the sole exception of the Inns of Court Regiment which is a territorial Hussar regiment attached to the Household Cavalry.

Streamers

These have no military significance in our history and were simply strips of material of no particular material, colour, or length, which were, and for that matter still are, used to lend colour to an occasion. I shall, however, refer to them again in a moment when dealing with terms used by our friends in the United States.

I should like to conclude this chapter with a few remarks concerning the use of the terms colours, standards, guidons, streamers, etc, used by the Americans whose President honoured the Gloucestershire Regiment and Troop C, 170 Independent Motor Battery, Royal Artillery, with a Distinguished Unit Citation for service in Korea.

Units which perform an outstanding act of gallantry may be awarded either of the following: A Distinguished Unit Citation, A Presidential Unit Citation (Navy), A Meritorious Unit Citation or a Navy Unit Commendation.

Let us deal with each in their order of precedence.

Distinguished Unit Citation

This award, sanctioned in 1942, is given to units of the United States' armed forces and her allies for acts of outstanding heroism. Commanding generals of the forces are authorized to make the award either immediately or up to a period not exceeding a year after the action.

The award carries with it permission to attach a blue streamer to the pike or lance. Embroidered in white letters on the streamer is the name of the action for which the award was given.

Individuals who were on the strength of the unit at the time of the action are allowed to wear a Distinguished Unit Emblem on the right breast as a permanent award. Those who subsequently join the unit may wear one during their period of actual service with it. The emblem consists of a blue ribbon in a gold metal frame which is worn on the right breast in the outside position when other citation emblems are worn. What is termed an oak leaf cluster is worn on the emblem to denote a subsequent award. When five of these bronze clusters have been gained, they are exchanged for a silver one.

Two British units received this award for an action that took place near Solma-ri, Korea, on 23rd–25th April, 1951.

Presidential Unit Citation (Navy)

This is a naval award on the same lines as the Distinguished Unit Citation to the army and carries with it the same permission to attach a streamer, in this case of blue, gold, and scarlet, to the unit's pike.

The emblem consists of a tri-coloured ribbon of blue, gold, and scarlet with the stripes running horizontally in that order. Subsequent awards allow the recipient to wear a bronze citation star on the ribbon, and the same qualifications as regards presence with the unit as those just mentioned with the Distinguished Unit Citation apply.

Meritorious Unit Commendation

This is awarded for meritorious service in fighting zone for a period of not less than six months. Several factors which have nothing whatever to do with bravery are concerned with its award such as the least number of absentees, court-martial offences, and the smallest percentage of men who have contracted venereal disease. Members of a unit gaining this award wear a golden laurel wreath mounted on a small square of cloth four inches above the right sleeve. Subsequent awards are recorded by the appropriate numeral inside the wreath. The previous qualifications as regards authority to wear the emblem apply. The unit is entitled to carry a suitably named scarlet streamer on its pike.

Navy Unit Commendation

This is the naval counterpart to the above. The colour of the streamer is green. The ribbon is of blue, yellow, and green. The commendation star is of bronze with five points.

Early English Armies

In giving an account of the early English armies, one is faced with problems similar to those of laying out a racecourse. A large area must be surveyed and then a decision made as to the exact location of the course and where to have the starting and finishing posts. Where, therefore, in the whole history of Britain shall we have our course and where shall we start and finish? I suggest that it starts at Canute and ends at Cromwell, which will make it about 650 years long. I chose this location because that bit beyond Cromwell is overcrowded with regimental historians, while that before Canute is so interesting and little known. As the course is so short we will allow flying starts so perhaps the reader would care to come with me while I warm up before I speed down the Canute-Cromwell Military Course, or CCMC as it would be styled under the modern craze for initials.

There are various definitions to describe what is meant by an army. John Locke, the philosopher and psychologist, who died in 1704, described it as being, 'a collection of armed men obliged to obey one man'. We can, of course, tear this definition to shreds by saying that if it is correct an armed mob which is obeying the directions of a mutineer is also an army. It has also been described as an instrument to enforce the will of the people. This definition seems to me to be more applicable to the hydrogen bomb. Let us, therefore, deal with the term in its generally accepted sense.

An army has no specific strength for there have been those of millions and others which have hardly exceeded the strength of a modern division or two. Such expressions as a large army, or small army, are completely meaningless unless one knows the resources of the nation supplying it. If, for instance, we were told that the Russians had an army of 200,000 men in Switzerland, that would not be a large one when judged by their standards but quite a different proposition from the point of view of the Swiss.

Armies, as we speak of them today, were unknown in early English history and, one might add, in that of continental countries. The whole male population and the army were one and the same thing; every male, from the age when he was old enough to lift a small club until relegated to boiling the water to make what corresponded to the modern 'cuppa', was a soldier every twenty four hours of the day.

A tribe was judged by its warlike strength as those of us who can still remember our early struggles with Latin will remember. Who does not recall that bit about, *Gallia omnia divisus est in tres partes, fortissimi sunt Belgae*?

For political reasons into which we have not time to probe, Julius Caesar made two raids into Britain, the first in BC 55, the second in BC 54. In both cases he found that the Britons were not quite as soft as he thought and, having negotiated terms and taken captives and hostages, he withdrew completely. For nearly 100 years the island was left in peace, but in AD 41 the Emperor Claudius launched an expedition and the Roman occupation had begun. The Roman occupation has given archaeologists a great deal of pleasure in unearthing various remains, but I doubt whether any single event has ever done more harm to a country than the Roman occupation of Britain.

Stamp out the soul of a nation and it is obliterated though not a man has been physically injured. That is precisely what the Romans did here by enforcing submission and maintaining garrisons to repel further invasions. Even if the will to defend the islands remained, the right to do so was forfeited with the result that the militant spirit and the will to fight for freedom was extinguished. The instinct of every living being is to defend his property and only hunger, pain, or some unusual twist of the mind such as is found in criminals, Hitlers, and rogue elephants makes them consider aggression first. What may seem like aggression in an animal is not originally derived from that spirit but from fear. He thinks extremely quickly – so quickly in fact –

that the act of thinking that he is being attacked and deciding to attack first follow each other so speedily that we forget the first process and only think of the latter. I cannot for the moment think of any wild animal that will attack without the vestige of a reason (though we may not notice what it is at the time), except the wild pig. Either his reactions are so swift that they cannot be separated, or he is too brainless to stop for a fraction of a split second to think. I have heard both suggestions and prefer the latter.

I must agree that the Romans gave the Britons roads, drains, and baths and failed to put up any signboards directing the natives to them for they look as if they could have done with that schoolboy's dread – a good wash.

The *Notitia* or, for those who hate abbreviations, the *Notitia dignitatum omnium, tam civilium quam militarium in partibus Orientis et Occidentis* gives an account of the garrisons of the Roman army and details of their troops in Briton. It was their policy to recruit their forces among the tribes they had conquered (though I think 'recruit' expresses the process rather mildly), and then despatch them far from their native soil. This fact accounts for the reason that remains have been found in England that owe their origin to such far away places as Spain and Portugal. In the same way, remains of some of our early tribes have been found on the continent. The object of this procedure is obvious because, with these islands denuded of their menfolk, fewer troops were required to keep the remaining inhabitants in a state of subjugation. The feelings of Mr Hutholder at being told what to do by a barbarian from the Baltic were not considered neither was the fact that the barbarian hadn't the foggiest notion of what his presence was supposed to imply. He was probably whisked away from home and was just as disgusted about the whole business as some of the Chinamen in the First World War who worked as dock labourers in Rouen and elsewhere and who, when on their own, groused incessantly at the idea of having to do our dirty work, and often having to eat with those diabolical instruments known as spoons and forks.

During the fourth century, the Empire was in decay, and gradually the Legions and the fighting men disappeared across the channel in the wake of Governors making their personal bids for power.

By 410, the Roman Empire had had its day. Its very heart, Rome, was being threatened so that all available forces had to be collected for its defence. The only part of that story that concerns us is the fact that the Roman Emperor, Honorius, recalled his few remaining garrisons stationed in Britain and so left the country to fend for itself.

Their departure was just what the Picts, Scots, and Saxons were waiting for. With the departing Romans went the men and means for protecting our shores. The number of different people arriving so bewildered the inhabitants who, as already explained, had all fighting spirit knocked out of them that they sent an urgent request to Rome for protection, known by the strange title of 'The Groans of the Britons'. The request received no reply so Vortigen, then King of Kent, finding that he was not strong enough to resist invasion, sent for help from two of his pals, Hengist and Horsa, who came at once with a strong following of Jutes. Having driven off the invaders they refused the rewards offered them and turned against Vortigen. Horsa was killed in the Battle of Aylesford, but Hengist established himself in Kent. It was from him, though some say that a hengist (horse) was only his badge, that the White Horse of Kent is derived which is the badge of the Queen's Own Royal West Kent Regiment.

All this happened in 449; the next notable event was the coming of the Saxons in 477 under their elderman Aella. Then came Cerdic in 495 with his landing at Southampton and founding of the kingdom of Wessex.

With all these landings going on the Briton soon disappeared with the result that the Saxons, Jutes, and Angles united to form the present English race, though the country was divided into kingdoms. A strange, or seemingly so, reversal now took place in that these united tribes called the original Britons foreigners who replied by calling the others Sassenachs (Saxons). Among themselves the Britons called each other Kymry, or comrade, so the Russians will have a job to say that they originated that term.

We shall stray too far from our subject if we deal with the historical events too much, but the period of the Saxon ascendancy has much to interest those looking for early military matters.

The different kingdoms organized their manpower in much the same way, which was as follows.

Witans were appointed which, in addition to their other duties, saw to it that men were always available for fighting. A witan was a body of wise men who occasionally held witan-moots – or meetings of wise men – to deal with major affairs, lesser ones were dealt with at shiremoots, and those of a parochial nature by tunmoots. The last-named were the forerunners of our town and borough councils.

A witanmoot had originally appointed a kinsman (from which we derive our word king and that of king's man) to rule them and, when he died, decided whether his successor should be of his family, and if so whom. Their king commanded them in battle but, to relieve him of some of the responsibilities of raising and maintaining an army, they also appointed eorls, later known as thanes, each of whom was made responsible for producing a body of men when wanted. Under the eorls came the ceorls. The members of the tribe, together with any prisoners they had, formed the rank and file. Here, then, in about 500, I find the origins of what later became known as a militia. I have described how all able-bodied males were the army, but here we find an effort made to supply officers and not only officers for battle but special people made responsible for a body of men, which they were to lead themselves should occasion require.

We must now skip the period from about 620 to 800, which was near the end of that which is sometimes referred to as the Heptarchy, or seven kingdoms, and, I admit, leave the realms of purely military history so as to get a better idea of the state of affairs in this island for the two hundred years immediately before the Norman invasion.

I dislike this term heptarchy because it signifies a government of seven people. We infer from that that they formed the same parliament when, in reality, the country was divided into various kingdoms and I doubt – seriously doubt – whether there were ever an exact seven in existence at any one time. They swallowed each other and split with such frequency that, if at any one time there happened to be exactly seven, it was a pure fluke. However,

1. A fully accoutred mediaeval knight, Arms of d'Abernon. Model by Charles Stadden. Courtesy Norman Newton, Ltd.

2. *Richard Neville, the Kingmaker.*
Model by Charles Stadden. Courtesy Norman Newton, Ltd.

let us not worry too much about whether this island was a heptarchy, or any other kind of archy, but get back to the year 800 and see why I think it an important one.*

Hiding in the court of Charlemagne, or Charles the Great, King of the Franks and Emperor of the Romans, was a decendant of Cerdic (whom I have mentioned as landing in 795) called Egbert whom the Witan of Wessex considered to have a right to the throne after the death of Brihtric. They sent for him and he was elected and so became King of Wessex from 802–39. He spent the first twenty-five years of his reign conquering the other kingdoms till he was acknowledged to be Bretwalda, a term signifying overlord. He was acknowledged to be Bretwalda of Britain which I can best describe as being the senior king. He called a meeting of the Witan at Winchester in 829 which decreed that henceforth the whole country should be called England. He is generally credited with being the first Anglo-Saxon king to style himself King of the Angles and of England. The whole story has a complete ring of authenticity about it and agrees with bits and pieces which we can fit in from sources other than those dealing with him personally so, until someone can produce to my satisfaction a carefully documented account to prove otherwise I shall continue to believe that the term 'England' originated as I relate, and that Englishmen started to be called such at the same time. The title of England (from Angles and lond, meaning land) remains (at the time of writing), but that of British Empire has, alas, gone. It is a sad thought for some of us older birds that that title, which meant exactly what it said, should no longer be considered applicable and that the future may find the word Commonwealth replaced by something like the Amalgamated Society of. . . .

I often wonder what my father, and the fathers of others of my age, would have said and done to me, or them, if we had insisted that in a few years' time we should not be allowed to use the term British Empire.

Never mind about the probable future, let us return to the certain past where we find that Egbert engendered a feeling of

* The seven kingdoms were: Northumbria, Mercia, East Anglia, Essex, Wessex, Surrey and Kent. *Editor*.

D

trust and respect. It is true that he appointed kings to rule the kingdoms he had conquered in the same way that Napoleon found jobs for his favourites nearly a thousand years later.

One might have hoped that Egbert's efforts would lay the foundations of a prosperous and peaceful era, but the story of invasion and reorganization was to start all over again in a few years' time.

The means that brought about the next upheaval can be described in two words – sea power.

What has sea power got to do with an account of military history? I should think that the answer that most people would give is 'nothing whatever'. How wrong they would be. Those who do not care to go too far back in history in the world at the time have been beaten in the end by sea power. The lack of which eventually beat Napoleon, the Kaiser, and Hitler.

The creeks and western shores of Denmark, Sweden, and Norway were inhabited by large numbers of sea-pirates who were collectively called creekmen or Vikings who, in their long oared and sailing craft, by superb seamanship continually raided our shores. They took, or destroyed, what they wanted on exactly the same lines as did the many commandoes during their raids in the last war. These Vikings probed along our shores to find the weak places in the defences. Whenever they did more than tip and run raids in the south they were defeated, but had better luck in Northumbria and Mercia. Having banded together and adopted, or been given, the general appellation of Danes, by 877 they had conquered half the country. By The Treaty of Wedmore, 879, the Danes were to control the eastern half and Alfred the western. He reintroduced the fyrds and in so doing earned himself the title of 'Father of the English Navy' though it would seem that he did little more than revive an idea.

Once again we think we are coming to a long settled period but are wrong. A succession of weak kings of Wessex encouraged the Danes to further efforts with the result that in 1017 Cnut (or Canute) became King of England in succession to his father, Sweyn, who had been king of both Denmark and England.

Here we are at what I said would be our starting point. Canute was King of England without any mitigating clauses as one might say. Egbert, as we have seen, called Wessex England

and styled himself king. This is little better than a play on words for there were other kings in Britain at the time. Cnut saw to it that there were not any more than himself by dividing the country into four earldoms – Wessex, Mercia, East Anglia, and Northumberland.

In case I have indulged in playing with words to please my own ends I had better clear up this question of kingship. Sweyn was King of Denmark and England (note the order). Cnut was King of All England, and of Norway, Denmark, and Sweden.

Cnut left three sons, Swegan, Harold, and Harthacnut. Swegen took Norway, which from then onwards leaves our history; Harthacnut took Denmark. England again became divided for the West Saxons chose Harthacnut to be their king too so he became King of Denmark and half of England. Harold was chosen as king of all the territory north of the Thames. Harold died in 1040 whereupon Harthacnut claimed the kingship of the whole country and brought with him from Denmark, where he was at the time of Harold's death, a large Danish army and fleet.

At the time of these numerous Danish incursions there was a tax known as the danegeld about which I wish to say a few words because I feel that the loud pedal is used when referring to the Feudal System as if it were rather a clever novelty introduced by William the Conqueror. I suggest that it was nothing more than a continuation of the danegeld with a few twiddly bits added. I will go further and admit that I do not know when the feudal system actually took priority for they were both in existence at the same time! If this is not so then how came it that one of the clauses in the coronation oath of King Stephen (1135) was that he should repeal it. Where I will agree is that the danegeld referred to money only, whereas the feudal system included both service and payment clauses. You know, if you really take both apart, to use a Canadian expression, there is very little difference is there? 'Fined £100 or three months imprisonment' is the sort of thing we hear in court today. The danegeld said, in so many words, ten pounds or three months service; the Feudal System said three months service or ten pounds. We hear something rather like this today and all too frequently in the incessant demands of labour for **x** quid a week or you all go without. The title of Feudal System is now out of date but we have another for which I leave the reader to give a name.

In 1042, the Witan chose the weakling Edward the Confessor as king. He was styled 'Confessor' for his supposed love of piety and religion, but he was a double-crosser if ever there was one. He was elected to be King of England yet toadied to the Normans and even, so it is said, promised the throne of England when he had finished with it to William, Duke of Normandy. When he died he was succeeded by Harold which annoyed William who, as everyone knows, came over and took by force that which he was not entitled to otherwise.

The danegeld started by being nothing more than a tax which was offered to the Danes as a bribe to keep away. This is exactly the same as the rackets I knew in the United States before the First World War when, in the large western town where I lived for some while, gangs of hooligans used to come round and demand payment unless we wanted our milk bottles smashed, and other such annoyances. The tax was later also put towards paying for an army to defend the coasts. As is invariably the case with all forms of blackmail, as soon as the victim had paid the first demand he received a second. Eventually the sum raised was not sufficient so that the witanmoot found it necessary to impose first a tax of one Saxon shilling, and later two more, on every hide of land. The tax, first said to have been levied in 991, eventually reached seven shillings and was used by the Danish kings on our throne as a source of income. At the time of Cnut it amounted to about £71,000 which, together with the £11,000 levied on the City of London, must have been a very large sum for the times.

William the Conqueror, as every schoolboy knows, used the Feudal System to obtain men and money. I use the word 'used' intentionally for the general impression that one gets from some books is that it was a bright idea of William's – that he invented it, in other words. Such is not the case as it had been in use on the continent before he introduced it to England but, as there is some doubt as to its date and place of origin, I do not intend to say more on the subject. I feel, however, especially in view of the trouble it subsequently caused, that it is advisable to enlarge on the subject further than just to say that it supplied men and money.

The word 'feu' is still used in Scotland to denote an estate held by a feuar for a term of years providing that feu-duty is regularly paid. This is the English equivalent to saying that an estate is held on lease by a tenant as long as he pays his rent regularly.

One must remember that all land belonged to the king who gave his barons large tracts of land as feuds; they in their turn subdivided their tract into fiefs, the holders of which were known as vassals and the service they rendered as vassallage. It was obvious that if a particular baron was given a large and well-populated tract he might become too powerful to manage. This was avoided by giving him bits in various places. Many of them were jealous of each other so they took good care that the out-lying men of any particular baron did not cross their land to give him a united force which he was quite likely to use against them. William did, however, make three exceptions to this rule by creating three palatinates – those of Durham, Shropshire, and Cheshire. This meant that the palatine earls had complete control as regards the laws and government of their palatines. The idea was sound when one visualizes the state of communications at the time. The palatines of Shropshire and Cheshire were responsible for guarding the rest of the country against the incursions of the Welsh, that of Durham for guarding the northern border against the Scots.

In the first instance every baron had to give an oath of allegiance to the king that he would faithfully carry out his contract which, though generally concerned with rendering military service, occasionally varied, as did what was held in feud. For instance, certain rights were given, but it would take us too far off the track if we went into all the details.

The last war showed how a certain balance in manpower must be maintained if the country is to function at all. You can lose a war and ruin a country just as quickly by calling up too many men as by calling up too few. If every able-bodied man is called up the land, the factories and hundreds of other functions will cease. William was not such a fool that he did not realize this so he introduced the payment of fees in lieu of service, and in so doing killed two birds at once for he ensured that he got some money and did not cause too much dislocation.

In a rather round about way, the system gave a sense of security to the vassals for they expected protection from their lords. If someone came and stole their cattle they could run to 'Muvver' and pour out their woes. If a baron, or for that matter a vassal, misbehaved himself he would have his feud or fief forfeited and, in addition, he would receive personal injury which made him toe the feudal line so to speak.

The idea was sound in theory but based on a fallacy for no man can serve two masters. When it comes to a decision he will decide which to follow after weighing up his personal likes and dislikes and noting which side his bread is buttered. It is difficult to be too loyal to somebody you have never seen and who does nothing for you when it comes to deciding between him and the other fellow to whom you owe almost everything you possess. In course of time the barons became self supporting with views of their own as to how things should be done. The oath to them proved stronger than their's to the king. The result was that the tail began to wag the dog – especially if two or more barons joined forces.

Let us now examine the system by which men were mustered for service.

The first thing that happened was that the king issued a proclamation under his seal. These proclamations were under the care of the Keeper of the Pells, or Keeper of the Rolls, a title which was subsequently altered to that of Master of the Rolls.

These titles are interesting and call for some explanation before we proceed.

There was no paper in those days so that all writing was done on either parchment or vellum. The differences between these two terms is. I expect my reader already knows, that parchment is made from the skins of lambs or kids, while vellum is made from that of calves.

The word 'pell' is derived from the French 'pel' or the Latin 'pellis', meaning a skin. The Keeper of the Pells was, therefore the keeper of the skins on which royal proclamations had been written. We still have a Master of the Rolls.

The pells which bore the names of those liable for service

were comparatively narrow and long, like (forgive me for saying so) toilet rolls. They were usually wound over a short stick so that they could be easily undone and allowed to roll over the hands of the caller.

The arrangements between the king and his barons were, as regards military service, private or close. The rolls which bore the names of the senior nobles were, therefore, called Close Rolls.

The calling out of the army was done by the sheriffs who were of two kinds, those appointed to the country by the king and those elected by the inhabitants. The resident sheriffs were sort of garrison commanders. These garrisons must not be confused with those which we have today in which men are housed in either ultra-modern or super-old buildings from the area of which bugles may be heard when the inmates are hungry, or tired and want to go to bed. The garrisons of the times with which we are dealing were more in the nature of localities over which certain nobles had control, and were responsible for the production of a stated number of soldiers whose particulars were recorded by the sheriff. The representatives which the king sent to each county were known as his lieutenants. Lieutenants of counties were appointed for the first time in about 1549, but it was not until after the Tudor period that every county had its own Lieutenant.

In addition to the men raised in England for service abroad the king employed mercenaries whom he hired with money from the King's Purse, which is another way of saying that, if he wanted mercenaries, he had to pay for them out of his own pocket.

It will be seen that the military forces available were made up to those furnished by the nobles, those compelled to serve under the orders of the sheriff (*posse comitatus*), and mercenaries.

The posse comitatus was the man power of the country and comprised all fit males between the ages of fifteen and seventy. From the point of view of liability to serve in the army the age limit was sixty. On being summoned by the sheriff, whether personally or by proclamation, all men were bound to attend the muster under penalty of severe and brutal punishment. As we are only dealing with the military aspect of the calling out, we need not go into the details of the duties which the sheriff could order to be carried out. It was pertinent to say that men so called up could not be used for service abroad and only in very exceptional circumstances outside their own counties. As a matter of fact their obligations were almost identical with those of the Home Guard of the last war.*

When the sheriffs summoned the men to muster for war, but not for training, they also issued orders that a certain number of horses, tools, provisions, clothing, etc, should be taken to the churchyards and placed at the disposal of the clergyman who was responsible for their custody until taken over by the sheriff in person. There were terrible penalties for those who did not comply with this order and even worse for those who stole from the accumulated stock. It is unnecessary to enumerate all the punishments, but it is interesting to note that for what were described as petty thefts consisted of having pitch poured over the head and body and then being covered with feathers. It is also worth noting that no guards were placed over the accumulated stores which were only protected by the fear of dreadful torture.

The clergy were paid a commission on the value of all that they collected so that what with the sheriff's men and the clergy making thorough searches that nothing that might possible be of value was overlooked, we can surmise that the wretched inhabitants had a busy and anxious time. The bishops were especially charged with producing the finest horses so there must have been some compensation for those with a sense of humour watching and listening to the local bishop turned knacker.

We have seen how armies were raised when required and have been able to form our own opinions as to the time lag that must have ensued between the issue of the first order and the mustering at the port of embarkation, or the place where the operation was to start. Though there has been no mention of a standing army I think that it is reasonable to suppose that the king took care to see that he had a small body of men available though doubtful whether they were the same ones for any long period. Though his power was strong he had to gang warily so as not to annoy the many powerful factions in the country.

* The general idea of sheriffs and posses in the maintenance of law and order will be familiar to all lovers of Western movies.

Another sobering factor was that he had to pay for such men out of his own purse so that if he kept more than the bare minimum continually at his call there would be little in the kitty should urgent need arise. The power of money has been a powerful factor with both kings and commoners since the days of barter.

It would be wearisome in the extreme to give more than a few examples as to what happened in our early history but I think that it would be a grave omission not to mention any.

The king convenanted with certain persons to serve him on varying monetary terms with a specified number of followers on specifically named expeditions.

Let us look at one or two examples which I have taken from *Baronage of England* written by Sir William Dugdale in 1675–76 We can hardly choose a better person from whom to quote for he had been Clerk of the Pells in the Exchequer and so had access to authorative information.

A Man-at-Arms c 1450.

An interesting example of the payment in kind to which I have made reference is contained in the agreement between Edward III and Michael Poynings. He was to serve the king with fifteen men at arms, four knights, ten squires, and twelve archers, having an allowance of twenty-one sacks of the king's wool for his wages.

In 1349 the same king engaged Sir Thomas Ughtred to serve him in his wars beyond the seas, with twenty men at arms and twenty archers on horseback, with £200 as his wage per annum during the continuance of the war.

In 1400 Henry IV contracted with Sir William Willoughby to serve in his expedition into Scotland, with three knights and sixty-nine archers, and to continue with him from 20th June to 13th September.

Henry V retained John Holland to accompany him to France and to serve for one whole year, with forty men at arms and one hundred archers, whereof the third part were to be footmen, and to embark at Southampton on the following 10th May.

We will conclude these examples with what is probably the strangest of them all, and I confess that I am unable to understand what is meant.

In 1497 Henry VII retained John Grey to serve in his wars in Scotland, under the command of Giles Daubeney, captain-general of the king's army for that expedition; with one lance four demi-lances, and fifty bows and bills, for two hundred and ninety miles; with one lance and four demi-lances, and fifty bows and bills, for two hundred and sixty-six miles; and with two lances, eight demi-lances and two hundred bows and bills, for two hundred miles.*

The first permanent force – we cannot call it an army – in these islands, except for the House Carles of Cnut, was the bodyguard of Henry VII which is the origin of the Yeomen of the Guard.

The first standing army in Europe in anything like modern times was that formed by Charles VII of France who died in 1461. One must remember that the Channel seemed very wide in those days and formed a barrier which has been shrinking in

---

* A lance, when used in this sense, was a body of men which corresponded with our present platoon, but I have been unable to trace its exact composition. *Editor.*

width, not by any act of Nature, as invention succeeds invention. In these days water is not measured, in the military sense, by width but by time. A river is a natural barrier whose effectiveness is judged by the length of time it will take to erect a bridge over it. Even the North Atlantic is only four and a half hours wide at the time of writing.

A Bowman c 1340.

There was no need for a standing army as a protection against overseas invasion. If, however, we wished to go over we could take our time. Another factor which somewhat tended to make a standing army unnecessary was that there were no scientific weapons which called for special skill and training to obtain the best results. Mr Brown, the blacksmith, could drop his hammer and take up his battle-axe and, after a few practice twirls, be a real danger to anyone within range. All he wanted was showing which way to go, and the colours worn by his friends and foes so that he knew which to clout. A few blacksmiths going in the right direction must have wanted some stopping!

The reader is probably wondering from whence came the

large number of archers who are credited with having played such important parts in our early victories. The answer is that archery was the chief, and almost only, sport in the country for the yeomen. As soon as a boy had developed sufficient strength to draw a bow he was taught how to use it, so that all men were primarily bowmen and the other qualifications were added.

It was the introduction of scientific weapons which brought about the need for a standing army as opposed to the advantage of having one. As they became more complicated, so the time taken to train men in their use became longer. There are two things to be learnt about every weapon. One is how to use it; the other how to avoid it, or its effects, when used by the other fellow.

Before a standing army could be introduced in this country, there was a greater difficulty than the advancement of science to be overcome. This was the inherent love of personal liberty. The Englishman would not tolerate the state of affairs under which he had to down tools every time the sovereign had belicose intentions, and he saw only too plainly that, if the king had a standing army under his complete control, he could enforce his will on the people. A bodyguard for ceremonial occasions was one thing, but armed might was something quite different.

We have now come to the beginning of the Civil War, which I always think is best described as the Great Rebellion for it was a rebellion of the people against the despotic rule of the sovereign backed by his control of the army.

The story of the First Civil War, with its battles of Edgehill, Newbury, Marston Moor, Newbury (again), and Naseby, with Charles I's eventual surrender to the Scots at Neward are quite outside our story except to point out that Cromwell noted that the Parliamentary forces which he commanded, though not in person at all the above places, required improvement. His reorganization started in 1645 when, as he put it, he collected men of religion to combat the Royalist forces whom he described as gentlemen of honour.

As neither side knew much about either religion or honour the results were much as to be expected. Much has been written about Cromwell's God-fearing New Model Army* but if the stark facts of history signify anything at all then Cromwell, in his religious guise, was an imposter.

A pikeman of Cromwell's New Model Army.

During his campaign in Ireland he murdered (the term today is conveniently watered down to liquidated) the whole garrisons of Drogheda and Wexford which sounds to me very much on par with the crimes committed by some of our enemies in the last war, and for which they were executed. It would seem that the enormity of a crime, or whether a crime has been committed at all, depends on which side wins!

This is conjecture so, having completed the Canute-Cromwell Military Course, let us, so to speak, unsaddle and go and find something else to interest us.

* The new model army was not Cromwell's. It was commanded throughout its existence as a separate force by Sir Thomas Fairfax with Phillip Skippon as Second-in-Command and responsible for its training and organization. Cromwell did not have an independent command till 1647 and did not become Commander-in-Chief of the Parliamentary Forces until 1650. *Editor.*

Cavalry

The earliest use of cavalry, therein called horse, that I can trace is to be found in Joshua XI. If it is true to say that the account given in the Bible refers to a date about 1450 BC, then it is also true to say that cavalry were used on battlefields for 3,389 years. I do not propose to make an attempt to give an account of its use over that period even were it of interest, and in my power to do so.

The word is derived from the Latin caballus, a horse.

Most of the wars of the ancients were for plunder for the carrying away of which the horse, owing to the absence of transport, was a necessity. It served, therefore, the dual role of being a mount and a beast of burden.

As the art of war, and the invention of new weapons, improved and increased so did the value of cavalry diminish.

The Greek and Roman armies were based on the foot soldiers, as every army has been ever since. In making this statement I have not forgotten that history is studded with examples of how battles have been won by the intelligent use of cavalry, and I have no doubt that historians of the future will be able to show exactly the same results when discussing the use of machine guns, tanks, aeroplanes, artillery, and so on.

It seems strange, but I firmly believe true, to say that pageantry and wealth supplanted the infantryman during the period of our Saxon, Norman, and Plantagenet kings. It was the appearance of gunpowder on the field that made the nobles realize that, however wonderful they might look in all their regalia, they were no match for the common man armed with a primitive firearm.

I show elsewhere how the lack of funds prevented our earlier kings from keeping standing armies, and say enough to let the reader see that soldiering was far from a profession likely to attract any man who could find employment out of it. The princes and nobles were almost continually fighting so, as they were invariably mounted, it stands to reason that they were the only ones with any military experience of cavalry. The foot soldiers were recruited from undisciplined yokels who were summoned from their work, badly clothed and fed, seldom paid, and more or less herded on to the battlefield. The same was equally true of their opponents so that one can say that all infantrymen of the period (except, perhaps, the few bands of mercenaries) were little more than armed rabbles. Strong words I agree, but how can anyone make out a case for it being otherwise?

The first English sovereign to organize his cavalry into formation was Edward III who, in 1324, divided them into small bodies each of which was commanded by a constable. I first traced the word 'troop' in Grose's account of the army before St Quentin, in 1557.

The days when the size of a victory was judged by the number of pennons captured were now nearly over. Apart from the lack of wealth thinning the ranks of mounted men there was the perfecting of artillery which fired balls which did not swerve when they found their way impeded by the body of his lordship. An attempt was made to decry this body-line bowling. but it was to no avail. The full tosses, first-bouncers, and downright sneaks had come to stay.

I cannot see that any useful purpose would be served by following the history of cavalry from the time of St Quentin to the First World War, but I do think that it would be of interest to say a few words about the origins of the various kinds which exist today, though alas only in name. When it comes to war they are all hidden in their steel juggernauts.

The two regiments which form the Household Cavalry are the Life Guards and the Royal Horse Guards and King's Dragoon Guards, all of which were raised by Charles II. The Life Guards were formed from the Cavaliers who fought for Charles I, whilst the Royal Horse Guards were recruited from members of

Colonel Unton Crook's Regiment which had fought for the Parliamentarians.

The famous historical authoress, Mrs Catherine Macaulay, in her monumental work *History of England from the Accession of James I to the Elevation of the House of Hanover*, published about 1781, has the following interesting things to say about the early history of the Life Guards.

> *The Life Guards, who now form two regiments, were then distributed (i.e. in 1661) into three troops, each of which consisted of two hundred carabineers exclusive of officers. This Corps, to which the safety of the King and the Royal Family was confided, had a very peculiar character. Even the privates were designated Gentlemen of the Guard. Many of them were of good families, and had held commissions in the Civil War. Their pay was much higher than that of the most favoured regiment of the line, and would in that age have been thought a respectable provision for the younger son of a country squire. Their fine horses, their rich housing, their cuirasses, and their buff coats, adorned with ribands, velvet, and gold lace, made a splendid appearance in St James's Park. A small body of grenadier dragoons, who came from a lower class and received lower pay was attached to each troop in 1685. In 1687 another body of Household Cavalry, distinguished by blue coats and cloaks, and still called the Blues, was generally quartered in the neighbourhood of the capital.*

The original names of the three troops to which she alludes were the King's Own, the Duke of York's, and the Duke of Albemarle's. One troop was raised in Scotland, and is found mentioned by Sir Walter Scott in his *Old Mortality*.

The Life Guards have the unique distinction of having supplied the country with a famous admiral, George Monk, Duke of Albemarle, who defeated the Dutch off Dunkirk. We, as a nation, are renowned for our powers of improvization but seldom can the Royal Navy have received such a strange order as, 'wheel to the left' from their admiral and yet won the day.*

* The present Colonel-in-Chief of the Life Guards is the famous sailor Lord Louis Mountbatten. *Editor.*

3. An officer of the 7th Hussars, 1808.

4. *Officers of Hussars, Horse Guards, Life Guards and Footguards, 1828. Courtesy of the Marquis of Cambridge.*

The colonels of the former two regiments were known as Gold Sticks. It was their duty to attend the Sovereign on all ceremonial occasions. They did duty for alternate months and whilst so doing were styled 'Gold Stick in Waiting'. The field officer of the same regiment as the colonel doing duty was known as 'Silver Stick in Waiting'. The colonel of the Royal Horse Guards was added to the duty roster in 1820, so there are still two Gold and Silver Sticks in Waiting.

The two regiments of Life Guards were amalgamated in 1921.

The Royal Horse Guards received the prefix 'Royal' in 1690, and in the same year the title by which they are best known, 'The Blues' or to be precise, 'The Oxford Blues'. This last

A Horse Grenadier, c 1687.

title was given to them at the Battle of the Boyne to distinguish them from the Dutch Horse Guards which also wore a blue uniform. They were amalgamated with the Royal Dragoons in 1969 to form the 'Blues and Royals'.

Dragoons were introduced into the English army at the time of the Civil War though cavalrymen taught to fight on foot, and suitably armed to do so, had been in existence for some years on the continent.

E

The date of the introduction is 1645 though the first regiment to be formed was the Royal Scots Greys, in 1681, now the Second Dragoons. The First (Royal) Dragoons was raised in 1661 when it was known as the Earl of Peterborough's Tangier Horse, but it was not incorporated into the army till 1684. Their first colonel was John Churchill, later to become famous as the Duke of Marlborough.

Historians are divided as to the origin of the word 'dragoon' and their views are so diverse that I had better give both. One

Dragoons c 1680.

group say that the origin of the word is to be found in the name of the old standard which had a representation of a dragon on it. They have taken their view from the writings of Marcellinus Ammianus, who wrote the history of Rome in about 390. I am inclined to the belief that it was taken from the dragon which was the pistol with which they were armed.

The senior regiment of Hussars in our army is the Third

(King's Own) Hussars, which was incorporated in 1685. Actually I suppose one must say that the Third Hussars no longer exist for they are now part of the Queen's Own Hussars. (In the same way the 5th Lancers are now part of the 16/5th Lancers.)

Here again there is a difference of opinion as to the origin of the word. The general one seems to be that it is derived from the peculiar cry of the men in action. If this is so, and regiments were named after the remarks of the men in action, I shudder to think what would be the titles of some of our regiments named after the remarks that I have heard in action.

Lifeguard, c 1900.

In my opinion the word is of Hungarian origin, or Polish perhaps, as this species of light cavalry constituted the national militia of these two countries.

Corvinus Matthias, King of Hungary (1458–90) ordered that every twenty houses were to provide one horseman for his army; hence from 'huzz' meaning twenty, and 'ar' meaning pay, we get, if my contention is correct, the word hussar.

The senior regiment of Lancers is the Fifth (Royal Irish) Lancers which dates from 1858 though they owe their origin to the Fifth Royal Irish Dragoons which was formed in 1690 and later disbanded.

The cavalry regiments still retain their titles and some have amalgamated but I hope that no Government ever tries to find an excuse to deprive us of those wonderful spectacles which can be seen on royal occasions, and others of a more light-hearted nature such as tattoos, etc.

We have institutions which have taken us centuries to perfect which could be obliterated almost by the stroke of a pen. The band of the Household Cavalry is one; the Sovereign's mounted escort is another. In them, and others like them, are to be found the very roots of our heritage which are unique the world over.

Let those who prefer it have their processions in which their head of state goes by in a mass-produced motor car surrounded by motor cycles.

The British Army will for ever owe the horse a very deep sense of gratitude – the civilian as well for that matter – and, in my view at any rate, it would be a disgraceful action to allow that fact to be forgotten by replacing him on state occasions.

Artillery

The origin of the word is uncertain. The French philologist, Ménage, in his *Origines de la Langue, Française*, published in 1650, says that it is derived from 'artiller', to fortify; whilst Vossins, the Dutch classical scholar, writing two years later, attributes it to 'arcus', a bow.

The term in its original sense referred to the weapons and what they fired, but today we use it to denote the weapons and the personnel that man them.

The employment of instruments to throw heavy objects is of very early origin. In 2 Chronicles, Chaper XXVI, verse 5, there is an account of how Uzziah (1000 BC) made, in Jerusalem, 'engines invented by cunning men to be upon the towers and upon the bulwarks, to shoot arrows and great stones withal'.

Artillery is really the evolution of the sling used by David. As the weapon for throwing stones became more efficient so the size of the missile increased till it became so large that it had to be mounted on some form of framework. Archery is nearly as old as the Creation for we read in the Book of Genesis, Chapter XXI, that Abraham dwelt in the wilderness and became an archer.

The bow was succeeded by the long-bow, cross-bow, and arbalist (or arbalast), which was in use till the battle of Bosworth, 1485. The arrows which were shot from cross-bows were known as quarrels, or bolts (hence the expression 'to shoot one's last bolt). They were additionally weighted at the head with heavy or sharp pieces of metal to destroy gateways and other entrances to fortifications.

Vegetius, writing in the fourth century, refers to such strange-sounding instruments as scorpiones, arcubalistae, fustibuli, and fundae as 'engines of artillery'. Balistarii and arcubalistarii, who might be considered as the forerunners of artillerymen, are mentioned in the Domesday Survey.

The advent of gunpowder did not mean that the old weapons were immediately scrapped any more than that the jet engine immediately replaced the piston one. The weapons employing explosive had to show their capabilities before the older ones were proved to be out of date. The arrival of gunpowder did, however, alter the art of war and, as this changed, so did the role of the older weapons gradually lose importance so they had to go.

The invention of gunpowder is generally credited to the Franciscan monk, Michael Schwartz, of Goslar, near Brunswick, in about 1330. This may be true as regards gunpowder, but it is said that explosives of some sort were known to the Chinese for centuries prior to its use in Europe. The embrasures in the Great Wall of China, built two centuries before Christ, are said to have been made to accommodate artillery of some sort though this may well have been of the catapult variety. Accounts relate that the Arabs used explosives during the siege of Mecca in 690 AD. It is also known to have been used during the war between the Chinese and Tartars in 1232. The first use in Europe that I have traced was during the siege of Seville, 1247. Roger Bacon, the philosopher, who died in 1294, mentions gunpowder so that it is almost more than certain that there was an explosive propellant in use before the battle of Crecy. The idea, however, that this was the first occasion in which cannons (then known as bombards) were used is so fixed in the minds of those who have any ideas on the subject that it seems almost heresy to dare to suggest that it could be otherwise.

Let the following accounts from the Grafton Chronicles speak for themselves and the reader consider whether he is still of the opinion that artillery, using some form of explosive, were first employed during that battle.

Henry III 1267.   In the rebellion which was led by the Duke of Gloucester, the King approached London with his army, which made daily assaults during which guns and other ordnance were shot into the city.

Edward III 1322.   The King fought the battle of Leydale, in

Northumberland, where he lost his ordnance which was conveyed to Scotland.

Edward III 1338.   In this year it is recorded that the King crossed over to Flanders with his army and artillery intending to attack France.

Edward III 1342.   The Scots besiege the castle of Estrevelin using engines and cannon.

Edward III 1343.   The King, together with his army and artillery, besieges Vannes.

Edward III 1344.   In this year we find mention of 7 armourers, and 12 artilleriens and gunner.

Artillery developed considerably from 1400 onwards and special pieces were made for special purposes as was the case with the pre-explosive weapons.

Before dealing – very briefly indeed – with the early cannons, a few words of explanation are necessary concerning what was known as Greek fire, and fire balls, in case they are confused with early artillery.

Little, if anything, is known as to the composition of Greek fire which was kept secret by the Greeks of the Byzantine Empire for war use. It is, I think, reasonable to suppose that naptha played an important part in its composition. Whatever it was made of, it is recorded as being able to burn both on land and water so must have been most effective against wooden fortifications and ships. There is an account of how it was used to destroy the Saracen fleet which attacked Constantinople in about 670 AD. It was discharged from engines invented by Callincicus, but they are not described. The casualties to the attackers are given as 30,000 which gives some idea of the whole-hearted way these people did things with what we would now call primitive weapons.

Fire balls were something quite different altogether and did not, in their first use at any rate, have anything to do with artillery. They were balls fixed to arrow-heads which were wrapped in some material that had previously been soaked in tallow which was ignited before being discharged. The same sort of thing was done with missiles thrown by balistas, catapults, and similar weapons.

The earliest cannons were made from lengths of iron banded with metal rings with the centre left open to take the charge and shot. The whole was mounted at the end of a stout piece of timber which was pivotted along its length to allow for elevation and depression. Their accuracy must have been precisely nil so that their effect was moral rather than actual. The science of making cannons was first taken seriously during the fifteenth century during which the barrel and the contrivance on which it was mounted were co-ordinated so that the two became known together as the weapon, or piece. In this century, too, an attempt was made to make cannons mobile by adding small wheels to the carriage so that the whole looked somewhat like the cannons on early men-of-war. The wheels were later enlarged so that the pieces could be drawn along the road by special horses or, in the case of the heavier ones, by oxen.

These earliest weapons must have been a danger to friend and foe alike for a fragment from one which exploded struck James II of Scotland during the siege of Roxburgh Castle, in 1459, and he died from the wound.

The method of casting was introduced towards the end of the fifteenth century when a mixed metal known as font-metal was invented.

Stowe tells us in his Annals, published in 1580, that John Owen, the first Englishman to make artillery, began to make brass ordnance known as cannons and culverins (which was the name given to the heavier pieces) in 1535. The actual design did not alter much in the succeeding century though it was found that a greater diameter of the bore did not necessarily increase the range so that the thickness of the metal was increased to withstand a greater charge and, subsequently, it was found that the length of the barrel had an effect on accuracy so that was lengthened.

A fine example of one of these early guns was known as Queen Elizabeth's Pocket Pistol which is 24 feet long. This was cast at Utrecht in 1544 and is to be seen in Dover Castle. Another, and earlier, example is Mons Meg which is said to have been cast at Mons in 1485, though I prefer to believe that it was cast nearer my home town by the M'Kim brothers, in 1455, and given by them to James II, whom I have just mentioned, to assist in the siege of Thrieve Castle (now in ruins) about two miles out of Castle Douglas, Kircudbrightshire. This piece was in London till

1829 when, at the special request of Sir Walter Scott, it was presented to Edinburgh.

In mentioning John Owen as the first Englishman to cast cannon in this country I am aware of the claim of John Hugget. He, however, unless I am sadly mistaken, did not commence making cannons at Uckfield, Sussex, till 1543 – eight years after Owen.

Muzzle loading weapons continued in use till the end of the nineteenth century. The first efficient breech-loading and at the same time rifled artillery piece, was invented by William Armstrong in 1859. Its first use in war was at the bombardment of the Chinese entrenchments at Sinho on 12th August, 1860. Muzzle-loading rifled artillery was first used by us in action on 17th October, 1854, against the forts at Sebastopol, during the Crimean War, but they were not a success.

In somewhere about 1836, a Mr Tucker proposed a method of breech loading guns which intrigues me. The barrel was to be bored completely through from front to rear. A hole was then bored vertically through the barrel some distance from the rear (or breech) end. Into this a sort of tap was to be fitted exactly like those on a beer barrel (probably why the idea fascinated me!). The ball was then placed in the breech end of the barrel followed by the charge. Both were rammed beyond the tap which was then turned. The priming hole being immediately in front of the tap, the gun was then fired in the normal way. I like the final sentence of the description too. It reads, 'A practical objection to loading cannon, or even fowling-pieces at the breech is, that however well the joints may be made they do not long continue tight, the powder inevitably finding its way through.'

I have probably given the impression that all cannons were the same size, shape, and mounting which, of course, they were not. I do not propose to give descriptions of each improvement as they came, or of each size. I trust, therefore, that the following table, which gives the names, weight of shot, and bores of the pieces in use between about 1550–1820 will suffice. So as not to give the expert a heart attack when he reads the last sentence, I want to make it quite clear that not all the weapons I list were in use all the time, also that I have omitted to mention some. Students of early naval weapons will also have something to say about the weights of shot that I give unless they realize that weapons of the same name in the two services did *not* fire the same weight of shot.

Name of piece	Weight of shot	Bore
Falcon	2 lbs	2 ins
Mynion	4 lbs	$3\frac{1}{2}$ ins
Saker	$5\frac{1}{2}$ lbs	$3\frac{1}{2}$ ins
Demi-Culverin	$9\frac{1}{2}$ lbs	4 ins
Culverin	17 lbs	$5\frac{1}{2}$ ins
Demi-Cannon	32 lbs	7 ins
Cannon	—	—

Anything larger than a demi-cannon was referred to as a cannon, and they most certainly varied in size! There is, for instance the old Mooke-e-Maedan at Beejapoor with a bore of some 27 inches. I am very loath to mention Indian place names for I have found that my spelling of them never seems to be the favourite one of the reader. In one book I spelt the name of the place where I was born as given on my birth certificate. I now know that it has various ways of being spelt each of which is correct. I feel that the truth is that anyone who argues about the spelling of place names in India is admitting that he knows precious little about the country as, for instance, this place Beejapoor might well be spelt Bejapur, Bejapoor, Bejirpur and so on. I have four atlases and, strange to say (as though proving my point), it is spelt differently in each!

I believe I am correct in saying that this piece is the largest cast cannon in existence. Its name means 'Lord of the plain', and it was cast to commemorate the capture of the town by the Emperor Alum Greer, in 1685. I am open to correction as regards the exact size of the bore and length, the latter being, if I remember aright, about fourteen feet. An iron shot for this weapon would have weighed about 1600 lbs.

So much for cannons, now let us pass on to howitzers which may be described as coming half way between the gun and the mortar.

I suspect that such a piece was in use before it received the name, which is derived from the German word 'häufen', to fill. It was, if my surmize is correct, called a short cannon, or short gun. The description of its being filled, rather than loaded, is correct as regards its early use. It was intended to be a short-range weapon with a wide danger area, so that it was filled with slugs or case-shot, which I will describe later. It was then, as it was in the Great Wars, primarily a weapon for use against troops in the open. It stands to reason, therefore, that the enemy is only in the open when his attacking troops are close, or when they have been blasted out of their defences and are on the run.

Short guns, by which I mean guns which were made specially shorter than the normal ones in use at the time, were used in Italy in 1618. They were introduced into France in 1683, which is about the same time as they were used in England. In the early part of the nineteenth century both iron and brass howitzers were in use and it is interesting to note that they were named differently. There were two kinds of iron ones which were referred to as the 10 inch and 8 inch howitzers; whilst those made of brass were designated by the weight of shell which they fired and calibres, viz, 24-pounders, 12-pounders, $5\frac{1}{2}$ inch and 4 inch (though the exact measurement was 4.4 ins).

In 1830, or thereabouts, the French, at the suggestion of Colonel Paixhans, and the English, under the recommendation of General Millar proposed that howitzers firing case-shot should be mounted in naval vessels. The weapons that both suggested were not exactly the same as the army ones for they were to have slightly longer barrels and use a heavier charge. The idea was that the penetrative power should be just sufficient to enable the shot to lodge in the side of the ship, or deck, so that the whole force of the explosion should catch those in the open. I cannot trace such weapons having been used in action by us, but one can well imagine that they would have been extremely efficient and that a few of them landing on the deck at the same time would have given the literate members of the crew something to write home about.

Mortars are really only howitzers that have been to a better school and so received a higher education, or, in this case, elevation. The first record of their use that I can find was by Charles VIII, of France, when he captured Naples in 1495. I don't think there is much need for elaboration as regards these weapons which were of large bore and very short range. Here I am open to every form of correction when I say that I think the largest mortar ever made was that known as the Mallet (after its inventor Robert Mallet). In 1857 it fired, at Woolwich, a shell weighing 2250 lbs a distance of 2,500 yards. This must have made some of the housewives along the river front wonder what the next war would be like.

I cannot leave the subject of mortars without mentioning Menno van Coehoorn. He was a Dutch military engineer who, in 1674, invented something which was to cause many of us considerable inconvenience in the years to come – the hand, or trench, mortar. An early description described it as 'capable of being carried about and served by one man; consequently it can be readily brought up to a convenient spot, and rapidly fired when it is intended to drive the defenders from behind the parapets'. These weapons were called coehorns. Its missiles were termed grenades, and I think that it must be agreed that it would be difficult to find a better description for our 2 inch mortar and rifle grenade. The French for stone is pièrre, and they had a small weapon, known as a pièrrier, for throwing small stones, as late as 1840, but I cannot say when it was first used, or discarded.

Another interesting type of mortar was known as the partridge. This is rather a difficult weapon to describe so I must ask the reader to imagine a cannon with an exceptionally thick barrel, so thick that it had thirteen small bores drilled round its circumference. The central, and larger, bore was loaded with shot, the thirteen smaller with grenades. The shot and grenades were discharged at the same time.

A unique type of mortar was the rock-mortar, of which one was made at Gibraltar in 1771, and others in Malta. These were holes made in the rock face about four feet long and three wide at the opening. They were loaded with a charge of 27 lbs of powder and 1,470 stones (so the account says). The discharge sent a quarter of the stones a distance of 100 yards; but, we are left to wonder what happened to the remaining 1,102.

A petard was really a mine so should not find a place in this chapter. They were a Huguenot invention of 1579 which were used most effectively by Henry IV in the taking of Cahors, in

1580. 'Hoist with his own Petard' is an expression used by Shakespeare in Hamlet.

So much for the weapons, now for a few words about the propellants.

The gunpowder invented by Swartz was known as black powder which remained in use till the early nineteenth century. It had the great disadvantage that a certain small residue was left behind after each explosion so that there was always the danger that a particle might be still alight when the next charge was loaded.* It was followed in turn by white powder, protected gunpowder, pellet gunpowder, and, by the Germans at any rate, brown, or cocoa, powder.

Gun-cotton, which owes its name to the fact that it was made from shredded cotton soaked in a mixture of nitric acid and sulphuric acid in equal proportions, was invented by a Swiss, Professor Schönbein, in 1846. It was one of the first explosives which was ignited by detonation instead of ignition. In 1855 the government set up a factory to make the stuff at Stowmarket and called the manufactured article patent safety gun-cotton. In 1871, however, the factory was blown up. As far as I know the product was never used as an artillery propellant but, when mixed with camphor, was used in the manufacture of imitation ivory billiard balls. Cordite was invented in 1889 by Sir Frederick Abel working with Professor James Dewar, and gets its name from the fact that it is in strips rather like macaroni.

Having dealt with the pieces and the propellants, we now come to the projectiles.

The earliest were known as shot or cannon balls, the latter term being used till the time of their discontinuance. Then came chain, grape, cannister, shrapnel, and so on, and this list is far from complete of all the names used to denote what was fired from weapons of various kinds.

The earliest shot, sometimes also referred to as bolts were probably made from anything handy that would go down the barrel. We know that Henry V, in 1418, ordered his Clerk of

---

* For this reason the barrel was sponged out with a wet sponge before reheating. The sponge was on one end of the ramrod, and a water bucket could often be seen either hanging from the gun axle or beside the gun when in action. *Editor.*

the Ordnance to have 700 stone shot made from the quarries at Maidstone. The last solid shot to be used were known as Palliser's chilled metal shot which was introduced in 1866 but, owing to the introduction of the rifled gun, had a short life.

Chain shot consisted of two iron balls joined together by a length of chain eight to ten inches long. They were mainly confined to naval use for cutting masts and rigging.

Grape shot was an assemblage consisting of a cylindrical container in which there were nine balls, which varied in size according to the bore of the weapon from which they were fired. Will the reader imagine that he is looking at one of the skewer-type receipt files, with a circular base and the hook at the top cut off. The diameter of the base is made to fit the gun as it is this base which comes next to the charge and takes the force of the explosion. He now puts nine balls in a net bag and threads the skewer through the centre, and then ties a cord round it so that its total external diameter does not exceed that of the base of the file. This, then, is what the grape shot looked like before being slid down the muzzle. The force of the explosion broke the cord so that the balls dispersed with what we would now call a shrapnel effect. It was most effective at short range against the massed columns that were considered the fashion for so many years until the Boers, and the advent of the machine gun, proved its stupidity. As a matter of fact grape shot was really only a variation of case shot. This consisted of a very light case filled with pellets. The base of the case was made strong enough to withstand the force of discharge, but the sides were very thin so that they disintegrated as soon as they left the muzzle.

General Shrapnel invented his famous shell in 1785. This was a cylindrical container fitted with a time fuse and filled with balls. The discharge ignited an internal fuse which set off a small charge which was just sufficient to expel the steel balls from the case whilst the latter was still in flight.

The artillery parachute flare and smoke shell were invented by Colonel Boxer in 1860.

A bomb, or what was sometimes called a carcass, is, in its general sense, very difficult to define for the term has come to be used so loosely. We say that a bomb was thrown at a carriage when we really mean a grenade, so that in the next few lines I refer to the term in its original use and sense.

A bomb, which is thought to have derived its name from the sound made at its discharge or bursting, was a hollow globe of iron filled with gunpowder, or some slow-burning material fired with a high trajectory so as to go through roofs and then ignite the interior of the buildings.

It is said by Strada in his account of the wars in the Low Countries, that they were used for the first time by Ernest, father of Charles, Count of Mansfeldt, in 1588 at the seige of Wachtendonk, near Gelders. He states that they were invented by an inhabitant of Venlo a few days before the seige. So keen were the inhabitants to exhibit the idea in the presence of the Duke of Cleves that they fired one and burnt down three-quarters of their own town.

In a translation of a work by Valturinus, made in 1555, there is a print representing a cannon which has just fired showing an ignited ball in the air and another on the ground alongisde the piece. As the first edition of this author's work is dated 1472, it would seem that Strada is about a hundred years out. Blondel, in his *L'Art de Jetter les Bombes* says that they were first used by the French at the seige of La Mothe in 1634. So, having laid this information before the reader concerning when they were supposed to have been invented, I pass!

The term bomb-proof was used to describe buildings and structures generally whose roof was considered strong enough to withstand the entry of the largest bomb. Incidentally, in my researches into the early use of bombs, I came upon the term blindage of which I had not previously heard. It meant the art of constructing bomb-proof buildings.

Having dealt with the weapons and how and what they fired, we must say a few words concerning the personnel and organization.

The first mention that I can find of any sort of organization as regards artillery dates from the reign of Edward III, who, in 1344, formed an ordnance train of 340 men which was composed of twelve artillerymen, the rest were artificers. In 1415, at the seige of Harfleur, there is mention of twenty-five master gunners and fifty servitour gunners. In this connection one must remember that the term ordnance included everything that was carried on wheels, so that the numbers given as representing the strength must not be taken to mean that all the men were employed with something to do with artillery. In 1455 Thomas Vaughan Esq was referred to as the Master of Ordnance, and in the next year John Judd was commissioned as Master General of Ordnance. In 1483 Raufe Bygood (some authorities give the name as Rauf Bigod) was appointed Master of Ordnance with John Stoke as Clerk. The wages of the latter were fixed at sixpence a day for life, so he becomes, as far as I am concerned, the first military man with an assured future. The style of Master of Ordnance was not abolished till 1852, but in 1519 another, known as Master of the Armoury, was instituted. In 1555 Sir Richard Southwell was appointed Master of the Ordnance and Armoury. There is evidence that the posts of Provost Marshal and Master of Ordnance were somewhat intermingled and it is difficult to decide which were the exact duties of each. During the sixteenth century, when operations were impending, Ordnance Traynes (Trains) were formed suitable for the operation in mind. These were sub-divided in various parts which were made responsible for the artillery, supplies of all kinds, baggage, and all the other items necessary for an army in the field.

The term train has now given way to that of column, for we speak of Ammunition Columns, Ration Columns, Petrol Columns, and so on.

In 1683 a Royal Command appointed five principal officers of Ordnance in addition to the Master-General. They were Lieutenant-General of Ordnance, Surveyor-General of Ordnance, Clerk of the Ordnance, Keeper of the Stores, and Clerk of the Deliveries.

On 16th June, 1685, James II commanded Lord Dartmouth, then Master-General of Ordnance, to instruct the Store Keeper at Portsmouth to prepare a Train of Artillery to oppose the Duke of Monmouth. The personnel required was carefully worked out on a basis of one gunner and one matross to each piece. A matross, which rank was abolished in 1783, assisted the gunner in loading, traversing, and cleaning the piece.

The person in charge of the weapons and crews was known as a fire-master, and he was responsible for seeing that the men were efficient in gunnery and in the use of the petard, which was the forerunner of what we in the last war called a sticky grenade, or limpet mine.

Prior to 1685 artillery pieces were allotted to infantry regiments who were made responsible for conveying them to the required positions – in other words the artillery had to rely on the infantry to move it if no civilian contractors were available.

In the next year, 1686, the ranks of bombardier and petardier were instituted to assist the fire-master.

Artillery of the time of Malborough.

In the important year of 1685 another interesting innovation took place in that two regiments were formed whose duty was to guard the artillery train. They were styled Our Regiment of Ordnance, and Our Regiment of Fusiliers, which later became The Second Battalion The Royal Fusiliers (City of London Regiment).

As a result of complaints made by the Duke of Marlborough concerning the unsatisfactory state of the Ordnance, and the difficulty of raising Artillery Trains when required for service, His Majesty issued a Royal Warrant, dated 26th May, 1716, which authorized the establishment of two Artillery Companies, each to consist of a captain, 2 lieutenants, 3 serjeants, 3 corporals, 3 bombardiers, 30 gunners, and 50 matrosses. On 11th June, 1720, a second company was added, and a colonel, lieutenant-colonel, and a major added to the establishments. In

F

1727 the number of companies was increased to four, and later further companies were added.

By an order dated 1st April, 1722, the companies were grouped and granted by George II the title of The Royal Regiment of Artillery, and appointed Colonel Albert Borgard, a Dane, who had previously served in both the Danish and Prussian armies, to be its first Colonel.

In the following years the number of companies had so increased that on 11th August, 1757, the King commanded that

Royal Fusiliers, c 1700.

the regiment be divided into two battalions, each with its own Colonel Commandant, field officers, and staff. The first battalion consisted of twenty-one companies under Colonel Commandant William Belford, the second of twenty-two companies under Colonel Commandant Borgard Michaelson.

The Royal Irish Artillery was formed in 1755 under Captain John Stratton and served with distinction in Holland, America, and the West Indies before being amalgamated with the Royal Artillery in 1801.

The artillery in our former Indian Army was formed in 1784, when the East India Company formed an artillery company in each of the three Presidencies, each of which was to be composed of 115 officers and other ranks as follows: 1 second captain, 1 captain-lieutenant and director of laboratory, 1 first lieutenant fire-worker, 1 second lieutenant fire-worker, 1 ensign fire-worker, 4 serjeant-bombardiers, 4 corporal-bombardiers, 2 drummers, and 100 gunners. In the following year Benjamin Robins, the philosopher and mathematician who was responsible for much research into the flight of projectiles, was appointed Engineer-General and Commander-in-Chief of Artillery. This extraordinary man was offered the choice between this post and that of one of the commissioners for settling the boundaries of Acadia (the former French colony in North America). Having accepted the former, he landed in India in July, 1750 but died exactly a year after from fever at the early age of forty-four. The rapid promotion from civilian to this high-sounding rank overnight is even better than the jet-propelled promotions now in vogue, but even today the rank commander-in-chief means very little, especially in the navy, wherein a fleet is now little more than a squadron probably led by a 7,000 ton cruiser.

The need for mobile artillery caused, in 1793, four troops of Horse Artillery to be formed which were originally named after the first four letters of the alphabet. It was at Egmont-op-Zee, in Holland, in 1799, that the 15th Hussars won renown in recapturing the guns of 'A' troop.

The idea that the guns should be drawn by civilian contract was realized to be absurd in 1794, when a unit known as The Driver Corps was formed whose title was changed to that of Corps of Gunners and Drivers and, finally, to that of The Corps of Artillery Drivers, which was disbanded in 1822 and the members transferred to the Royal Artillery.

The term battalion gave way to that of brigade in 1859, when that of troop was altered to battery. The term troop was, however, retained to denote a subdivision of a battery.

The title of 'Right of the Line' was bestowed on the King's Troop, Royal Horse Artillery by the younger son of George II, the Duke of Cumberland, on 15th April 1756, whe he ordered that they take the right of all foot on all parades, and likewise of dragoons when dismounted

Engineers

Trying to trace who was the first military engineer would be like looking for a needle in a haystack without being certain that the search was being made in the right stack.

The ancient armies must have had men with a very sound knowledge of engineering in many of its branches, for how else did the masses of men manage to cross the rivers and similar obstructions which have always impeded movement?

One of finest, and best organized advances in history, at any rate to my way of thinking, is that of Hannibal who left New Carthage in the late spring of 218 BC and crossed numerous rivers, and both the Pyrenees and Alps with an army of some 60,000 foot and 12,000 horse. In the next year he defeated the army, under the Roman consul Flaminius, near Lake Trasimenus; and, in the next year, annihilated some 70,000 Romans near Cannae, in Apulia. How could a man maintain a campaign for sixteen years and fight the numerous actions that he did without engineers? You cannot go on a safari in Africa without either yourself, or one of your members, having some idea how to build things. We know that Hannibal used some form of explosive, or had a method of disintegrating rock, probably with a form of vinegar, so that he must have had men trained in this art.

However, let us leave the period when we know that there must have been engineers and see if we can trace the first person whom we might be justified in calling the original English military engineer.

I have seen it stated that the first was the Earl of Derby, in 1340, but I think that we can go back farther than that and still be reasonably certain of our ground. We must remember that we are not looking for the term engineer but ingeniator – which strikes me as a delightful name for one who has to think up ways and means of doing so many different things.

In 1086, one Waldivus Ingeniator was given nine manors in the County of Lincolnshire for his services to William the Conqueror during the Norman invasion. Now, if Waldivus is called an engineer, and rewarded for his services during the invasion, are we expected to believe that they were other than of an engineering nature?

Gundulf, a Norman prelate, who was made Bishop of Rochester in 1077, was architecturally responsible for, among other buildings, the White Tower in the Tower of London, started in 1078; and might be called an engineer in the old sense for the terms architect and engineer were used somewhat indiscriminately.

During the reign of Henry III (1216–1272) Corfe Castle, in Dorset, was used as a factory for making engines of war with Peter Ingeniator in charge.

In an account of the composition of the forces engaged at the seige of Calais, in 1346–7, the following are mentioned, carpentarii, fabrii, and ingeniatores; and, a manuscript of the time of Edward III (1327–1377) mentions that he retained 57 engineers in his Ordnance.

The title of the senior engineer varied during the sixteenth century for in 1562 Sir William Pelham was appointed to the post with the rank of trench-master; twelve years later the rank was altered to that of camp-master-general. That of chief engineer originated in 1660 when we find that Captain Thomas Rudd was Chief Engineer to the Royalist Forces, and John Lyon as Chief Engineer to the Parliamentarians.

At the time when those two first cousins, William and Mary, were on the throne the appointments to the senior engineering posts were made by the king and in this connection one must remember that they were not military. The persons chosen were attached to the various trains to act in an engineering capacity and, with rare exceptions, were demobilized (or whatever the expression was in those days) as soon as the particular campaign for which they were formed was over. The nomenclatures used varied so frequently that I consider it would be more confusing than helpful if I related them. Having travelled many thousands of miles on cargo vessels, I am forcibly reminded of those journeys when reading the appointments made by William which were, Chief Engineer, Second, Third, and two other categories which were called simply Engineers. There was also one known as an Extraordinary Engineer, whose salary was greater than that of the Chief, but I never discovered what was extraordinary about him.

In studying our military history one is amazed at the amount of improvization (some may prefer to call it last-minute organization) which has invariably preceded the getting of our armies to where they were wanted, and the collecting of all the bits and pieces which it would require. The same has applied with almost equal force as regards the personnel. Without getting involved in technicalities, one might say that everybody and everything not actually wanted on the battlefield formed part of one of the various Trains, one of which was the Ordnance Train to which the engineers belonged. These, as just stated, were disbanded as soon as the campaign was over so that the army was left with no engineers.

A Royal Warrant dated 24th May, 1698, remedied this defect by establishing the first Train to exist in peace time and so, as engineers formed part, it is obvious that the history of the first peace-time engineers is linked with the history of their parent body of the time – the Ordnance Train.

This state of affairs lasted for nineteen years – till 22nd August, 1717, to be exact – when another Warrant of that date separated the Engineers from the Ordnance so that became an independent organization. They were, however, still civilians who took precedence according to their grades which, in order of seniority, were known as Chief Engineer, Directors, Sub-Directors, Engineers-in-Ordinary, Engineers Extraordinary, Sub-Engineers, and Practitioner-Engineers. I can only wonder whether the difference between them was as ambiguous to those of the day as it is to me now.

The adoption of army titles was approved by a Warrant dated 18th November, 1782, when the different grades were abolished never, thank heaven, to reappear.

One of the landmarks in the history of the Corps took place

in 1787 when, on the 25th April, a Royal Warrant conferred the title of Royal Engineers.

Having mentioned that all who were not actually required to be in contact with the enemy were members of one of the Trains, it is necessary to note the important date 26th May, 1716, on

Engineer officers of the time of Marlborough. The figure on the left wears the special armour worn when tunnelling or mining.

which the artillery and engineers were divided into separate services, and after which we find no mention of titles which combine two or more of the terms ordnance, artillery, and engineers.

At the outbreak of the Crimean War (1854) the Royal Engineers had reached an establishment of seven battalions of forty-eight officers each.

The reader may have noticed that so far I have only mentioned officers and said nothing about the men. The reason is simple – there were none!

The other ranks side of the present Royal Engineers only dates from 6th March, 1772, when, at Gibraltar, a corps known as the Soldier Artificer Company was formed. It subsequently attained a strength of 116 made up of men of various trades; it was officered by the Royal Engineers but the two Corps were entirely separate.

The title Soldier Artificer Company was altered to that of Royal Sappers and Miners on 4th August, 1813, and it and the Royal Engineers were amalgamated under the latter title on 17th October, 1856.

The last medals issued bearing the name of the unit as the Sappers and Miners were to the twenty men who served under Lieutenant Nugent, RE, on board HMS Duke of Wellington, and Captain King RE on the transport Julia who sailed with the fleet to the Baltic to assist in the demolition of the shore defences.

In giving this very brief outline of the Corps I have, and must, leave out so much which is of interest to those who prefer a general rather than a particular knowledge. I am far from competent to do more than scratch the surface of the many fields in which Royal Engineers have distinguished themselves.

A certain section of those who have been Her Majesty's guests – as I believe the old lags call themselves – will be interested to know that Captain Joshua Jebb, RE, after his appointment as Surveyor-General, was responsible, or partly so, for the construction of the establishments at Dartmoor, Chatham, and Portsmouth in about the 1840s when, so I read, the most advanced sanitary arrangements and a separate cell for each resident were incorporated. Judging by the books written by ex-inmates many of these 'latest improvements' are still in existence, which only goes to show that none of the modern jerry building would pass Captain Jebb's eagle eye!

The field of archaeological and other exploration is studded with the names of Engineer officers: Murdoch Smith in Asia Minor, 1860; Gill in Persia and China, 1871–8; Gordon to Equitorial Egypt, 1874–6; Shepherd through Mongolia and Siberia in 1877, and so on.

The Royal Corps of Signals, which was formed in 1920, and the Royal Air Force both owe their origins to the Royal Engineers.

The first telegraph lines laid in war were the land and submarine ones used during the Crimea, but, though the efficiency of both were well proven, nothing was done after the war till 1870, when a Telegraph Troop of the Royal Engineers was formed. Two additional companies were subsequently formed and all the units were amalgamated into a Telegraph Battalion in 1884 and first saw active service during the Egyptian Campaign, though telegraphy was used in that in Ashantee in 1873–4.

I wonder whether it would be stretching the truth too far to suggest that the germ of the Royal Air Force could be traced to the magnificent sum of £150 given to Major Templer, a Royal Engineer in the Militia, towards his experiments with military ballooning, which had already proved a great success on the continent. The first use of them by us was in the Soudan in 1885.

The aeroplane had arrived before the outbreak of the First World War and many and varied were the opinions expressed as to its future in war. There must be many who, like myself, remember those early machines and the various races and competitions which some of the daily papers organized. It seems absolutely incredible that only a little over forty years separated the dates of the race from London to Manchester and that of England to New Zealand.

The results of the early competitions demonstrated beyond a shadow of doubt that, in spite of what the critics said, the aeroplane was going to play an important part in future wars. In this connection I often wonder why people persist in calling an aeroplane a weapon; it is no more a weapon than a sword scabbard. If the danger from the skies in future wars merely consisted of falling aeroplanes the prospects would not be so terrible. It is not the plane that we are frightened of but what it can carry.

The Royal Engineers could not, naturally, sit out whilst the early planes were being developed. A detailed account of what they did is outside our story, but I must conclude by saying that they left their mark in aeronautics – at any rate as far as I am concerned – in the name of one of the early machines, the RE8. I presume that the number signified something to do with the eighth model based on the original design; what the average quartermaster would hasten to call a Mark VIII.

Medical Services

It is difficult to decide when medical officers were first appointed
to the army, for before coming to a decision one must differen-
tiate between appointments made solely for the benefit of the king
and those for that of others. If the reader agrees with me that
where we have information that only one appointment was made
we may consider it a personal one, then 1345 is the first date on
which I can trace the army having been thought of from a
medical attention point of view. In this year a surgeon was
appointed to the king's household, four for the army of North
Wales, and three for that of South Wales. In this year, too, I
found mention of inferior surgeons, who were called barbers, and
others known as field shavers, and confess that my knowledge
of the early history of surgery and medicine is not sufficient to
distinguish between the roles of these people.

Early accounts of what we would now call medical attention
make most amusing reading, and I cannot refrain from giving a
few examples and extracts.

Henry V, in 1415, engaged Master Nicholas Colnet, a
physician, to serve him for one year in Guyenne, or France. He
was to bring three archers with him, and his wages were to be
forty marks for the period plus a further twenty for the archers.
In the same year Thomas de Moretede was appointed surgeon
and had to bring with him twelve other surgeons and three
archers. His pay was to be a shilling a day and half that for
each of his assistants. He was allowed two horses and a wagon
for his transport, but his request for money with which to buy
instruments was refused. In the next year a William Brede-
wardyn was appointed to assist Moretarde, with instructions to

impress as many more surgeons as he could, as well as artificers to make instruments.

The degree of medical skill reached on the Continent in 1536 is well illustrated by the following remarks made in papers published in 1619. They state that wounds made by fiery engines should be cauterized with oil of elders mixed with a little treacle.

A famous Turin surgeon of the time is said to have used a balm for wounds which, if variety is the spice of life, might have prolonged it on that score alone without whatever therapeutic value there might be in the ingredients. The balm was made from 'two young whelps, one pound of earth worms, two pounds of the oil of lillies, six ounces of terebinth of Venice, and an ounce of aqua vitae'. Having prepared this mixture, the surgeon then called on God to witness this balm which he used on all gunshot wounds.

It is a great pity that we have no statistics concerning the mortality rates during our earlier campaigns, for we could compare them with the remarkable figure of 6 per cent which was that published for the wounded after the landings in Normandy – a figure which does more to describe the efficiency and skill of the present Corps than many thousands of words of eulogy could ever hope to do.

In 1557, during the reign of Mary, surgeons were appointed to each of the generals at a salary of a shilling a day, and further on in the same account I read that they were appointed to the cavalry at two shillings a day, and to the infantry for one shilling and sixpence. We are left to form our own conclusions as to whether the price refers to the quality of the service administered to, or that of the service itself!

During the reign of Elizabeth I (1558–1603) there was a fixed charge of twopence a week for all troops to pay for their medical attention as and when required. An abbreviated extract of the regulations reads as follows:

'Surgeons should be men of sobriety, of good conscience, and skilful in that science, able to heel all sores and wounds, especially to take out a pellet. All captains must have such surgeons, and ought to fee them to have all their oils, balms, salves and instruments, and necessary stuff . . . allowing and sparing carriage for same. That every soldier, at the pay day, to give unto the surgeon tuppence, as in times past has been accustomed, to the augmentation of his wages; in consideration whereof, the surgeon ought readily to employ his industry upon the sore and wounded soldiers. . . . Regard that the surgeon be truly paid his wages, and all monies due to him for cares that by the same he may be able to provide all such stuff as to him needful. Such surgeons must wear their baldriske, whereby he may be known in time of slaughter, it is their charter in the field.'

The mention of the baldriske is most interesting, for, in feudal times it was a belt, or band, normally worn round the waist, but sometimes over the right shoulder. It was an article of military dress, occasionally used to support the sword, which signified the dignity of the wearer, as may be noted in Westminster Abbey on the figures of the Earls of Pembroke and Lancaster. I have found a baldric (note the difference in spelling) described as a roll of material, or a roll of different bits of material, so that it may have served two purposes at the same time, one to distinguish the wearer, and, secondly, as a supply of material for bandages. The latter suggestion is, of course, merely surmize on my part.

By 1620 the pay of surgeons had risen considerably, and so had their numbers, for we find that one was appointed to every troop of a hundred men at a salary of two shillings and sixpence a day. Physicians to the General's Train received six shillings and eightpence a day, and those appointed to the General Officers of Horse four shillings. The Ordnance and Pioneers were allotted one barber surgeon at two shillings a day, and two inferior surgeons at sixpence. The latter were what we would now call medical orderlies.

I am in no position to judge the standard of medicine and surgery of any era, but, when reading between the lines of such accounts that exist concerning medical attention in the field, there can be little doubt that the wounded man was considered little more than a damned nuisance, so much so that for many years in our history the badly wounded were given a small sum of money and told to find their own way home!

The Royal Army Medical Corps, as we know it today, dates from 1660, when Charles II formed a standing army. In its initial stages it was very dispersed, for both treatment and hospital service were on a regimental basis. Every regiment had its own doctor and orderlies who wore the badges of the regiment with which they served; that of the Corps today was adopted when it took its present title in 1898.

In addition to the regimental medical staff there were garrison medical officers and hospitals, the doctors for these being specially appointed. The rest of the staff was supplied from local units, with special enlistments for dispensers and clerks. The three senior officers of the Corps were known as the Surgeon-General, Physician-General, and Apothecary-General. The medical equipment and stores were under the control of a Purveyor, who combined the duties of paymaster and quartermaster. The few 'other ranks' were known as hospital mates, hospital assistants, apothecaries' mates, and deputy purveyors.

A study of the conditions after the battles of the next few years would lead one to believe that very few of the wounded were evacuated from the scene in anything approaching the modern sense. Picked up from where they lay, yes, but only to be removed to some near-by house or barn where they were left to the mercies of the local inhabitants. It would, in my opinion, be grossly inaccurate to call such places hospitals, for on no single occasion have I found mention of the slightest effort to prepare any building with even such elementary requisites as a supply of clean (let alone hot) water. Of sanitation and hygiene there was none – in fact these were conspicuous by their absence quite apart from anything to do with the care of wounded. We must, however, be fair – or at any rate as fair as we can – and realize that there were no railways and only few and primitive roads, and that, with medical knowledge as it then was, it might well have been best to leave the wounded alone rather than complicate their injuries by a lot of inexperienced handling and jolting. It would, for instance, need a cast-iron constitution to withstand the application, whose ingredients I have just mentioned, followed by a bumpy journey which ended with being thrown on a damp and dirty cow-barn floor. One might add, having mentioned the tuppence contribution, that the wounded, having paid their money, could take their choice, and one can hardly blame them if they preferred to be left alone.

The credit for being the first to organize an ambulance service in war must be given to Baron Dominique Larrey, a French man, who joined the French army in 1792 at the age of twenty-six. He introduced what were called *ambulances volantes,* which were light vehicles that carried the necessary equipment to attend to the wounded on the field and then, when the situation permitted, removed them to what really were prepared places for giving them further attention. He went to Egypt with Napoleon in 1798 and on his return published, in 1803, what was the first account of a campaign dealing entirely with its medical aspect, with the title *Relation historique et chirurgicale de l'Expedition de l'Armée d'Orient en Egypte et en Syrie.* He had already, in 1796, published a work with the long title of *Dissertation sur les Amputation des Membres à la suite des coups de feu, étayée de plusieurs operations* in which he points out the necessity of operating as soon as possible before gangrene sets in. He foresaw the wisdom of having what in the last war were called Advanced Surgical Centres, and it seems extraordinary that such did not appear till 168 years after – which figure I arrive at by thinking that these advanced centres did not come into being till after the landing on the Normandy beaches in 1944. In this I stand to be corrected by a year or two, but I most certainly cannot recall them at the end of the 1914–18 war or, for that matter, their use during the many operations that took place in India and elsewhere between the two Great Wars.

A contemporary of Larrey was Baron Percy, who formed a corps of *brancardiers,* from whom we probably got the idea of our Bearer Corps. Percy's men were specially enlisted and trained as such, whereas ours were obtained by detailing sixteen men from each regiment to act as stretcher-bearers, which is unsound as it weakens the trained fighting strength at a time when it is most needed. That the man is a bandsman in peace time and plays boogie-woogie to perfection may be economical, and even to some an asset, but there must be a sacrifice in training and skill in one of these two extremes.

Though Marlborough had considered his wounded, I think what might be termed the first British attempt to organize a system for the care and evacuation of casualities occured during the Peninsular War, when 'Collecting Posts' for the wounded were formed which were the forerunners of the Walking Wounded

Collecting Posts of the First War. Their disadvantage like those of the Peninsular War, was that many men staggered to them and there collapsed with shock, which I imagine can be – and in many cases often is – as serious as the wound.

The surgeons present, such as Guthrie, McGrigor and Millingen, to mention only three, realized the ghastly treatment which the wounded had to endure, but could not overcome the anger of Wellington at the thought that vehicles, and a certain number of men, should be allocated to their care. The commander-in-chief was the commander-in-chief and his wishes, also his biases, ruled the day however absurd they may have seemed to the *cognoscenti* of the times.

We have never been a warlike nation so we treat wars rather as we do our weather – a beastly nuisance about which there is little that we can do, and the sooner the storm is over the better. When war breaks out we must, undoubtedly, do something about it. This something generally consists of sending the flower of our manhood to fill the gap while we do a bit of improvization, followed by large purchases of out-of-date equipment at exorbitant prices, followed again by a perfect spate of production just before the show ends and nicely in time for the stuff to be sold at knockout prices as war surplus. At any rate, who would deny that something like that has not been the case in, and after, both the two Great Wars?

To read of the state of affairs after Waterloo one would think and quite rightly so, that nothing had been done. The wounded were left to hitch-hike their way to Brussels; others, so I read somewhere, were lucky enough to have been carried on stretchers. It not only seems incredible, but is incredible, that after nine years of almost continuous fighting this state of affairs should still have existed. Sandwiched in between, or added to if you prefer, the actions from Maida (1806) and Waterloo there was the ghastly expedition to the island of Walcheren, on which some two hundred casualities were received from enemy action and nearly 24,000 from disease during the few months they were there in 1809!

In 1815 the fighting stopped and medals, for the first time in our history, were awarded to officers and men alike, but what did we do about improving the lot of the wounded and sick in any future war? The answer is simple and simply nothing.

There had been considerable fighting in Africa against the Kaffirs between 1843–5, 1846–7 and 1853–4 in which some fifteen British regiments, not to mention colonial units as well, had been engaged, but all this was a long way off, and as the medals for the first campaign were not awarded till nine years after it finished, it is more than probable that even the few who troubled to read about it cared very little what happened to the quick, the dead, and much less the wounded.

If this is not true, then it is difficult to explain how it was that, when the Crimean War broke out in May, 1854, there had been no advance whatever in the military medical situation. I find it difficult not to laugh at the true situation which prevailed during that war. It has been glamourized by a somewhat inaccurate poem, *The Charge of the Light Brigade,* in which we are told that cannons volleyed and thundered to right and left of them, being left to infer that they were firing at them, though one side of the North Valley, down which the charge took place, was in our hands. However, in a campaign during the latter part of which the commander of the Light Brigade slept on his yacht *Dryad,* which was moored in Balaklava Bay, with the permission of the commander-in-chief, it is impossible to be surprised at anything that happened. Incidentally, Lord Cardigan, the commander of the Light Brigade, came ashore on the morning of 25th October, found that he was wanted, mounted his horse, led the famous charge and then, after capturing the Russian guns, walked his horse back down the same valley, leaving his men to fend for themselves, and returned to his yacht. We often read about the *sang-froid* of the English in battle, but though I have read a good deal about our military history, this episode surpasses all the others with a large margin to spare.

When one reads this sort of thing can one wonder that the horse took precedence over medical equipment when they were re-embarked at Varna for the final stage of the journey to the peninsula?

I have made a careful study of the impedimenta that were disembarked and can only trace four vehicles which appear to have been allowed for medical use, but not a word concerning any horses to draw them! A unit designated the Hospital Conveyance Corps had been hastily scraped together – the word enlisted is hardly correct, for many of the men had not the faintest idea what they were supposed to do when they arrived at what they facetiously called the crime centre. I suspect that the whole idea behind the raising of this corps was a sort of face-saving device of the high-ups who suddenly realized how slack they had been during the last few years. I humbly apologize if I am wrong, but I have failed to find any mention of their services on any of the fields of battle. I have, however, found mention of the heroic efforts of bandsmen and the fighting personnel, under the guidance of the regimental medical officers, performing deeds of valour and self-sacrifice of which the members of the present Corps may be more than justly proud.

As a matter of strict fact, my grandfather, as CRE, was intimately connected with the building of the base hospitals at Scutari, 350 miles away from the scene of the fighting, and the state of affairs there was so terrible and outside our subject that I will leave it out. Miss Florence Nightingale, as all the world knows, did much to relieve the suffering, and it was through her writings and efforts, supported by Queen Victoria, that a Royal Commission was formed in 1857 to go into the whole matter of the care of the sick and wounded.

We must now retrace our steps so as to obtain continuity. In 1854, as already noted, the Hospital Conveyance Corps was raised, which on 21st July of the next year was amalgamated with the Land Transport Corps, which changed its title to that of the Military Train on 11th August, 1856, with the strange arrangement that the other ranks drew their pay at cavalry rates whilst the officers drew those of the infantry.

A Royal Warrant dated 11th June, 1855, announced the formation of a Medical Staff Corps, which can hardly be described as a military unit as the personnel carried no ranks in the military sense. This Corps, which had its headquarters at Chatham, was primarily responsible for the care of the sick and wounded after their return to England, though one of its companies landed in the Crimea. The rank and file had such titles as stewards, wardmasters, barbers, orderlies, cooks, and even

G

washermen. The whole Corps was a hotch-potch and it is not surprising that it did not last longer than 1856.

On 1st August, 1857, the Army Hospital Corps was formed the members of which were given army ranks and wore the same insignia. On the same date exactly seven years later the name was changed back to that of Medical Staff Corps.

The present title dates from 23rd June, 1898, when the Medical Staff Corps and the Army Medical Staff were united to form the Royal Army Medical Corps, which first went on active service as such with the Nile Expeditionary Force in the same year.

I would now say that the tables have been turned in the field of surgery as regards the civilian and military doctor, for the knowledge gained by the latter in dealing with the casualties of the two Great Wars must have been of innestimable value to the former and, I suppose, the same must be true to a certain extent as regards the prevention and cure of diseases.

I am not conversant with the numerous fields of medical science with which the Corps has had to deal since the beginning of the First World War, each with its own specialists and directorate.

Dentistry was, till 1921, a branch of the Corps, but in that year the Army Dental Corps was formed, which had the prefix 'Royal' added in 1947.

The record of the Royal Army Medical Corps is truly brilliant, for I find that up to 1945 it has gained no fewer than twenty-six Victoria Crosses, and two of the only three to which bars have been awarded.

That is a truly remarkable record, but the Corps has another which I am quite sure is very little known. It concerns the Distinguished Service Order, instituted by Royal Warrant dated 6th September, 1866. The first ever awarded to an officer was gained by Deputy Surgeon-General Stewart Lithgow. It is, of course, necessary to include the qualification 'to an officer' because, as with all Orders, the Sovereign is the first recipient after its institution.

The doctors will, I am sure, not mind if I end this story with a few words about those without whom it is inconceivable that they could work – the nursing sisters.

The early story of the part played by women in the care of the wounded is gained by inference rather than detailed knowledge. We have seen how in the primitive stages of the development of an ambulance service the idea was to get the wounded back to some village where, it is obvious, the army, so to speak, washed their hands as regards what happened to them afterwards. It is equally obvious that the maternal instinct found scope, for history is studded with various accounts of how women helped the wounded and then assisted them to find their way home. I would even go so far as to say that their help was taken for granted by both friend and foe alike. Though there are a few mentions in our early history of doctors being appointed to the army, there are none concerning women to care for the sick and wounded.

The first person who seems to have realized that women had a part to play in the care of their menfolk was Florence Nightingale during the Crimean War. She, as already mentioned, organized a team of devoted women who performed near-miracles with the slender resources available, and under conditions which would give the members of the Farmers' Union apoplexy if they heard of the same on a farm.

In spite of all her efforts, it was not till 1881 that an Army Nursing Service was formed which on 27th March, 1902, was replaced by Queen Alexandra's Imperial Military Nursing Service. Though, as I say, a regular nursing service was not formed till 1881, fourteen ladies were awarded the South Africa Medal, 1877–9, for their services during the Zulu War.

In 1907 a unit known as the First Aid Nursing Yeomanry was formed, and the ladies looked extremely becoming in their scarlet tunics, blue skirts, and forage caps. In 1936 the name was changed to that of the Women's Transport Service with the intials FANY added in brackets after it. This, much to the disgust of those serving in it, lost its identity in the ATS (Auxiliary Transport Service), though they were allowed to wear flashes bearing the words 'Women's Transport Service (FANY)' on their shoulders. In the last war they changed their role to that varying from general dogs-bodies to car greasers alternating with the duties of the ATS and became completely divorced from anything to do with the medical service except, perhaps, to drive ambulances.

In 1941 the Queen Alexandra's Imperial Military Nursing Service and the Territorial Army Nursing Service were incorporated into the temporary women's forces. This lasted till 1949 when the QAIMNS was organized into a Corps of the army with the title of Queen Alexandra's Royal Army Nursing Corps, and nurses were granted regular commissions.

Personal Firearms

It is difficult to give the complete story of the evolution of the modern rifle in strict chronological order for our knowledge is based on existing documents which were written at different times by different authors who have not gives the dates of the origins of the weapons they describe. However, I think that we shall be near enough for our purpose as regards the early firearms.

The exact date of the invention of gunpowder is undecided. It is said to have been used in China about AD 85 and its uses learnt by the Arabs and then the Crusaders who brought it to Europe. It is known that it was employed by the Arabs at the seige of Mecca in AD 690, but they claim to have learnt about it from the Indians. We see, whoever claims the credit for inventing it, that it was known a long time before it was applied to lethal purposes though I suspect that the Chinese, who invented fire-works, had a few casualties with their early catharine wheels and rockets, or whatever their special attractions were called. I am restrained from giving any particulars of its composition in case they are closely related to Greek fire, about which Gibbon gives this warning, 'the Historian who presumes to analize this extraordinary composition should suspect his own ignorance'.

Hand firearms were introduced in the fifteenth century, and their first use that I can trace was in 1430 when they were used by the Lucqueses when beseiged by the Florentines. In making this statement I have ignored the writings of Anna Comnena, the Byzantine princess and historian (1083–1148), who wrote the fifteen-volumned Alexiad in which she mentions that soldiers 'blew artificial fire upon their enemies' because she forgot to give the year in which these unfriendly acts were performed.

The hand-cannon, dating from about 1450, was the first

weapon in the long line that leads to our modern magazine rifle. It consisted of a tube with a moulded rim at the mouth, for additional strength, which was fitted to a perfectly straight piece of wood, about three feet long, like a stout broom handle. There was a hole, called a touch-hole, about an inch from the bottom for priming purposes. The cannon was fired by applying a lighted taper to the powder exposed in this hole. The later models were fitted with a small tray, or pan, in which the priming powder was placed. This pan, the precursor of the gun-lock, was placed at the right side, so as to allow a clear view down the barrel for sighting purposes.

The next weapon was known as the hand-gun which was modelled on the first. It had a longer barrel and was made of brass instead of cast iron. For those of us who are looking for origins, the most interesting thing about this particular gun is the ring which was fitted at the end of the barrel to assist in aiming – in other words the first foresight. In addition to this innovation the pan was fitted with a hinged lid to keep the rain out, and also enabled the carrier to have the gun charged at some time prior to its immediate use. The Greeks made use of such a weapon in 1453 and I have seen mention that it was found in England before this – in 1446 – but I suspect that the historian used the term hand-gun instead of hand-cannon.

We are indebted to Phillipe Comines, councillor to Louis XI, who, in 1488, wrote his 'Cronique et Histoire', in which he describes the battle of Morat. It was here, on 22nd June, 1476, that the Swiss defeated Charles the Bold. In his account of the fight he mentions the arquebus which was a species of hand-gun fitted with what we would now call a butt. This butt was, of course, crude by modern standards in as much as it was simply a curved piece of wood which enabled the firer to hold the weapon to his shoulder while he looked along the barrel. This, then, was the first firearm to be fitted with a butt. When this weapon was introduced into England it was variously called the haquebut, hakebut, hagbut, or hagbush and one or more of these terms are to be found in accounts of the fighting during the reign of Richard III. In that of Henry VIII there were troops known as haquebutters. In accounts of the various wars during the reigns of Mary and Elizabeth I one may come upon the mention of a currier which is best described as a larger and heavier haquebut.

The next hand firearm was the demi-haque which was a long pistol with an almost semi-circular butt. The barrel had a smaller diameter than the haquebut and was, as far as I have been able to trace, the first weapon to fire something specifically called a bullet. It is also said to have fired half-shot but, unless this means small shot, I cannot imagine what it was. In any case we are dealing with smooth bore weapons so it makes little, if any, difference what term we use for the missile. At the time we used the demi-haque there was a weapon in use on the continent known as an esclopette which appears to have been much the same thing. It is specially mentioned in a decree of the Council of Tarragona, in 1591, as being forbidden to the clergy. I cannot find any particular reason why this weapon should have been mentioned to the exclusion of the others so it seems probable that it was used as a general term in much the same way as we refer to a rifle without designating any particular pattern or bore. It is rather surprising to note that the clergy did carry arms of this nature and one suspects that their presence was to encourage prompt payment of such things as tithes, and it is gratifying to note that the modern borough treasurer does not arrive at the door armed with an automatic weapon to demand the rates!

I estimate that the era of the demi-haque and esclopette to be somewhere between 1534–1600 – I am not prepared to go nearer than that.

In Sir Samuel Meyrick's account of the war in Picardy in 1559 we find mention of troops called carabins, who were light cavalry, armed with carbines, in the service of Henry II of France. The origin of this weapon could form the subject of a lengthy and endless argument in which I do not propose to get involved. The Calabrians, who lived on the toe of Italy, armed their boats, known as carabs, with small weapons and some say that the word carbine owes its origin to this fact, and I must say that the story is feasible.

The carbine was a large version of the arquebus and was employed by the French, who named the troops who used it carbiniers. These troops fought in a rectangle with a short side towards the enemy. The front rank fired first and then went to the rear to reload, so that by the time each successive rank had fired they were ready to perform again. This sounds an excellent idea in theory and presupposes that the enemy will be too enthralled by this tattoo-like performance to take, what the airmen now call, evasive action.

The next weapon is the musquet which was adopted by the Duke of Alba (or Alva) when he took over the governorship of the Netherlands in 1567. The Spanish musquets had straight stocks, those of the French were curved. This weapon was, again, a heavier and longer version of the haquebut – so long and so heavy that it required supporting by a rest. I do not envy the musketeer for these reasons. To start with he had to carry the weapon, which weighed goodness only knows what, on his left shoulder. The rest was carried in his right hand with a strap round the wrist similar to that on a polo stick. He had a large powder horn, dangling from a cord, at about the level of his right knee; a leather bag containing bullets attached to a wide belt (or in a bag hanging down his right side); a small leather horn with a brass funnel which contained specially fine powder in his left hand, with which he also helped to support the weapon, he carried a long tinder which looked like a dressing gown cord. In case he got attacked whilst juggling with all these things he also carried a large sword down his left side. If ever an infantry-man had a cause to grouse this fellow had and he did so to such purpose that firearms were very nearly discarded in favour of the bow! The situation was saved by the introduction of the caliver, a light arquebus, which has the distinction, so I believe, of being the first firearm to be standardized in our army. It had a larger bore and considerably shorter barrel than the arquebus and was fired by means of a match-lock.

Here I must mention three other weapons known as petronels, dags, and pistols. They are practically contemporaries in that they came into favour during the reign of Henry VIII. There is no need to give a detailed description of each as they were all a species of pistol which owed their origin to the Italians. They varied in size, weight, bore, shape of butt and methods of firing but were all intended to be single-handed weapons for use at close range.

We now come to a piece whose name is probably the best known of them all – the blunderbus, which I shall couple with the dragon and hand-mortar. Their introduction dates from about 1600 – I say about 1600 advisedly because I have not searched through German history. The word blunderbus is a corruption of the German 'donderbuck' derived from the two words 'donder', meaning thunder, and 'buck' (Americans please note), a gun. These weapons, which came into use about the times of Charles II, were short with a wide bore and had somewhat bell-shaped muzzles. They were usually made of brass though I have seen one of iron. The object that I can see in the introduction of this weapon was to fire grape shot, or canister shot. It was loaded with several carbine balls (sometimes referred to as slugs) so that the range was short though the lethal area was wide. It had what we might call a short-range-shrapnel effect which was most useful against the thugs who attacked coaches as one charge would drive off several attackers.

At about the same time as the blunderbus was in use the most effective cavalry in Europe were the German reiters who were armed with a short pistol. To counteract their superiority Mareschal de Brisac introduced a piece which he called the dragon. This name is derived from the fact that every piece was ornamented with a small dragon. The troops so armed were calleed dragoneers. In 1661 the Earl of Peterborough raised the Tangier Horse which in 1684 became the First (Royal) Dragoons. The dragon, from which it is reasonable to suppose the troops so armed received their name, was a small blunderbus. Though pistol-like it was just that bit too heavy to be fired with one hand by other than the strongest men – especially when mounted. It was a weapon of somewhat mixed parentage that took after its father as regards looks and its mother as regards size, and neither of them were outstandingly handsome, so that the Blunderbus-Pistol marriage was not a great military success.

We may dismiss the hand-mortar for it was little more than a variation of the dragon without the ornamentation.

The next weapon is the fusil, which was invented in France in 1630 and introduced into this country during the reign of Charles II. In a book called the *Traites des Armes*, published in France in 1688, the fusil is described as being, 'of the same proportions as the musquet, although by couching the cheek you can take better aim, yet it often misses fire from the use of the flint'.

As the fusil gave its name to some of our famous regiments I propose to digress so as to give the story as to when and why this came about. This will necessitate mention of the Monmouth Rebellion.

James Fitzroy, Duke of Monmouth, said to be the illegitimate son of Charles II and Lucy Walters, commanded the forces sent to help the French in the Dutch Wars (1165–7) and later, 1675–9, those who fought against the Scottish Covenanters. In 1679 he went into exile from which he returned to associate himself with the Whig leaders, but soon became so unpopular that he had to escape to France.

As soon as James II came to the throne he (Monnmouth), together with the Earl of Argyll, planned an invasion – Argyll to land in Scotland, and Monmouth on the south coast.

At this time there was no artillery regiment; the guns were kept in the Tower of London and only brought out as and when needed. Though gunners and matrosses were allotted to each gun, the remainder of the crews were drawn from other units, or hired for the purpose. The draft horses were obtained from tradesmen or wherever else they could be procured. What one might call the absurdity of this state of affairs was attended to in 1685 when, on the 11th June, a Royal Warrant authorized Lord Dartmouth, then Master-General of the Ordnance, to raise two regiments to be known as Our Regiment of Fusiliers and Our Regiment of Ordnance whose duties were to look after and guard the guns. Need I add that the former were armed with fusils?

Argyll duly landed in Scotland, was captured and hanged in the Grassmarket in Edinburgh. Monmouth landed at Lyme, marched to Taunton where he proclaimed himself James II on 20th June, 1685. He was defeated at Sedgemoor, soon after which he was captured and beheaded on Tower Hill on 15th July.

I cannot continue without giving a short extract from George Monk's *Observations* which were published in 1671. He, the reader may remember, was the general-cum-admiral who later became the Duke of Albemarle. He says, 'It is very fit likewise that you have in each company six good fowling pieces, of such length that a soldier may well be able to take aim, and to shoot off at ease; twelve of them being placed in a day of battel (sic), when you bring a division of foot to skirmish with an enemy, on the flanks of a division of foot. Those soldiers that carry the fowling pieces ought to have command when they come within distance of shot of that division of the enemy that they are to encounter with, that they shoot not at any but at the officers of that division.' I'm not quite sure if I know what he means as regards the tactical handling of fowling pieces but there was a time that I heartily wished the powers that were had read Mr Monk's inferred allusion to the conspicuousness of officers. Nude chorus girls could not hope to attract more attention than officers did in the beginning of the First World War with their Sam Browne belts, swords and different uniforms than the men. It was not till many valuable lives were lost by this stupidity that orders were given that officers were to make themselves less conspicuous – at any rate those who were near enough to the enemy to get hurt.

In about 1680 a short-range carbine that employed a fire-lock instead of a wheel-lock, called a mousquetoon, was in use in France, but I don't think that it was ever adopted as a military weapon.

The latter end of the seventeenth century witnessed the introduction of the rifled musket on the continent. The flint-lock musket, which became familiarly known as the Brown Bess, was introduced into the British Army in about 1705. At that time it had a barrel forty-six inches long which, in 1750, was shortened to forty-two inches. In about 1770 it was further shortened to thirty-nine and as such was used in India, Egypt, The Peninsular, and at Waterloo. There were many minor variations, such as the light fusils for officers, and a sea service pattern in use at the same time. The Rifle Brigade was formed in 1800 (as Manningham's Rifle Corps) and armed with the Baker rifle. The King's Royal Rifle Corps, then known as the Royal Americans, were issued with the same weapon shortly afterwards.

I cannot see that any useful purpose would be served by

enumerating all the different firearms that have been used since the introduction of the first rifle and those now in use. There was no strict dividing line between the introduction of one and the discarding of the other. When, for instance, the Crimean War broke out in 1854 the Minié Enfield, Brown Bess flintlock, and the percussion system converted musquets were all in use, some regiments having one, some another.

So far I have only dealt with the weapons as a whole and said nothing about such things as triggers, locks, and so on. Let us, therefore, now see how they kept pace with the development of the weapons to which they were fitted.

Strange though it may seem, till one stops to think, the first trigger was formed by the forefinger and thumb! When bowmen pulled back their strings they held the arrows between finger and thumb till they were ready to let them go with the great disadvantage that the bow had to be held at full stretch until the moment of release. The crossbow was introduced to circumvent this. This weapon was a bow fixed at right angles to a frame which was held against the shoulder in much the same way as we hold a rifle. It was cocked by pulling back the string and then fixing it over a peg, or some similar device, so that when it was pushed out of the way the arrow was released. Whether the crossbow was small and carried by one man, or some huge affair more in the nature of a catapult made no difference, for the principle which released the arrow, or rock, was the same.

When firearms were introduced, the trigger had to perform an indirect function for it had to release something which in turn ignited the charge. The first firearms had no trigger of any kind but were fired by the application of a flame to the touch-hole from which a small amount of powder was left exposed for the purpose. There were many disadvantages to this, the chief of which was that it took one hand to hold the gun and another to apply the flame – quite apart from the fact that it may not have been too easy to keep the flame alight. In all this we have presumed that the soldier had a lighted taper handy. Let us just pause for a moment and imagine what must have happened between the time the firer saw his target and that when he got off his first 'round'.

The first thing he had to do was to find something with

which to light the taper. We will not make his task more difficult so take it that we have handed him just the thing he wants. Now, is he to load the gun first or light the taper? We will assume that he loads the gun first and leans it against a tree whilst he gets the taper really going. Having done that, he picks up the gun and gets into his chosen firing position. Now comes the superb test of skill whilst he sees where he is aiming and ignites the charge. It is quite possible that his nicely laid trail has fallen off so he has to poke about till something happens. Perhaps the reader will now join me in wondering whether they ever hit anything. I would be inclined to prefer the good old battle-axe! Interesting as the books on the early weapons are with their detailed descriptions of the shapes, etc, they leave the practically minded reader completely in the dark as to how all the different bits and pieces that were necessary arrived on the spot, and the process which put them all together so as to get the weapon to work. In the above imaginary situation I have said enough to let the reader see that it was one thing to have a hand-gun, and another to get it working with an irate enemy standing by ready, and albeit only too willing, to disembowel you with nothing more complicated than a nicely balanced heavy sword.

The article used for igniting the charge was called a match — not taper, which I have just used rather loosely — and in case the reader confused this with the modern word, as well he might, I must describe this article a little more fully.

The first matches were twisted pieces of hemp made into a rope of anything from a yard long. They were of two kinds known as slow and quick. The slow ones were made by soaking the rope in a solution of saltpetre and boiling water and then allowing it to dry. This match burnt at the rate of about four to five inches an hour. The quick-match was made by soaking the rope in a solution of spirit of wine, saltpetre, rainwater, and very finely ground gunpowder. The rate of burning was regulated by the amount of gunpowder in the solution. Old prints of men armed with any of the earliest firearms show them with a cord hanging in a loop from the left hand; this is a length of slow fuse which, as just explained, he could have lit some while before.

The reader is now probably wondering why I made such a point about lighting the taper in the case of the man supposed to be loading and firing the first hand-cannon. The answer is that I have yet to see an illustration of the firing of one of the earliest – note this word earliest, not early – weapons with anything other than what appears to be a taper. Later illustrations depict the cord-like match which I have just described. I am quite prepared to be corrected but, as we are really dealing with the weapons I feel that we would be justified in not wasting too much time in trying to decide when the match displaced the taper.

Matches as we know them today were originally called lucifers from the Latin luciferus, meaning light. They were small bits of wood the ends of which had been dipped in sulphur and allowed to dry. When dry, the extreme tips were dipped in a solution of glue, chlorate of potash, and phosphorus. After this had also been allowed to dry the head would produce a flame if rubbed on a rough surface. The safety match is a Swedish invention and, like so many others that seem extremely clever, very simple. In this case the phosphorus is on the side of the box so that when the match is rubbed against it the 'formula' is again complete and causes a flame.

Having described the early matches, which we would now call tinders, let us return to the weapons. Two things are now obvious, first that we can dismiss the quick-match; the second, that we have only a smouldering match. The advantage of the latter, as already explained, is that it could be lit some while before required, but it also has two great disadvantages in that rain would put it out, and having to blow on it immediately before use would give away the position of the firer.

Captain Walhuysen, a Danzig soldier, in his *Art Militaire pour L'Infanterie*, published in 1615, has something to say on this subject which is both to the point and rather amusing, so here is an extract.

It is necessary that every musqueteer should know how to carry his match dry in moist and rainy weather, that is, in his pocket or in his hat, or by some other means to guard it from the weather. The musqueteer should have a little tin tube, of about a foot long, big enough to admit a match, and pierced full of little holes, that he may not be discovered by his match, when he stands sentinel, or goes on any expedition.

A brass case of this type may be seen worn on the left belt on the breast of Grenadiers throughout the eighteenth century.

Owing to futility of trying to keep matches dry in the trenches, we used to use something rather like Walhuysen describes. The end of the tinder fitted into a sort of lighter which one twiddled and then blew to get the thing going. They were quite entertaining, especially as they did not always go out when the lid or cap was put on, or whatever it was called, for mysterious smells of burning clothing would arise. In the northern sector it was even impossible to keep the tinder dry so someone had to be detailed to do a bit of chain smoking so that a light was always available! What with this performance and keeping the rats down both sides had much to worry about besides each other.

Walhuysen's idea was subsequently introduced and became known as a match-box, and one was carried by grenadiers as well to enable them to ignite their grenades.

It will be seen that, although they had got over the problem of keeping their matches alight, they still had not got instantaneous ignition.

The next step in the progress was to groove the pan holding the priming charge and think of something that would strike it in such a way as to produce a spark. The first step towards achieving this was the introduction of a somewhat large and crude affair, called a hammer, which was pulled back against a spring and held there by means of a sear. On the end of this hammer was a claw, similar to the end of a pen used by draughtsmen to draw their lines, in which a flint was held. When the trigger was released, the hammer came down sharply and the flint rubbed against the grooves in the pan and caused a spark. This mechanism was called a flint-lock. It was later improved on by replacing the claw and flint by a wheel which gave exactly the same result as the modern cigarette lighter and was known as the wheel- or rose-lock.

Though these two ideas were a great improvement on the former match, they did not overcome the problem of what to do in the rain, and this remained unsolved till the arrival of what was known as the percussion cap – the cap which is to be seen in the centre of the end of the modern cartridge.

This was the invention of the Reverend Alexander Forsyth of Behelvie, Aberdeenshire, who, in 1807, patented the principle of percussion cap ignition. This, stripped of all technicalities, is a small tube filled, in those days at any rate, with nitrate of silver Now, instead of either of the devices which have just been described, a small tube stuck out onto which the cap was pressed. When the hammer was released it struck this cap and thus caused a flame to pass down the tube on to the charge.

In order to round off the account of the progress of the systems of ignition I have run ahead of my story so we must now go right back and say a few words about the actual charge which we have been so busy trying to ignite.

Both the charge and the primer were of gunpowder with the difference that the latter was ground considerably finer. The former was carried in a powder-horn, the latter in a powder-flask, sometimes referred to as a touch-box or touch-flask. The word 'touch' being used, of course, because the small amount of powder in the pan was called the touch, and it had to be touched off – the expression which preceded that of our's to ignite.

The horns are illustrated in old prints worn from a cord round the neck, or hanging down the right side; in later ones it is shown hanging from the belt together with the flask. Both were usually made of leather and often very nicely ornamented with silver or engraved designing. They were subject to several improvements as time went on. The first were just containers, then they were fitted with pipe-shaped funnels for easy pouring, then a stop was fitted at each end of this pipe so that by turning the flask upside down the length of the pipe would be filled with powder. When this was done the stop at the rear was shut, the flask applied to the weapon, and the top stop opened. In this way the same amount of charge, or priming, was loaded at every filling.

Here we are again up against the same old problem as to what to do when it was raining. The answer was extraordinarily simple – wrap the charge in paper, or put it in specially

5. *Changing Guard. The 6th Dragoon Guards, 1832. Dubois
Drahonet.*

6. *Madras Light Cavalry c 1835, Officer, Indian Officer and trooper.*

made small paper bags. The arrival of this idea was the cause of the introduction of bandoliers which were also called patrons – protectors in other words – for they protected the charges. These were made of leather and worn slung over a shoulder or round the waist. Though the first models do not appear to have had flaps, the ommission was soon rectified. I am not prepared to be didactic as to when bandoliers were first introduced beyond saying that I believe they were a French idea which came into popularity during the reign of Henry III of France in about 1580. There are several early examples in existence which differ quite considerably in design and I am not going to say in what sequence the patterns were evolved, or the countries from which each came.

We have now briefly discussed the early weapons and how they were fired so, to complete the account, we should know something about what they fired.

Rifled weapons have been with us for a long time, and show every sign of remaining for a while yet. This fact, must, therefore, be my excuse for being somewhat long-winded in what is going to follow for I am a great believer in explaining how and why whenever possible. I want to make things as easy as possible and avoid all technicalities, questions of ballistics, wind, temperature, etc, etc, and above all I want the reader to imagine that when we fired whatever it is I am referring to, that we are able to retrieve it in exactly – yes, exactly – the same shape and size as it was when we first put it into the barrel. He must imagine that absolutely nothing affected it in any way – no chips, no getting out of shape on hitting the ground, and so on. The whole of what I shall soon be saying will be absurd if he does not bear this continually in mind.

If we dismiss the early missiles too summarily we shall omit mention of the need that caused the invention of – or the introduction of – shot. If you place an odd-shaped piece of metal in a round barrel you will note that it only touches the latter in a few places. Now, explosions are 'lazy' in that they like to avoid doing more work than they have to – they are almost human in fact! If, instead of exerting an effort to push the odd-shaped bit of metal out of the way, they can find an unhindered way out they will take it, from which we see that the more accurate

H

the fit of what we put in the fewer the gaps will be round the side and, consequently, the more work the explosion will have to do before it escapes.

Now let us get an odd-shaped piece of metal and put it down a barrel and fire it three times using the same charge and elevation each time and note the distance that it travels. Twenty-five yards, a hundred, and sixty. Why all this difference? The answer is that the range must vary according to the amount of surface that actually took the explosion. If, for instance, you laid a sixpence flat on the charge it might go quite a long way; put it edgewise and it may hardly leave the barrel. Now let us get a lot of small odd-shaped bits of metal and shove them down, then fire them three times, and see what happens. The maximum range, and the amount of spread, will be different on each occasion. The reason in this case is that they didn't all fit in the same way each time, so that the spaces left for the explosion to escape are different. When the different pieces of metal left the barrel they had different faces facing forward so that their speed and direction of flight must vary. We have now seen that, if we want anything like consistency, we have got to start with something the same shape each time so the solution seems to be in making balls of identical sizes. This sounds easy enough at first thought, but it isn't. Before I describe how these were made I should mention that it is absolutely impossible to promise the same result with the balls which are identical when placed down the barrel for they cannot be round by the time they leave it. A ball in a cylinder only touches the latter on two tiny places on its circumference. The explosion being, as I have already said, 'lazy' will go for the places which, with the friction along the barrel and the damage caused by the explosion, will be worn. When the ball starts its flight it will be slightly out of shape so the result will vary for the same reason as already explained when dealing with the odd-shaped single piece of metal. However, this is the best we can do with a ball.

In these last few lines, in discussing what is obvious to us now, we have covered centuries and arrived at the year 1782.

In this year a strange combination of a dream and a church paved the way to the introduction of a method for making a large number of balls of exactly the same size. A workman living in

Bristol dreamt that by pouring lead from a height he could obtain sperical globules. He proved the practicability of his dream by pouring a quantity from the tower of the church of St Mary Radcliffe in that city. Though the drops which he obtained were of the same diameter they were pear-shaped so no use for muskets. In order to ensure that they were completely **circular** arsenic was added to the lead in the proportion of about one **in** sixty. Later a small quantity of mercury was added to counteract the poisonous effect of the arsenic. When the practicability of the whole method was proved, shot towers were built, the most famous of which was the one that was in the grounds of the site of the Festival of Britain held in 1951. It has now been demolished.

At the top of each tower was a melting room wherein the mixture was melted in a sort of large cauldron with a furnace at the side. Some of the dross from the molten mixture was first poured into a sieve with holes slightly larger than the diameter of the shot that it was intended to make. This dross allowed the mixture to cool slightly before it fell through the holes in the sieve and then down the height of the tower into a tank of water. The water served two purposes in that it prevented the shot from getting damaged and also cooled them. They were then taken out of the tank and graded for size in a machine similar to those that do the same to apples and potatoes. Now we have, shall we say, four different sizes of shot which are not absolutely round but very nearly so. We take the ones that are a size larger than those which we eventually require and put them into a circular drum, like that found on the top of wells for winding the bucket, and revolve it till the shot have become completely circular and, what is equally important, polished.

This completes the story of the ball-firing weapons, though I shall have to refer to the reason for their inaccurate firing again in a few moments.

We now go back to take up the story of the rifle, which takes its name from the rifling in the barrel. The word is said to have been derived from an Anglo-Saxon one signifying to rive, or to tear. A weapon which had its barrel grooved, whether straight down or spirally, was said to have been rived. We now, of course, refer to such a weapon as being rifled and call the rives rifling.

It is uncertain when rifled barrels were first used in war, but Père Daniel in his *Histoire de la Milice Française* written about 1720, states that the carabiniers of the French cavalry were armed with such weapons and adds that they had been used some time before as he had seen them prior to the formation of the carabiniers into a regiment. He gives the date when he first personally saw them as 1692 so that it seems reasonable to assume that they were in use on the continent about the middle of the seventeenth century. He refers to them as carabines *raycés* (grooved) and describes how they spiralled down the barrel.

Rifling was introduced to counteract three main defects inseparable from the smooth-bore firearms. The first was that however accurately the ball fitted the barrel it was never really tight enough; the second, that the force of the explosion flattened a portion of the surface of the ball so that the centre of gravity was upset with the result that it developed a slight wobble when going through the air; the third, is rather more difficult to explain so that we must carry out a little experiment in our minds.

Roll a ball down an inclined plane on to a level one and note that it has attained a rotation, which has been imparted by contact. Now imagine that we had fixed sides to our inclined plane and rolled the ball down in such a way that it did not touch either side till just before it left. You will note that it went off in the opposite direction – in other words it bounced off the side. The opposite result will be obtained by using the other side. Right, now put an imaginery lid over your chute and shake it while letting the ball roll down and then tell me which side the ball hit last. By seeing where the ball went you might be able to guess. Now shut your eyes and do the same performance again and predict which way the ball will go. You can't can you? If you agree it is impossible to do so, you have now seen that the ball-firing muskets just could not be accurate. The lengthening of the barrel does not quite meet the case (even if we can guarantee an army of giants to hold them up) for the longer the distance the ball has to travel the greater it is subject to friction, so you come up against the problem of which is the better, an 'accurate' barrel and 'inaccurate' bullet, or vice versa.

Frankly, I don't know and, to use a modern expression, I couldn't care less, so we will return to the rifle.

As I have already remarked, it seems uncertain when rifled weapons were first used by any troops, and, strange to say, as to who first thought of the idea. The general consensus of opinion is that it was probably a Viennese gunsmith, Gaspard Kollner in about 1520 (which ties up rather well with what Père Daniel said); others favour Augustus Kotter of Nurenberg at a much later date. I cannot find any mention of the exact date accredited to Kotter so that having started off the hare I propose to leave him running and deal with their introduction into the British army.

The first seems to be that known as Baker's Rifle with which he armed his Rangers that fought in the War of American Independence in 1778. They were quite successful, but for reasons which I cannot trace were not adopted at home till 1800 when they were issued to the 95th Foot. The fact that there was this delay in adopting a rifle is difficult to understand for, in addition to the Baker's rifle, some of German origin were used by German mercenaries hired for service in the same war and the accuracy of their shooting was specially commended.

In 1836 the Brunswick rifle was introduced and issued to the Rifle Brigade and to the Kings Royal Rifle Corps soon after. They were not a success due to the difficulty in loading them and their short accurate range. They were replaced by another which was invented by Captain Minié, an instructor at the military school at Vincenne, in 1849. They were made under licence in the small arms factory at Enfield and became known as the Minié-Enfield and were used during the Kaffir War and in the Crimea. During the latter the factory at Enfield had designed its own rifle which was produced just in time to be tested in the field during the latter part of the Crimean fighting. This was subsequently adopted and remained in service for the next twenty years.

I do not propose to risk boring the reader with a detailed description of the improvements which had taken place as regards bullets and cartridges so will confine my remarks to saying that the year 1867 marked the introduction of breech-loading weapons and needle-firing. The latter expression meant that the cartridge had its percussion cap in the centre and that it was struck by a needle, which we now call the firing-pin.

The changes in the rifles used by our army between 1867 and the standardization of the Short Magazine Lee-Enfield (now superseded by a Belgian F/N of .300 calibre) are bewildering in the extreme.

The principle of the needle mechanism originated with a Mr James Whitley of Dublin, in 1823, but I cannot trace his patenting of the idea so we must start with Abraham Adolf Moser who patented his needle-gun in England on the 13th December, 1831. He offered the patent to the British Government which would have nothing to do with it, so he took it to the Prussians who immediately noticed its many advantages. They improved on the original model under the direction of one of their leading gunsmiths, Herr J. N. Dreyse, of Sömmerda, and issued it to their infantry in 1848. It proved a tremendous success in their war with Denmark in 1864, in that with Austria in 1866, and in the Franco-Prussian War of 1870.

Having noted the success of this rifle in the war with Denmark, the Home Government thought it had better do something about it as it was obvious that the breech-loading needle-gun had come to stay. The usual committee was formed and told to keep an eye on the financial side of whatever they suggested. This is generally another way of saying that they must not recommend the scrapping of anything, so what about a bit of conversion? Such proved to be the outcome for a sort of round robin was sent out asking for suggestions which resulted in those of Eugène Schnieder (or Snider), a French manufacturer from Nancy, being accepted. All the existing Enfield muzzle-loaders were converted to breech-loaders together with the new metal cartridge case as redesigned by Colonel Boxer. Though we went rather a long way about it, the result was that we were the first nation to adopt breech-loading rifles using all-metal cartridge cases. No one man, or firm, seems to have been able to design a complete rifle, so we find a series of hyphenated names appear from now onwards.

Martini invented a breech mechanism, and Henry a seven-grooved barrel and in 1871 the Government introduced the Martini-Henry rifle.

Whilst we were experimenting with the breech-loading single-shot rifle the Americans were one step ahead and thinking about a repeater or, as we would now say, a magazine weapon. Several names appear among the early models but the first note than I have concerning their use in war was at the battle of Kars in October, 1877, when, in the Russo-Turkish war, the Turks did tremendous execution with the American Winchester magazine rifle. The strange location of its use does not mitigate the possibility of its being correct for the Turks had no armament factory and might just as well have bought their rifles from America as anywhere else. There were probably arms magnates in those days willing to sell anything to anybody even if there were only a few millions in the deal!

The Martini-Henry rifle had a calibre of .45 in. which not only had the disadvantage of making it heavy but made the ammunition heavy also. Experiments were set on foot to see whether something smaller could be found. Nothing came from the home market but did from the Swiss. The Rubin rifle, with a calibre of .303 was tested and found satisfactory as regards the size but rather a poor view was taken of the barrel and the bolt! The outcome was that a hybred affair known as the Lee-Metford was adopted in 1888. The barrel was designed by Metford; the bolt action and magazine, which held eight rounds, by Lee. Three years later the number of rounds was increased to ten.

The Enfield factory was not content to have its name omitted from the service rifle and so came into the picture again with an improved barrel. This led to the introduction of the Lee-Enfield Magazine Rifle which subsequently had a bit taken off the barrel and so became the Short Lee-Enfield Magazine Rifle known to millions of us.

The Short Lee-Enfield Magazine Rifle was replaced by one of Belgian origin with a high rate of fire. This was, in its turn, replaced by the self-loading 7.62 automatic, which is today's standard NATO weapon. This can be fitted with an infra-red sight to enable snipers to use it at night. As its weight is considerable, ie about $14\frac{1}{2}$ lbs, its use is more likely to be confined to fitment to machine guns.

History, as regards personal firearms, has gone full circle for in 1450 we had hand-cannons and now we have recoilles infantry guns.

In my younger days I recall a period of either fighting or endless fatigue parties carrying ammunition. It is all very fine giving the modern infantryman weapons that will fire a few hundredweight of ammunition in a matter of minutes, but I am left wondering how, or when, he will get his next lot when he has disposed of his first!

Military Music

The first mention of a musical instrument that I have traced is in Exodus 19, verse 16, which reads, 'And it came to pass on the third day, in the morning, that there were thunders, and lightnings, and a thick cloud upon the mount, and the voice of the trumpet exceeding loud; so that all the people that were in the camp trembled.'

My first record of the word music occurs in the Lamentations of Jeremiah in which, in the third chapter, the prophet prayed to be avenged of his enemies. In verse sixty-three he laments, 'Behold their sitting down, and their rising up; I am their music.'

I am unable to say when the first mention of musician occurs in the Bible, but I do know that the Fourth Psalm was dedicated to the chief musician on Neginoth and that succeeding Psalms were dedicated to others. The term did not signify a person whom we would now call a conductor, or leader of an orchestra, but overseer.

To trace the first occasion on which a collection of musical instruments played simultaneously to make what could be called the first martial music would lead us into the jungle of early military history from which we might never return! Let us, therefore, start with William I whose army of invasion was accompanied by minstrels, as professional musicians were then called.

These ministrels were treated as officers and allowed to wear a feather, the insignia of nobility, in their caps and were supplied with horses and grooms by the king, or the noble by whom they were employed. They remained in personal attendance on their masters so as to sound fanfares, or any required call, on their trumpets. They were, in other words, the heralds. The head minstrel was accorded the rank of King of the Minstrels. Minstrels employed by the sovereign were referred to as the King's Minstrels, and the leading player of each instrument was known as the King's Trumpeter, the King's Drummer, and so on.

The number of minstrels employed by each of the Norman kings varied from about fifteen to twenty. The majority were trumpeters. They are so connected with our early history that a brief account of them cannot be out of place before going on to discuss military music.

The word minstrel is derived from the French 'menestral' which probably came from the Latin 'minister' signifying one who amused his patrons. During the middle ages they went from place to place giving what we would now call concerts as they combined music with amusement. These concerts provided the entertainment in the same way as the theatres do today. No festivity, or public event, was considered complete without them. The minstrels composed their own tunes and songs and took good care to see that the latter were topical so that, travelling from place to place as they did, they combined the rolls of news carriers, but more probably gossip-mongers, with their other accomplishments. Their songs were composed to fit the occasion whether it be convival or martial. In the course of time they specialized so that some became more in the nature of military minstrels and others just entertainers.

The imported minstrels were the successors of the early bards who figure prominently in the histories of Gaul, Britain and Ireland, and, indeed, all early Europe. In contemporary Danish history they are referred to as scalds signifying that they were smoothers and polishers of language or, what we would now term, poets. Their knowledge and work was respected.

Poetry and song were combined by the Angles and Saxons as complimentary arts so that when the latter came to these islands they brought them with them. In course of time the Saxons adopted Christianity and their minds inclined more towards poetry and reading than music so that literature gradually became disassociated with music with the result that the poet and musician developed into individual specialists. Poetry thrived in the quiet of the monastries, whereas the minstrels continued to earn their livlihoods by giving entertainments in villages, or baronial halls, for many years after 1066.

The Normans used the term minstrel to describe a variety of entertainers such as the bard who composed, the harpist, the dancer, the mimic, and the general entertainer. They introduced the title of mimic and joculator which are mentioned in the Domesday Book.

In the Domesday Survey of Gloucestershire mention is made of the Joculator Regis who, incidentally, owned three vills (houses) thus showing that he was a man of substance.

The term juggler owes its origin to the joculator, or juglour of the Normans. The King's Juggler was a man of note in the royal entourage. In the twelfth century the title of Rex Jugulatorum, or King of the Jugglers, was conferred on the chief of the company. The title remained in use until the reign of Henry VII. The juggler fell from royal grace at the same time as the minstrels owing, no doubt, to his increased skill. He was gradually shunned by descending stratas of society and became known as a hocus pocus and eventually found his way to fair booths.

The King's Minstrel was also a soldier as is seen by the accounts given by historians of Taillefer who rode in front of the invading army at the Battle of Hastings, throwing up and catching his sword, singing the song of Roland. A similar performance is now carried out by the drum-major with his staff though, mercifully perhaps, we are spared his singing.

It would be wearisome to trace minstrelsy through all the reigns but I might remind the reader of the intimate connection between the King's Minstrel and the Sovereign by mentioning that it was his minstrel, Blondel de Nesle, who found Richard I in captivity; and another who rescued Edward I from a Saracen assassin when on his expedition to the Holy Land. When Henry V went to France in 1415 he was accompanied by eighteen minstrels, whilst Henry VI was so keen to have them that, when told none were available, he ordered the impressment of youths to make up their numbers. I often feel that some of the modern orchestras that broadcast are recruited in the same way immediately before a concert! The expressions on their faces obtained by roaming television cameras does not give the impression that the artists are always happy in their work.

The crusades had a profound effect by introducing to Western musicians such novelties as kettle drums, cymbals, bells and reedpipes, exerting an influence very similar to that to be found currently by the introduction of Indian instruments.

The title of King's Minstrel was discontinued during the reign of Edward IV and that of Serjeant-Minstrel substituted. There is an account in Sprott's Chronicle which, when referring to this king, says, 'And he was in the north contray, in the moneth of Septembre, as he lay in his bedde, one named Alexander Carlisle, that was sarjaunt of the mynstrallis, came to him in grete haste, and bade him aryse, for he hadde enemys comming.'

At about this time another title known as the Serjeant-Trumpeter came into being and it was he who had the sole authority for granting licences to perform music in London and Westminster without which it was a very serious offence indeed to annoy the populace with trumpet voluntaries, or any of the other beastly rows occasionally inflicted on town dwellers today. O si sic omnia!

I share the feelings of Elizabeth I who, in 1597, published a statute which proclaimed that minstrels, jugglers, bear-wards, fencers, tinkers and pedlars, were to be considered rogues and vagabonds and were to be punished accordingly. This act sounded the knell of minstrelsy and divorced it from royal favour as such.

I cannot mention the reign of Elizabeth I in connection with entertainment without risking a slight digression to refer to another origin which appeared in her time, ie that of Her Majesty's Servants.

It was the custom of persons of rank to have their own company of entertainers and Sir Francis Walsingham persuaded the Queen to do the same. To this she agreed and twelve performers were engaged for her and given the titles of Her Majesty's Comedians and Servants. After the Restoration a few of the old actors at Drury Lane Theatre were honoured with the style of His Majesty's Servants.

I have shown how the connection between minstrelsy and military music came about by association as the king, who was also commander-in-chief, was invariably accompanied by his minstrels who were, therefore, members of the headquarters staff. Later the barons employed their own so that they were found, singly or otherwise, at all headquarters. The barons had their own trumpet calls and so, without too great a stretch of the imagination, one can, perhaps, see the origins of regimental calls and tunes.

Though music was undoubtedly more popular on the continent the supply of minstrels, to use a modern expression, exceeded the demand with the result that many found their way over here. It was those who roamed the country earning a precarious living alternatively playing and begging who got the profession into disrepute. When the individual minstrels were outlawed, as previously explained, they banded together in various towns and formed guilds which we would now call town bands. Even this banding did not take up the whole supply so that others became waits. The word 'wait' is derived from the Anglo-Saxon 'weccan' which means to wake or to watch. These waits were employed by corporations and their job is described in Rymer's Foedera thus: 'A wayte that nightelye from Mychelmas to Shreve Thorsday pipethe the watche within this courte fower tymes, in the somere nyghtes three times, and makethe bon gayte at every chambre doare and office, as well as for feare of pyckeres and pillers; he eateth in the halle with the mynstrells.' There is also an account which says that there was a 'yeomanwaighte at the makinge of knightes of the Bathe, who, for his attendance upon them by the nyghte tyme, in watching the chappelle, hathe to his fee all the watchinge clothing that the knight shall wear upon him.' I am not sure if I know what all this means but, it is interesting to note how the spelling of the same word varies in the account.

It will be seen from these extracts that some waits performed the duties of a sort of human Big Ben-cum-night watchman. Other waits formed themselves into travelling musical bands (though this term had not yet been introduced) and toured the country giving performances and offering themselves for hire for special occasions such as fêtes, weddings and other celebrations. It was the custom for a suitor to serenade his lady-love with the aid of waits until, I presume, the in-laws-to-be clubbed together to stop the habit as it must have been very trying to have a miniature band competition in the court yard if their Mary attracted more than one suitor.

The appearance of bands of waits brings us back to military and, incidentally, naval music. We will dismiss the latter with the single remark that the Waits of Norwich were on board Sir Francis Drake's ship at the time of the Armada.

Kettledrums and trumpeter of the Lifeguards c 1700.

The first mention of the term military band that I can trace relates to the year 1661 when Charles II introduced military musicians, as distinct from civilians employed on military duty. The earliest military musicians could be styled as semi-official because, though they were not shown on military strengths, authority allowed one ficticious name to be added to each company so that pay could be drawn for the musicians who, as a matter of fact, received considerably more than anyone else as they were not liable to have to pay any of the many stoppages and other forfeitures deductable from the men's pay.

Those who have made a special study of early military music do not appear to agree as to the dates on which the first bands and instruments were introduced, but my research has produced the fact that instruments, presumably oboes, were issued to the Horse Grenadiers in 1678. I also note that in 1681, when regiments of dragoons were raised, each troop was allowed an oboe and two drums. The Foot Guards and line regiments introduced bandsmen at about the same time. Though accounts mention military bands in the reign of Charles II the expression would seem to have been used accidentally because one can hardly describe a few musicians as a band unless, or until, they had practised together which the earliest troop and/or company oboists and drummers did not do.

The first military bands in anything approaching the sense we mean today originated in Germany where some regiments had their own which were paid for by the State; others were paid for by the officers from their own pockets. It is true to say that regiments at home had produced bands for special occasions which were composed of waits but, this a different thing altogether from being able to say that every regiment had its own band.

The reader must be careful to distinguish between the introduction of an instrument and the first band. If he, or she, gave each of his, or her, fifteen children, ranging in ages from four upwards, a different instrument the resulting cacophony is unlikely to be classified as music by the neighbours and your offspring taken collectively would probably be called all sorts of names before anyone thought of the word band!

The first regimental band was owned by the Royal Artillery whose commanding officer issued special instructions concerning its pay and discipline in 1762. It is interesting to note that in these instructions is an order which states that each musician (there were only eight of them) was to contribute $5\frac{1}{4}$d a month to the regimental surgeon. Did this famous regiment inaugurate the National Health Scheme?

From this date onwards every regiment obtained its own band, first on a private basis then paid for from public funds. There is, I think, no useful purpose served by a study of the dates on which the different regiments obtained their bands, but it is worthy of note that some played during the battles of Talavera (1809) and Busaco (1810) in the Peninsular War.

Band of the Foot Guards c 1750.

Now, having traced the story of military musicians, let us retrace our steps and deal with musical signals, musical instruments and the ranks of musicians.

The first instrument used as a signal was a drum, then came the horn and the trumpet. The earliest signals were merely sounds and not in any way tunes. For instance, the order to charge would be given by a pre-arranged beat, or beats, of the drum, or the blowing of a trumpet irrespective of what note, or notes, were sounded. The ears were used to assist the eyes, so that musical instruments were used for signalling.

7.   *The 17th Lancers in 1839. Courtesy of the Marquis of Cambridge.*

8.   An Officer of the 7th (Queen's Own) Hussars, c 1835.

The minstrels were ordered to place themselves alongside the standards and play hard so that the men in the heat of battle could hear, as well as see, the location of their commander.

I have been unable to trace the exact dates of the introduction of the various calls but, by inference, I would assume some of them to have been standardized in, or about, the reign of Henry VIII. The calls played on the drum were the Assembly (also known as the Gathering and the General and Fall In); the Troop (or Battalion); the Preparative; the March; the Battle (or Charge); the Retreat; the Tapto (or Tattoo); and the Revally (or Reveillé). The calls for the trumpet were the A la Standardo (To the Colours, or Troop Call); Boutez-selle (Boot and Saddles). This as an order and not as two nouns); Mont a caballo (Mount); Tucquet (March); Carga (Charge); and Auguet (corresponding to Tattoo).

The most interesting of these is the tattoo which owes its origin to the Dutch expression 'doe den tap to' meaning, turn off the taps, and, in slang, 'shut up'. It came into military use in the seventeenth century at a time when soldiers were quartered in private houses and was, therefore, the signal for the inn-keepers to stop serving drink and for the soldiers to return to their billets. In an old book, written in 1644, I read, 'If anyone be found tiplinge or drinking in any taverne, inne or alehouse after the hour of nyne of the clock at night when Tap-too beates, hee shall pay 2s 6d between then and revelly has beaten.' In this brief extract we find ususual spelling for the time, and the fact that fines had to be paid promptly.

It would take too long to deal with the history of all the instruments but a brief account of some of them might be of interest.

The drum, horn and trumpet have their origins in the earliest history of mankind and there are accounts of how they were used to frighten the foe serving any other purpose. These instruments were, originally, almost weapons – noise weapons as opposed to lethal ones.

The flute is probably the first instrument introduced solely for music. Plutarch attributes it to Apollo, whereas Lucretius infers that it invented itself in the form of hollow reeds which gave out musical sounds in the wind. The word is derived from

129

I

the Latin 'fluta', a species of eel which has holes lengthwise down its side. The earliest flutes had two tubes and were played by the Greeks and Romans at religious ceremonies as well as for entertainment and military purposes. On its introduction to this country it was called the 'flute à bec' from the resemblance of the mouthpiece to the beak of a bird.

The fife established itself in England in 1540, or thereabouts, though it had been popular in Germany some thirty or forty years before. The original fifers in this country were importations and served, strange as it may seem, as spies as much as musicians. The reason was that by playing a foreign instrument they were able to approach enemy positions and thus ascertain dispositions. One essential qualification was that they had to possess a knowledge of languages so that they could be employed as interpreters and message carriers.

At the time of the Commonwealth musicians were considered to be the pampered luxuries of royalty so they were banned except for drummer and trumpeters who alone remained to give military signals. It is amusing to read that it was necessary to have a permit to play a trumpet during the Commonwealth!

The pipe did not return to military popularity until, some say, it was reintroduced by the Duke of Cumberland into the Guards in 1745. The first line regiment to adopt it was the Green Howards in 1747. Before passing on to the next instrument it might strike a chord in the memories of my readers if I say that the original name of the fife was the Allemaine Whistle. The Royal Regiment of Artillery also claim the reintroduction of the fife and quote a manuscript by a Colonel Forbes Macbean as saying that the first fifers in the British service were established in the Royal Regiment in 1748. This account may well be true as I cannot trace any mention of fifers of any regiment of Guards prior to 1797.

The oboe first became a military instrument in 1678 when six oboeists were appointed to the Horse Grenadiers.

Lastly, but by no means least, the bagpipe. That this is an ancient Greek and Roman instrument appears evident from an old statue in Rome which depicts not only a bagpiper but one dressed like a modern highlander. The bagpipe was used by the

Germans, Swedes and French long before it came to Britain, the name itself is a translation of the German sackpfeife.

Chaucer mentions the bagpipes as supplying the music that accompanied the Canterbury Pilgrims and again when referring to his miller, 'A baggepipe wel coude he blowe and soune', almost, one might notice with a Scotch dialect!

The first mention of them in Scottish military history occurs in 1594 – the last in English (as opposed to Scotch) is at the battle of Fontenoy where Marshal Saxe defeated the Duke of Cumberland in 1745. The Scotch claim that they were played at the battle of Bannockburn in 1314.

We now come to the origins of the ranks of senior musicians.

The first mention of a drum-major appears in the reign of Charles I (1625–49) when it was the rank of a staff officer. The French at about this time had one known as a colonel-drummer so we, presumably not to be outdone, introduced a drum-major-general in 1685.

The original drum-majors were responsible for carrying out the punishments awarded in the regiment though it is difficult to see the connection between music and punishment except in the case of the modern pop groups where it is too painfully obvious.

In 1785 the Coldstream Guards appointed a music-major in charge of their band of twelve musicians.

Many of the early regimental bands were, as I have said, paid for by the officers, so the wealthier the regimental officers the better the band. The regiments of the Irish Militia were amongst the wealthiest in the Kingdom and it is to them we owe the first appearance of the rank of bandmaster. The first appointed to an English regiment was William Herschel who assumed the duties of bandmaster to the Durham Militia somewhere between 1757–59 after serving in the band of the Hanoverian Regiment of Guards. Herschel later became the famous astronomer noted for the telescope which he set up at Slough.

A distinction was made between cavalry and infantry bands in 1863 in that a bandmaster was appointed to the former and a sergeant-bandmaster to the latter. This date is the first on which all military bands and bandmasters were officially recognized.

Incidentally, the kettledrum was originally awarded to cavalry regiments as an honour, but in the last century and up to 1914, all regular British cavalry regiments had them.

Drum Major of a Line Infantry Regiment at the time of Waterloo.

Military Finance

The title of the person responsible for military finance has come through our military history under various disguises, such as Treasurer, or High Treasurer of the Army, and others which include the words paymaster-general.

The appointment, for it was a civil office and not held by a soldier, was instituted in 1662 when the holder was granted what was termed a Royal Sign Manual countersigned by the Treasury which can best be described as an authority from both King and Parliament to hold public money. He was made personally responsible for all sums entrusted to him and had to account for them to His Majesty's Auditor of Imprest.

There is a little point of interest here which appears to have escaped some historians in that the holder of the money to pay the army, whatever title he was given, paid other expenses as well. The army was, so to speak, not his only baby.

The system by which he accounted for his expenditures is interesting in that every time he made a payment he completed what was called a signed manual warrant, which we would now term a certificate, on which was given the name of the person to whom the money was paid, the date, and his signature. This warrant was placed with the accounts together with the receipt so that for every payment there were two signatures, those of the payer and recipient. The object of this double-signature system was, of course, to infuse some sort of honesty but, as I shall show later, it failed lamentably.

In every walk of life there are two kinds of payments that can be made which, for clarity's sake, I will call personal and impersonal. If I owe you ten shillings it is a personal debt and the repayment will be a personal matter. If, however, I owe ten people a pound each and give you the money to pay them, you have no direct financial concern in either the original debt or its repayment. The only interest that you have is in the producing of evidence that you have correctly disposed of the £10 and until you have done so you are in my debt and must account for what you did with my money. You are, therefore, an accountant. If you were my junior in a large business I might have received the £10 from the treasurer so that, as far as he is concerned, I am the accountant who has employed you as a sub-accountant. From the military point of view the treasurer is the Crown, the accountant the paymaster, and the sub-accountant is the squadron, battery, or company commander, or any other officers who holds an imprest account.

The origin of the term imprest account is quite simple to trace if we remember what is meant by an imprest which is money advanced on loan, or perhaps a sum deposited to show good faith. In other words the paymaster loans certain officers sums which are to be paid out as pay for the men or other specified purposes. Those officers are imprest holders, and the accounts which they keep are known as imprest accounts.

Let us return to the appointment of Paymaster-General and note that the writing out of all manner of warrants and receipts does not signify honesty unless the intention is there. As a matter of strict fact by 1702 the whole system had degenerated into one of such graft and malpractice that it seems incredible that nothing had been done about it before. Military accountancy had become the shuttlecock of politics with everyone distributing whitewash and dipping into the kitty for refreshers until, in 1705, two Controllers of the Accounts of the Army were appointed, one for the army at home and one for that abroad. The changing of a title and making two heads instead of one is not a panacea for all graft but, after the departure of Lord Ranelagh, things improved though I note that the accounts for 1706 show that a little sum of £299,000 odd appears to have been mislaid and so written off. There is a considerable improvement next year when there was only a deficiency of £135,000.

In an effort to prevent these losses a system of ballot auditing was introduced under which those who audited the army accounts were chosen by ballot. Their findings make interesting reading for one of their first discoveries was that the commander-in-chief had misappropriated £63,000 of the monies entrusted to him for the purchase of flour for the troops in the Netherlands. He had also managed to procure a rake-off of $2\frac{1}{2}$ per cent on the pay of the foreign mercenaries amounting to about £15,000 a year!

This was, on the surface, stopped so that the general (who had better remain nameless) started a secret service for the payment of which he claimed an allowance which had a remarkable resemblance in size to the other sums added together.

Most soldiers are familiar with the expression 'authorized establishment' which is another way of saying the maximum strength allowed for the unit with detailed figures as to the numbers of the various ranks, etc. Most soldiers also know that it is rare indeed for a unit to be anywhere near this strength in times of peace. I should add that there are war establishments and peace establishments but even the latter are seldom obtained and even more rarely maintained. In the early eighteenth century units were paid, or more strictly speaking money for pay was allocated, on an establishment basis so that we are left to make an easy guess as to what happened to the monies left over after the numbers present hed been paid. If these goings on had been confined to English troops only it might not have been so bad but when foreigners were employed the wretched tax payer's money left, shall we say, the sterling area.

In 1743 Parliament decreed that the post of Paymaster-General should be ministerial and in 1797 further decreed that he should make no payments without its consent. It was not till 1857 that the appointment was divorced from politics.

By 1783 the sums voted for the army were paid into the Bank of England from which the Paymaster-General could draw for certain clearly specified purposes.

The only one which concerns us is that dealing with the payment of the officers and men.

It had been the custom for a hundred years and more for every regimental colonel to employ a clerk to manage his accounts. In course of time this clerk became known as the regimental agent and was later officially recognized as such. The paymaster-general, therefore, paid these agents who held, as regards military financial matters, the colonel's power of attorney. To ensure that he remained honest he had to furnish a bond of security of £2,000 and he received no pay until his accounts had been audited by the paymaster. Paymasters were usually chosen from the regimental subalterns who, on appointment, resigned their commissions. Some, however, were civilians who, like all paymasters of the time held the relative rank of captain on appointment and then, after a requisite period of satisfactory service, received the honorary rank of major. In addition to other sources of income the paymaster received, by deduction, the sum of a penny a week from every soldier whose accounts he managed.

The position of regimental paymaster could be bought and sold, as could military ranks, so that the nett receipts were not necessarily as great as they would first appear. Sometimes the paymasterships changed hands for as much as £2,000 in addition to the surety which, as already mentioned, had to be deposited as a bond. We are entitled to presume that the jobs were lucrative ones as otherwise the sum of £4,000 was a heavy gamble.

The role of army agents is now carried out by certain banks as regards the pay and allowances of officers but that of all the other ranks is done by the man's immediate unit commander or other imprest holder.

For many years I used to instruct cadets and officers in the elements of keeping company accounts and invariably found confusion in their minds as to why sums which are paid by the account should be shown as credits, so I will give the same analogy which I used to use with them, and ask the reader to imagine that, in what looks like the not too distant future, he finds me penniless by the roadside. If he gives me a ten shilling note to go and buy him a packet of cigarettes he will expect the change and credit me with what I paid out. Until I return I owe him the whole ten shillings. If he gave me the money to go and pay a bill for five shillings he will credit me with the value of the receipt and I shall owe him the change. I shall, in other words, be in debt to him for the amount of the change. Let us assume that when we first met that I had no money and no debts. From the time I first held your ten shillings until I satisfactorily accounted for what I spent and handed you back the change I was ten shillings in debt to you. If you were a paymaster and I an imprest holder precisely the same state of affairs would exist between us and I should continue to be in your debt until I had accounted to you for all my expenditures and given you back the change.

Let us now turn to the many expressions, some of which are still in use, that have a bearing on military finance. As, in most cases, there is no real relationship between them, it matters not in what order they are taken, so I will deal with them alphabetically.

Acting Pay

This was paid to regimental officers performing the duties of paymaster, adjutant, or quartermaster. In the case of non-commissioned officers it consisted of the difference between the pay of their substantive rank and that in which they were now acting.

Originally, therefore, it will be noted that it was only paid to those who performed either one of the three duties mentioned. Today, acting pay is that which goes with the acting rank.

Beer Money

This was paid at the rate of a penny a day to all non-commissioned officers and men serving at home.

Blood Money

This was instituted in 1685 and was the forerunner of what we would now call a wound gratuity. It was paid to officers according to their rank and corps and the nature of the disability. The loss of a leg to a cavalry officer was a much greater disaster than to an infantryman – absurd though it may seem. In the case of non-commissioned officers and men it was usually paid in the form of a pension which was generally commuted by the recipient who then received a lump sum in cash.

As this sounds just a bit too honest for the early eighteenth century I must add that it was the custom to deduct half the pay due to a soldier for every day that he was off parade due to wounds or sickness so that what might otherwise appear as a very laudable transaction was in fact nothing more than handing back to him the monies deducted for absence due to no fault of his own.

Those who care to go back to the very early days will find that once a man was wounded he ceased to be of interest to anyone and he was left on the field to die or find his way home the best way he could. It was not unusual for the slightly wounded to form themselves into armed bands which roamed the countryside and made costly and confounded nuisances of themselves. Many soldiers on both sides were mercenaries with no interest whatever in the causes or results of the campaigns in which they were embroiled so, once the heat of battle had cooled off a bit, the slightly wounded of both sides became jolly good pals together and looted in unison.

Brevet Pay

A sum of two shillings, in addition to their pay, was paid to regimental captains holding a brevetcy except for those in the cavalry who received no extra.

Coat and Conduct Money

This payment was introduced during the reign of Elizabeth I but was mainly employed by Charles I. I use the word employed advisedly as it was, to put it mildly, one of his biggest rackets – so big in fact that it featured as one of the two hundred grievances which made up the Grand Remonstrance which was presented to the House of Pym and Hampden in 1641.

Charles I, as every student of our history knows, was continually at loggerheads with Parliament which, by depriving him of money, rather cramped his style and made it more difficult for him to raise an army. To assist in overcoming this, he ordered all counties, through their lieutenants, to produce men to whom he gave an enlistment payment of one shilling (hence the term 'Taking the King's Shilling'), and a further payment of fourteen shillings with which to buy a coat. For the purpose of this scheme, he termed his county lieutenants 'bringers' and allowed them to pocket a fee for each man produced. The combined expense was termed 'Coat and Conduct Money' which he told the lieutenants to claim from Parliament. If the lieutenants, or those whom they delegated to carry out the task, showed any unpleasantness or failed to produce the necessary number of men they were thrown into prison with a good fat fine. As the number of men they were supposed to produce was almost an impossibility the lieutenants usually paid a whacking great fine for a start and tried to think no more about it.

Command Pay

This was, and still is, given to commanders of certain units in addition to the pay of their rank. It was, but is not now, given to company and equivalent commanders on the reserve whilst commanding their units overseas.

Contingent Allowance

As originally introduced it was really a financial gamble between the paymaster and the battalion commander who received a fixed sum per annum according to the strength of his unit to cover the cost of burials, the non-payment of debts contracted by his officers and men, and minor repairs to arms and equipment. If the colonel had a bad year as regards burials and bad debts he had to fork up out of his own pocket. Though we can hardly expect him to control the number of deaths, it made him a keen business man as regards the obtaining of cheap funerals and, I imagine, a bit touchy over anything to do with the repairs to arms and equipment. The exact opposite to the intention was obtained and the turn out depended to a certain extent on the number of funerals.

In later years the account became what the civilian would call the Petty Cash Account and received, and still does, a grant on a per capita basis which is spent on office requisites which are not supplied by the Stationery Office in kind.

The first mention that I have traced of the item concerns the reign of Henry V who paid contingent monies amounting to 6d per day to those who supplied troops. This sum was to cover all contingencies such as pay, food, lodging, clothing and travel, in fact everything.

Corps Pay

This was an additional sum paid to officers of the Royal Engineers, Commissariat, Military Store Department, and Medical Service when on duty but not when on leave. It was not paid if the officer was already drawing other extra money such as staff pay.

Equipment Allowance

This was a sum ranging from £100 to £150 paid to non-commissioned officers on being granted a commission.

Fatigue Pay

This was an additional daily sum ranging from 4s for a subaltern down to 9d for a private which was paid whilst employed on any duty not of a military nature such as working for the Commissioner of Works, or helping the civil authorities. It is a sad commentary on the pay of soldiers that the military authorities admitted that they were really worth considerably more, or else why the difference in pay between digging a hole for the major and the mayor?

Field Allowance

This was, as originally granted, of two kinds known as ordinary and extraordinary. The former, varying from 1s to 50s a day according to rank was given to officers in camp in the United Kingdom. The extraordinary kind was given when on active service and was slightly more in the case of the junior ranks but the same for the senior.

Good Conduct Pay

This was an increment in pay awarded to non-commissioned

officers and men at, in 1860, the rate of 1d a day for every completed five years of service up to a maximum of 6d. It is still paid under a different name for varying periods of service in both commissioned and non-commissioned ranks.

Imprest Account

A certain amount about this has already been said so I will confine myself here to saying that it is the one from which all warrant officers, non-commissioned officers and men are paid.

The earliest of which I have a record is dated 12th October, 1347, which concerns the sum of £127,201 2s 9½d and I trust that Edward III agreed the figure without quibbling!

Length of Service Pay

This applied to officers, mostly quartermasters and surgeons, who could not get promotion beyond a certain rank so drew extra pay for each extra period of service above a certain minimum.

Lodging and Furniture Allowance

This was paid to all soldiers irrespective of rank for whom accommodation at the public expense was not provided.

The amount of furniture that was considered necessary for the various ranks makes amusing reading and many of the articles are no longer found in the best bedrooms.

Marching Allowance

This was a sum of five shillings a day which was paid to all officers who had no mess available whilst on the march. A sum of 3d a day was paid to infantry soldiers for every day they marched more than ten miles and cavalrymen received a penny for the same distance. These are the rates which were applicable in England; they were slightly more for Ireland, and abolished altogether in the case of service overseas.

Mess Allowance

This was paid by the Crown, and here I quote an order dated 1811, 'To enable officers of a regiment of every rank, but more especially the junior ranks, to enjoy the comforts and advantages of a mess without incurring expenses which their pay is not calculated to meet.'

It was paid at the rate of £25 per company so that it is doubtful whether it had much effect in the way of increasing the enjoyment and comfort of anyone.

When I joined, my pay did not cover my mess bills so that any assistance towards closing the gap would have been much appreciated but I knew of none that I could claim.

Non-effective Allowance

This strange name was given to the annual sum paid to the senior lieutenant-colonel and major in every regiment. It owes its origin to the practice of carrying fictitious names on the regimental roll. These imaginary men were called non-effectives and the pay drawn for them was used for various purposes such as pensions and others of not quite such a laudable nature. It was not unknown for the non-effectives themselves to be shown as drawing pensions!

Passage Allowance

This differed from what we now call travelling allowance in that it was paid before the journey began. In those days the recipient had to argue as to how much he should return instead of, as now, how much he should receive. I don't think that hansom cabs and growlers were fitted with meters – in my younger days they were not – so the paymasters must have been at a bit of a disadvantage for when taxis appeared they knew the distances from one station to another to the nearest foot.

Prize Money

This was the sum received by the individual as his share of the booty captured from the enemy.

In the early days, wars were the sport of kings so that any prizes won were his property which, when all is considered, was fair as he had arranged for the war and paid for it out of his Privy Purse. If he chose to distribute any of his winnings it was an act of generosity. During the time of the Dark Ages, which is another name for the Middle Ages, the whole cost of some of the wars was paid for by the sale of the booty. It was offered as a lure to tempt men to join up for a certain campaign and, during shortages of cash, portions were offered in lieu. If the king ransacked a town all was in order but, if the men indulged in a bit of scrounging, the most diabolical punishments were inflicted such as the cutting off of a limb or blinding the eyes. The thief was considered to have stolen the king's property so the punishment meted out depended on the royal mood of the moment which, on such occasions does not seem to have been particularly sociable.

It was not till 1793 that the whole question of prizes and the distribution of prize money was put on a legalized basis. On the 17th of April of that year the government decreed that all prizes should be sold, or the value of the article credited to the Prize Fund if ownership was retained by the State. This fund was then divided into eight equal parts, and at the same time all the army ranks from commander-in-chief to private were formed into eight categories. Each category had one part and shared it equally among the members. In this way a private might have got a forty thousandth of the eighth part and a captain one two thousandth – it all depended how many there were to share in each category.

In the early part of the nineteenth century the commanders appointed prize agents who were responsible for the whole business of collecting the monies and distributing them. A list of all entitled to share was sent to Chelsea Hospital by the commanding officers of all units present at the time of the capture of the prize. Three months after the obtaining of all monies due for distribution, the treasurer of the hospital had to make a notification in the London Gazette stating the amount available for distribution to every rank. The usual practice was for the total due to each regiment to be paid to it in one sum where it was left to the person appointed by the commanding officer to carry on with the distribution to the individuals. There were a few variations from this procedure but, in the main, this is what happened.

There were extraordinarily strict laws regards unlawfully claiming any money. The minimum penalty on conviction was seven years imprisonment and ranged up to transportation for life.

Prize money for the army has been abolished though it is still paid to the Royal Navy. The sums involved are small compared with the olden days as the booty, or prize captured, has not the commercial value that it had and, very often, there is very little of it that anyone would care to buy. Those of my readers who took part in the 1914–18 War will probably remember the condition of such places as Festubert, Achet le Grand, Albert, and many other places for which they would have hated to part with 100 francs for the lot. The job of converting a warship to private use in the days of sail was simpler than now. A submarine would make a poor house-boat whilst a cruiser, or destroyer, would be too expensive to run for most of us.

I had better add, for the sake of strict accuracy, that the word 'prize', when referring to property captured by the army, is inaccurate. Prize and prize money, are naval terms whilst the correct ones for the army are booty of war and booty money.

The High Court of Admiralty deals with booty and the Prize Court of the Admiralty with prizes.

Remount Allowance

This was a sum, usually the agreed value of the horse, paid to officers of non-mounted units on appointment (but not voluntary transference) to a mounted one. The animal had to be vetted by a member of the Army Veterinary Corps if the officer intended to use one of his own. As a matter of fact there were fixed rates for the approved types of chargers which varied according to the age of the animal and were not exceeded unless no other horses were available. The results usually were that the officer got cab-horse prices for beautiful beasts.

Riding Allowance

This was paid at the rate of £7 per troop to the riding masters and, at rates which varied with different units, to men who had passed the necessary tests to be styled a rough rider.

I have only come across the rank, or title, of rough rider in connection with medals to the Royal Artillery but I presume that there were also such men in cavalry regiments as the regulations do not confine it to gunners.

Stationery and Postage Allowance

The former is now issued in kind and postages paid from the Contingent Account but, prior to the introduction of this account a sum, varying from £55 for each battalion of Foot Guards to £40 for one of Infantry of the Line, was allowed.

From these sums one might infer that the Foot Guards were greater exponents of bumph than line regiments but this might not be correct because, strange to say, this allowance also covered the cost of hiring grooms and the provision of packing sticks to the drill sergeants though I would be the first to admit that I can see no connection between stationery, grooms and pacing sticks.

Stock Purse Fund

This was, in some ways, the Guards version of the line regiments' non-effective pay.

The fund received money for the payment of non-existing soldiers and yielded as much as £70–£90 to captains and above in the Brigade of Guards. It also received all the monies paid by men who purchased their discharge plus the 2s 2d which all guardsmen had to pay for medical attention every year. If they were admitted to hospital they were charged a further 10d a day.

It seems incredible that non-commissioned officers received a reward for obtaining recruits whilst officers benefitted by selling discharges, but such was the state of affairs as late as 1860.

Subsistence, Debentures and Tallies

I am taking these three together because the last two arose by the non-payment of the former.

K

Subsistence was money supposed to be paid (circa 1690) to both officers and men for their food but it seldom seems to have covered the cost. A particularly cruel way of swindling them was to reckon the basis of payment as a month which, for this purpose, consisted of four weeks of seven days each but was paid – on such rare occasions as it was paid – by the calendar month so that there were many days on which the men had to pay for their own food even if the calendar payments were paid promptly.

When money on account of subsistence was owing, the sum outstanding was called a debenture. These debentures were offered for sale at considerably reduced rates in the same way that debts can be sold today.

For instance, if a commanding officer was owed the sum of £1,000 for back subsistence and there seemed no immediate signs of getting any payment he (or his agent) would offer to sell this debt (in this case a debenture) for £600 cash. The buyer was left to collect what he could. I need hardly add that the records show that few debentures were sold for much over half their face value.

Even after making every allowance for roguery it still seems extraordinary to me that men would take up colonelcies when they knew that they might well have to pay for the feeding of their men out of their own pockets.

The normal time for paying the men was at the musters but here again graft crept, or plunged in, because the paymaster would say that he had not got sufficient money. For the balances owing he would issue tallies which were what we would now call IOUs. These were treated by the men in the same way as the debentures by the colonels. They seldom fetched more than 6s in the pound and, when considerably overdue, only fetched a few pence.

If the reader would care to study the period 1690–98 and to read the State Papers he will find that some regiments were as much as seven years in arrears and had not received one penny piece during the whole of that time.

It is so easy to condemn the soldiery of that period but it is those in charge that deserve censure. Before being shocked at the pilfering that went on, one should study the conditions under which the men served. Beer may have been only a penny a gallon for all I know but, to a man who seldom had that sum in his pocket, the price must have seemed heavy. Surely the praise due to these men for having even a vestige of discipline outweighs anything derogatory one could say of them.

I should complete this account by saying that officers also issued their own personal debentures for debts owed to them by the Crown. If an officer was detailed to conduct a draft from, say, London to Chester he had to pay for everything during the journey after which he could claim 'Keep and Conduct Money'. Having seen how such an important item as pay was treated, we don't have to stretch our imaginations very far to guess what happened as regards these claims.

There were so many debentures offered that a special fraternity arose who specialized in dealing in them and pay tallies.

Sutlers

These were the people who provided the food and forage for the armies of the seventeenth century. In modern parlance they would best be described as performing the joint function of the supply service and the canteen.

They were appointed by the colonel and were, in the case of the Life Guards at any rate, often females.

It is difficult to imagine how any other single name could cover so many varieties of graft. They were so crooked that it must have been agony for them to walk down a straight road.

They had a custom, to prevent which the authorities did nothing, of having special weights of their own. Their pound, for instance, varied from twelve to fourteen ounces. The actual weight depended in some cases on just how low the senior officers would allow it to be as they had a pecuniary interest in the matter!

A favourite trick was to say that no food was procurable so they would pay the men the value instead. When it came to making a cash payment the value was said to be about $1\frac{1}{2}$d per day but, naturally, they were short of money – and so it went on.

The same remarks apply concerning the provision of forage and fuel. They were expected to supply the fodder for the horses and fuel for cooking the men's meals, also illumination. At times no fuel was available; others no candles; at others no tents or quarters of any sort. When these commodities were not available the sutlers were supposed to give money with which they could be obtained. These sums were variously known as Fuel Money (or Allowance), Light Money (or Allowance), Lodging Money (or Allowance).

Table Money

This was given to senior officers to compensate them for the expenses of entertainment. The first mention I found of it was in the reign of Henry IV who would appear to be the first to realize that the various appointments made by the sovereign can, and often do, entail a fearful financial loss.

In 1858 the sum of £5,004 was authorized to cover the cost of dinners and wine for the officers of the Guard at St James' Palace and Dublin Castle. I should be interested to know when this payment was abolished as it was never brought to my notice and neither can I recall ever having a real beano of a meal at anyone's expense except my own!

Trophy Money

This was a fund chargeable to the public, as opposed to a military fund, from which company commanders in the militia purchased necessaries for his men. It was controlled by the lord-lieutenant of the county who could also pay small sums to non-commissioned officers for proficiency. I have also found that ammunition was purchased from it so presume that it could be used in any way to the advantage of the county's militiamen.

The title hardly seems consistent with these uses but the extra-ordinary thing is, to me at any rate, that I have been unable to trace the purchase of any trophies from the fund whose first mention I traced to George I. It may well be that the title was in existence before this reign when the money was used for a more appropriate purpose and then discontinued leaving a balance which was carried forward for use as described though the account's title remained unaltered.

Aeronautics

The word is derived from two Greek ones which mean sailing in the air of which there is mention in early mythology, but I think we should be indulging in the same sort of thing if we tried to connect these vague allusions with modern flight.

Bishop Wilkins in his book, called *Mathematical Magic,* published in 1680, suggested a carriage with sails, and much the same sort of thing is attributed to the Chinese. The only things in which this race does not appear to have taken a part in originating are the English climate and the battle of Waterloo.

Francis Bourgeois, better known for his inventions in regard to lanterns, wrote a book called *Recherches sur l'Art de Voler* which was published in Paris in 1784, that is three years after the author's death. In this he refers to the work of a Jesuit priest, Francis Lana, who, in 1670, suggested that a vessel be suspended from metal balls, from which the air had been extracted. He adds, however, that the Almighty would never allow an invention to succeed by means of which civil government could easily be disturbed. As a matter of fact Lana made predictions as to what would happen should balloons ever become really effective that is simply staggering in its accuracy. His description of the dropping of bombs on ships, houses, and cities is so exactly what happened between 1939–45 that it is extremely difficult to realize that it was written so long ago.

Let me give an example of their writings on the subject of aeronautics. Porta, Gassendi, Lana, Ramus, and our own John Wilkins, Bishop of Chester, one who assisted in the founding of the Royal Society, all give an account in their writings as to how John Muller Regiomontanus, bishop of Ratisbon, constructed an eagle which flew out from Nuremberg to meet the Emperor

Charles V and then flew back again over his head. It is significant that none of these writers describe this eagle and, alas, it would be difficult for Bishop Regiomontanus to do so either as the poor fellow died on 6th July 1476, and Charles V did not arrive in this world till 24th February 1500.

It would probably be easy to confuse the reader with a selection of names of those who fill much of the space of works on aeronautics, such as those who tried to fly with the aid of wings and various gadgets which proved quite useless. These remarks must not be taken to mean that we must scoff at what now seem absurd schemes. Every invention is the result of trial and error, and science is the richer by many discoveries which were made, almost we might say, accidentally.

I am quite prepared to give Lana the credit for suggesting that articles could be raised from the ground but, beyond that I cannot go.

An English chemist, Henry Cavendish, had discovered in 1766 a substance which he called inflammable air, later known as hydrogen, which I believe is something like fifteen times as light as air, but he did not realize the possible use of his discovery as an agent for raising articles above the ground. The idea did, however, occur to a Dr Joseph Black, professor at Glasgow University, who is known for his discoveries of carbonic-acid gases and latent heat. He, like Lana, had an idea which he did not try to put into practice. It is reasonable to assume that, if he had followed up Lana's ideas, he would have produced the first practical balloon. The fact remains that he did nothing and that it was left to two brothers to evolve the first, which rose into the air without the help of either Lana's or Black's discoveries or suggestions.

I refer to Joseph Michel, and Jacques Étienne Montgolfier who were paper manufacturers at Annonay, about 35 miles south-west of Lyons.

Before dealing with these brothers and giving a somewhat detailed description of their efforts and first flight, mention must be made of Tiberius Cavallo, a Neapolitan, born in 1749, who came to London in 1771 in order to learn something about the way mercantile transactions were conducted in this country. He abandoned his original intention and took up philosophy and developed great industry in the observation and experiment in the laws of nature. In 1781 he toyed with Dr Black's theory that, if a container could be filled with hydrogen, it would float in the air. He found that airtight containers were too heavy so turned his experimenting to the use of paper bags but found them porous. He had already used soap bubbles but came to the obvious conclusion that there was little future for floating objects as brittle as they were. His real interest was in the study of magnetism so, finding the solution of the problem as to how to contain hydrogen too difficult, he let the subject drop. Here, then, was the third person who so very nearly stumbled on the solution of the difficulty of inaugurating human flight. Let us now return to the Montgolfiers who not only thought of an idea but made it work.

In addition to their business of making paper, they were also interested in chemistry and philosophy. At about the same time as Cavallo was experimenting with his idea of filling paper bags with a substance lighter than air they were doing precisely the same thing and, strange to say, came to the same conclusions concerning the porosity of paper.

Their study of cloud matter gave them the impression that their elevation was caused by the presence of electricity, and from some of their previous experiments they came to the conclusion that electrified bodies weighed less than those not so treated. Joseph, in his memoires, states that after trying various other methods they hit upon the idea of lighting a fire under a balloon, not to rarefy the enclosed air, but 'to increase the layer of electric fluid upon the vapour in the vessel, as to divide the vapours into smaller molecules, and dilate the gas in which they are suspended'. The experiment succeeded. In these memoires he makes the statement that, 'Large balloons might be employed for victualling a beseiged town, for raising wrecked vessels, perhaps even for voyages, and certainly, in particular cases, for observations of different kinds; for reconnoitring the position of an army, or the course of vessels at twenty-five or even thirty leagues distant.'

As a matter of fact the idea of putting a balloon to observation uses was first employed by the French, under Jourdan, at the battle of Fleurus where they were saved from being surprised by the Austrians, under Coburg, on 16th June 1794 – the first military use of observation from the air in military history.

I wonder how many recall Thomas Gray's prophesy in his *Elegy Written in a Country Churchyard*, in 1751, which reads,

> *The time will come when thou shalt lift thine eyes*
> *To watch a long-drawn battle in the skies.*

This is a pretty good description of the Battle of Britain that was to take place 169 years later.

The first public demonstration of a balloon in flight was given at Annonay on 5th June 1783. An enormous paper bag, said to have weighed about 500 pounds, was taken to the town square and, on a fire being lit under the opening, it rose to the height of some 6,400 feet and drifted just over a mile before the fire died down and the enclosed air cooled. Machines employing this principle were known as 'montgolfiers' to distinguish them from hydrogen balloons which arrived soon after.

When the success of Montgolfier's demonstration reached Paris, it caused a tremendous sensation and a subscription fund was opened for the purpose of making a hydrogen balloon. On 26th August 1783, after a failure on the 23rd, a lutestring filled with hydrogen was released on the end of an hundred foot rope. On the 27th it was taken to the Champs de Mars where, in the presence of a vast crowd, it was released. It rose into the air and, after being wind-driven for a quarter of an hour, it descended about 14 miles away.

This constitutes the first free flight of a hydrogen balloon.

Joseph Montgolfier arrived in Paris during the next month and gave demonstrations similar to those at Annonay on the 12th and 19th. The latter is interesting as on that occasion the strange assortment of a sheep, a cock, and a duck were taken up and so became the first animals – human or otherwise – to fly.

On 15th October 1783, Monsieur Pilâtre de Rozier volunteered to go up in a tethered montgolfier and thus became the first aviator in any kind of machine.

On that day he was taken up to a height of about 100 feet, and on the 19th a further 200 or so.

The first people to offer to undertake a free flight were

Monsieur Rozier and the Marquis d'Arlandes; and this they did at the Château de la Muette, near Passy, on 21st November 1783. Though the marquis was the first passenger in a free balloon he is beaten by one ascent as the first aerial passenger by Monsieur Gironde de Villette who went up on a tethered ascent on the 19th. Actually, the two went up on the same day but the accounts record that Villette went up first.

In view of the state of aerial travel today, an account of the first free flight of man makes interesting and, if I may say so, amusing reading, so I propose to give an extract of the letter which the marquis wrote to his friend Monsieur de St Fond, dated 27th November 1783. To get the perspective as to time right, I would ask the reader to remember that the flight took place 22 years before the battle of Trafalgar.

Pilâtre was the pilot; the marquis the stoker; straw the 'fuel'.

The marquis had obtained permission to make the flight alone but, on the advice of Joseph Montgolfier, was persuaded to allow M Pilâtre de Rozier to accompany him and the account of that memorable adventure reads:

We set off at 54 minutes past one. The ballon was so placed that M de Rozier was on the west and I on the east. The machine, says the public, rose with majesty: I think few of them saw that, at the moment when it passed the hedge, it made a half turn, and we changed our positions, which, thus altered, we retained to the end. I was astonished at the smallness of the noise or motion occasioned by our departure among the spectators: I thought they might be astonished and frightened, and might stand in need of encouragement. I waved my arm with little success; I then drew out and shook my handkerchief and immediately perceived a great movement in the garden. It seemed as if the spectators all formed one mass, which rushed, by an involuntary motion, towards the wall, which it seemed to consider as the only obstacle between us. At this moment M de Rozier called out, 'You are doing nothing, and we do not rise.' I begged his pardon, took some straw, moved the fire, and turned again quickly, but I could not find La Muette. In astonishment, I followed the river with my eye, and at last found where the Oise joined it.

Here, then, was Conflans; and naming the principal bends in the river by the places nearest them, I repeated Poissy, St Germain, St Denis, Sève, then I am still at Poissy or at Chaillot. Accordingly, looking down through the car, I saw the Visitation de Chaillot. M Pilâtre said to me at this moment, 'Here is the river, and we are descending'. 'Well, my friend,' said I, 'more fire'; and we set to work. But instead of crossing the river, as our course towards the Invalides seemed to indicate, we went along the Ile des Cygnes, entered the principal bed again, and went up the stream till we were above the barrier La Conférence. I said to my brave associate, 'Here is a river which is very difficult to cross'. 'I think so,' said he; 'you are doing nothing'. 'I am not so strong as you,' I answered; 'and we are well as we are.' I stirred the fire, and seized a bundle of straw, which being too much pressed, did not light well. I shook it over the flame, and the instant after I felt as if I had been seized under the arms, and I said to my friend, 'We are rising now, however.' 'Yes, we are rising,' he answered, coming from the interior, where he had been seeing all was right. At this moment I heard a noise, high up in the balloon, which made me fear that it had burst. I looked up and saw nothing, but as I had my eyes fixed on the machine, I felt a shock, the first I had experienced. The shock was upwards, and I cried out 'What are you doing – are you dancing?' 'I am not stirring.' 'So much the better,' I said; 'this must be a new current which will, I hope, take us off the river.' Accordingly, I turned to see where we were, and found myself between the Ecole Militaire, and the Invalides, which we had passed by about 400 toises (a toise is 6.395 feet). M. Pilâtre said, 'We are in the plain.' 'Yes,' I said, 'we are getting on.' 'Let us set to work,' he replied. I heard a new noise in the machine, which I thought came from the breaking of a card. I looked in and saw that the southern part was full of round holes, several of them large. I said that we must get down. 'Why?' 'Look,' said I. At the same time I took my sponge and easily extinguished the fire, which was enlarging such of the holes that I could reach; but on trying if the balloon was fast to the lower circle, I found that it easily came off. I repeated to my companion that we must descend. He looked round him and said, 'We are over Paris.' Having looked to the safety of the cords, I said that we could cross Paris. We were now coming near the roofs; we raised the fire and rose again with great ease. I looked under me and saw the Mission Etrangers, and it seemed as if we were going towards the towers of St Sulpice, which I could see. Raising ourselves, a current turned us south. I saw on my left a wood, which I thought was the Luxembourg. We passed the Boulevard, and I called out 'Pied à terre.' We stopped the fire; but the brave Pilâtre, who did not lose his self-possession, thought we were coming upon mills, and warned me.... We alighted at the Butte aux Cailles, between the mill Des Merveilles and the Moulin Vieux. The moment we touched land I held by the car with my two hands; I felt the balloon press my head lightly. I pushed it off and leaped out. Turning towards the balloon, which I expected to find full, to my great astonishment it was perfectly empty and flattened.

Posterity is lucky to have such a detailed account of the first aerial voyage and, apart from its clarity, one can hardly fail to admire the sang froid of the two intrepid men who blazoned a trail which, 170 years later, was to lead to such aerial destruction that will take generations to repair, and cause a state of world tension to which I seriously doubt there will ever be an end.

The second balloon voyage is of note in that it was made in one filled with hydrogen. It occurred on 1st December 1783, by Professor Charles, a French physicist, and a Monsieur Robert who ascended to a height of two miles, stayed up for about two hours and covered a lateral distance of 27 miles.

The third was that made in a montgolfier on 19th January 1784. It was made to carry six people but at the last moment a seventh jumped aboard and so became the first aerial stowaway — though I rather doubt if that is quite the right term to use to describe an unwanted passenger in a balloon.

A flight made by Monsieur Blanchard on 2nd March 1784 is worth noting for two reasons. He added a pair of wings and a rudder to his machine in the hope of being able to steer it, but they proved useless. He was the first to carry a parachute, in this case described as an open umbrella, which he attached to the basket in case it and the bag parted company. Here, I might mention that the first recorded parachute jump was made from a tree by a French doctor named Sebastian Lenormand. The first jump from a free balloon by Jacques Garnerin; the first in September 1793, the latter in October 1797.

Four ladies ascended in a tethered montgolfier on 20th May 1784, but the first woman to fly in free flight was Madame Thible who did so over Lyons on 4th June, in the same year.

The first balloon to rise from Great Britain was a small hydrogen one launched by an Italian, Count Zambeccari, on 25th November 1783. It came down near Petworth. The first human flight was made by another Italian (or Neapolitan to be precise) who rose from the Honourable Artillery Company's ground at Moorfields. He took with him a pigeon, a dog, and a cat. The last-named probably made so much row that the balloonist, Vincent Lunardi, decided that he had had enough of it so he came down at North Mimms and let him find his own way home, and then went up again to finally come down at Standon, a few miles from Ware.

The 7th January 1784, is a memorable date for on it Monsieur Blanchard and Dr Jeffries, an American, set off from Dover and landed in the Forest of Guiennes, thus being the first humans to fly the English Channel. They only just succeeded in crossing the water and had to throw overboard all their ballast and provisions. Blanchard, very gallantly, threw away his trousers to lighten the load and must have looked a strange sight landing in France in midwinter in only his underpants. I doubt whether such a grave measure of sacrifice would be necessary in a modern aeroplane but, should such be the case, the disembarking of the passengers at Heathrow would be well worth watching!

On 15th June 1785, our old friend Pilâtre de Rozier and Monsieur Romain intended to cross the channel from east to west in a balloon which had a hydrogen bag at the top and another of the montgolfier pattern underneath. About twenty minutes after they ascended, and when some 3,000 feet high, the balloon caught fire and both occupants fell to their death near Wimereux, on the high ground above Boulogne, from which they started. These two men were the first aerial casualties.

On 22nd July 1875, Major Money ascended from Norwich but the balloon developed trouble over the North Sea into which he fell. He was rescued after floating for six hours and thus became the first aeronaut to be rescued from the sea. The first to do the opposite from landing below where he started was Jacques Garnerin, whom we have mentioned before. In 1807 he ascended from Paris and was dashed against Mount Tonnerre some 300 miles away. He, in 1802, had the distinction of making the first parachute descent in England landing near the Smallpox Hospital, St Pancras, London, on the 21st September. The height at which he jumped is not stated, but there is a record of the descent which includes the following, 'At first, namely before the parachute opened, he fell with a great velocity; but as soon as it was expanded, the descent became very gentle and gradual. The height from which he descended was so great that for a long time he could hardly be distinguished.'

I cannot leave the subject of parachutes without mention of two most remarkable descents. The first took place on 31st August 1785, when two men and a boy intended to try out a new type of parachute. Something, however, went wrong at the start and first one man and then the other were thrown out on to the ground before the balloon rose. Having discharged two of its passengers, the new parachute, and all the ballast, the balloon rose suddenly, in fact so quickly that the envelope could not withstand the sudden expansion with the result that it burst. By some freak the material formed a sort of umbrella within the netting surrounding the bag with the result that the wretched boy found himself alone and drifting parachute-wise. He eventually landed in the Thames off the Isle of Dogs none the worse for his remarkable experience.

In 1806, Carlo Brioschi, who at the time was the astronomer royal at Naples, ascended with Signor Andreani in an attempt to beat the altitude record then held by Messieurs Gay Lussac and Biot, who had reached 23,000 feet. They went so high into the rarefied air that the balloon burst. Its remnants checked the rate of their fall; and this, with their fall on to an open space, saved their lives: but Briochi contracted a lung complaint from which he subsequently succumbed.

To fall from a balloon that burst in the rarefied atmosphere and survive at all would be a remarkable escape in any period of the world's history but, to have done such a thing a few months after the Battle of Trafalgar which one is inclined to think happened long, long, ago seems, to me at any rate, to make it even more remarkable.

The first woman to fall from the air and be killed was Madame Blanchard who seems to have rather tempted fate by giving a firework display from her balloon on the evening of the 6th July 1819. I need hardly add that this exhibition did not last long before the balloon itself joined the illuminations.

To give the details of all the various balloon voyages and accidents that have taken place since this date to the present day would be far more likely to bore the reader than interest him so I propose from now on, as regards balloons, to concentrate on those events which have a distinct military connection either as regards the flight itself or some incident connected with it. I freely admit that by doing so I shall have to omit many remarkable flights which furthered the knowledge of the science itself and many others.

The first aerial bombardment – and here I use the word most grandiloquently – took place on Venice in August 1849, when the Austrians released a number of Montgolfier-type small balloons to which were attached small bombs. Some fell in the city and, the wind having changed during the flight, some among the Austrians so, in the words of the usual local papers describing a village fête, a good time was had by all.

Balloons were used by the French and Sardinian armies against the Austrians at the battle of Solferino, in Lombardy, though I think that this action is better known to historians on account of the fact that the Austrians claimed that their defeat was due in no small measure to the longer range of the French rifled cannon.

Balloons were used by the Federal army in Virginia during the American Civil War in the years 1861 and 1862. The Confederates made one of ladies' dresses which was, however, captured before it could be put to military use. Whilst on the subject of ladies' dresses, I might interpose that the Americans can claim originality – in this case imbecility – of inaugurating balloon weddings in 1865. One can well imagine that the receptions were somewhat difficult to arrange unless, as was probably the case, the balloon was tethered during the 'ceremony'. I have tried to find an account of one of these stunts as I should have liked to have read the reporter's description which, if truthful, must have read something like this: 'The bride went up looking radiant, and came down looking like nothing on earth.'

The first soldiers ever to fly as passengers were taken up at Paris on 4th October 1863. Accounts seem to vary as to their number but the average of the figures variously quoted is 29. One account, written at about the time, refers to the basket, or nacelle, as a cottage made of wicker work. I doubt, however, whether it was fitted with what even then would be called 'all modern conveniences'.

A Mr G. Shepherd is credited with having 'invented a balloon for postal purpose', but I can find nothing about it or any account of flights which he made. The first use of balloons for carrying what I should think were messages rather than ordinary letters was made by Monsieur Dufour who ballooned out of Paris during its seige in the Franco-Prussian War and landed at Tours, on 23rd September 1870. A few days after a similar flight in the opposite direction was made from Metz.

It was not till April 1879, that our military authorities began to take an interest in the possibilities of using balloons for observation. In that year the Royal Engineers were entrusted with all to do with the subject. On the 7th March 1885, the Royal Engineers Balloon Corps disembarked at Suakin for service in the Egyptian Campaign – the first during which we used balloons.

I think we can conclude our account of balloons by saying that they were used in the First World War as aerial observation posts fitted with telephones; and in the Second as a means of supporting a cable to entrap enemy planes, either moored to the ground or drawn by ships. The incendiary bullet signed the death warrant of personnel-carrying ballons in the same way that it did that of the dirigibles.

Dirigibles were of two types, known as rigid and non-rigid, the difference being that the former had a lattice framework over which the envelope was stretched, whereas the latter was merely kept in shape by the gas, or helium, inside it. As a matter of interest I might add that the envelopes in the latter dirigibles werem ade from gold-beaters' skins so that, although it may be true to say that cows have not flown (except, perhaps, as bovine passengers), vast quantities of their intestines have flown round the world!

I used the past tense advisedly in the last paragraph because, except for a few airships in use, at the time of writing, by the United States navy, airships are no longer considered practical propositions for civilian or military use. Their life was short and, with a few memorable exceptions, hardly a gay one lasting from 1898, when the first appeared, to 1937 when, except for those just mentioned, further construction was discontinued all over the world.

Two names predominate as regards dirigibles, those of the German Count von Zeppelin, and the Brazilian, resident in Paris, Santos Dumont. It is rather extraordinary that the first successful flights of these two men should have followed each other so closely – on the 2nd and 12th July 1901, respectively. The potentialities of the new form of aerial transport was brought home to the world by a flight round the Eiffel Tower, in Paris, by Santos Dumont on the 19th October in the same year.

To Count Zeppelin must unquestionably go the credit of being the world's premier designer and some of the performances carried out by his ships will remain as aerial landmarks – if I may be pardoned for using such mixed metaphors. He had, in his airship 'Hansa', a thirty-five passenger-carrying ship of remarkable reliability as early as 1910. She covered at total of something like a million and a quarter miles and carried 14,000 passengers during its service as did the Graf Zeppelin before she was voluntary scrapped in 1937, shortly after her sister ship had blown up at Lakehurst, New Jersey.

Christmas Day 1914 deserves a place in aerial history though I cannot recall having seen particular attention called to it. On that day of supposed peace, seven of our seaplanes made the first aerial raid in history – as distinct from attacks by solitary planes. It was made on the German warships lying in the Schillig Roads, off Cuxhaven, and the planes were accompanied by the cruisers HMS Arethusa and Undaunted which waited some way out to sea for the return of the planes. Whilst waiting they were attacked by Zeppelins but managed to pick up six of the machines before they were forced to retire. It is extraordinary that this event was the forerunner of many which ultimately altered the whole course of naval construction and made – at any rate so it would seem – the large capital ship obsolete.

An historic flight was made by a Zeppelin between 21–24th November 1917. It left Jamboli, Bulgaria, with the intention of taking twenty tons of medical supplies to the German troops fighting in East Africa, under Colonel Lettow von Vorbeck. When flying over Lake Victoria Nyanza it received a wireless message to return, so the supplies did not reach him, but this does not detract anything from the merits of the ship or its crew for the colonel was an extremely elusive man who, with a small part of his force, avoided capture throughout that war.

The Graf Zeppelin, which I have previously mentioned, made history on the 29th August 1929, when she landed at New York on completion of the first flight round the world which she did in 21 days with only three stops and an actual flying time of 12 days. Whilst on the subject of world circuits, I might mention that it was first done by an aeroplane, flown by an American, Wiley Post, who completed his flight on 22nd July 1933, having flown 15,596 miles in 7 days, 18 hours, 20 minutes and 30 seconds.

The British attempts to make airships are better remembered by those of my vintage by their failures, perhaps with the exception of the R100, than by their successes. The first disaster was the loss of the R38 over the Humber on 24th July 1921 and then on 5th October 1930, the R101 was destroyed at Beauvais, in France, when on her maiden voyage to India. Whilst a certain amount of official discussion went on as to whether experiments should be continued, the United States airship Akron crashed into the sea off New Jersey with a loss of 74 lives, on 4th April 1933. Incidentally, Mount Everest had been flown over three days before – twenty years and 66 days before it was climbed on foot.

Whatever the future of airships might have been from a commercial point of view, there is little doubt that they had no future in war. Not only was their cost enormous but so was that of their hangars. We have already noted that they were extremely vulnerable in the air, and it should also be remembered that they could not be camouflaged when on the ground. Owing to their vast size they were, too, at the mercy of the elements when up aloft or down below.

Though we had no large airships in service during the First World War we did, however, employ small ones which were called 'blimps'. These were used for patrolling the channel to spot enemy submarines and, as planes were not very substantially advanced beyond their capabilities, they did fine service. They always seemed to me to be sitting targets and I marvelled that the Germans allowed them to patrol so unconcernedly up and down the Channel so near their Belgium-based aerodromes. A friend of mine had an amusing experience in one of these 'blimps' when the bag sprang a leak the ship started to descend. They tried to reach the high ground near Dover but could not make the necessary height. They hit the very edge of the top of the cliffs with the result that the nacelle was torn off and fell to the beach whilst the balloon part drifted away and eventually came down on its own near Maidstone. Luckily they just managed to grab some tufts of grass before the nacelle fell and were able to drag themselves to the top. In these days, when flying machines disintegrate into small pieces when they crash-land, this adventure seems so quiet and peaceful – rather like cracking an egg on the edge of a basin and allowing the yolk and white to fall in whilst the two halves of the shell go their separate ways!

Mention must be made of autogiros – or helicopters as they are now called – before dealing with aeroplanes though their origin is not so early.

Little useful purpose would be served by delving into their early history so suffice it to say that the first time such a machine left the ground was in 1907. The first practical autogiros was made by a Spaniard, Juan de la Cierva who made his first flight in 1923. I am not sufficiently aero-minded to give a technical description of his machine beyond saying that he employed an overhead rotor (as seen on modern helicopters) instead of wings with an additional propeller to drive the thing along. It was, therefore, an aeroplane capable of rising and landing vertically from a standing start.

The first helicopter was made by a German, Herr Focke (of aeroplane fame) which gave a display in Berlin in 1938. It had two rotors and so was the forerunner of what I believe is now called the air-bus, or air-horse, which can carry one or more small vehicles.

The helicopters now usually seen were developed by a Russian (now a United States citizen), Igor Sikorsky. He showed the world the possibilities of his machine by doing a series of aerial hops, and then an endurance flight of over an hour, at Stratford, Connecticut, in 1941. The successors to this form of aerial transport are now familiar sights with their small propeller on the tail to counteract the turning movement on the body which the revolving rotor exerts.

These machines have, and I suppose always will have, their limitations. They are not fast when compared with aeroplanes, and neither have they a comparable endurance. They fill a niche so entirely their own that if they and aeroplanes were to compete it would be to the detriment of both. In an age of cold war – on the brink, perhaps, of a really hot one – it is pleasant to think that this machine has proved itself to be an agent of mercy rather than of destruction. In the fighting in Vietnam, wounded men were evacuated by helicopter to base hospitals within an hour or two, and, after disastrous floods or earthquakes helicopters take food and clothing to the marooned with a speed and efficiency quite impossible without them. The same remarks apply in the case of other accidents that have taken place in inaccessible places all over the world.

I suppose it is true to say that every invention – even the bath-chair, if that can be considered an invention – has its uses in time of war, but it is pleasant to know that there is one modern marvel which appears to have greater potential for the betterment of man than scope to help destroy him.

We must end this chapter with a few words on the subject of something of which, if really truthful, we are all afraid – the aeroplane. It is not the plane itself which frightens us but the terrible weapons of destruction which we know it has carried, can now carry, and might do in the future if another war should come.

The age of the aeroplane starts, for all practical purposes at any rate, with the memorable flight of the machine, appropriately enough named 'The Flyer', piloted by Orville Wright, at Kitty Hawk, on 17th December 1903. It was the creation of the Wright brothers, Orville and Wilbur, who also designed and made the engine of about 10 hp which took the plane off the ground and kept it in the air for 12 seconds at an estimated speed of about 30 mph.

The aeroplane age had started though, strange as it may seem, neither the Americans, nor the rest of the world, realized the fact. The brothers were treated to what almost amounted to derision by their fellow countrymen, so much so in fact that they left the States and came to Europe. As a mark of their appreciation of the help and hospitality which they received in this country they left their original machine to the Science Museum in London. This, however, has now been returned to the United States and an exact replica takes its place.

Their plane was a biplane – that means that it had two wings, one above the other – a type which lost favour after Louis Bleriot flew the Channel in a monoplane on 25th July 1909.

This memorable flight brings back nostalgic memories for I still remember being severely criticized for saying that I had seen an aeroplane fly over a tree only a little while before this event happened! How little did I realize that in another few years I was to be one of the targets for the arrows and small bombs which these sort of things dropped in the early days of the first war. Aerial warfare in those days was almost a gentlemanly affair with the opposing pilots potting at each other with revolvers, and then they took up a passenger who carried on with a rifle, or Lewis light machine gun, balanced on the side of the cockpit. The end of that sort of thing came when both sides introduced a syncronized machine gun gear to fire through the blades of the propeller.*

* The history of military bombing begins with the dropping of a bomb by an Italian aircraft on Benghazi in August 1911, during the Turko-Italian War. The first bomb dropped by an aeroplane in Europe fell on Vesoul on 13th August 1914. It was dropped by the Germans on this railway centre in Haute-Saone, Eastern France. The first English bomb was dropped during the famous retreat from Mons. It fell in a field on 10th September 1914, causing neither damage or casualties. The first English raid – as opposed to operations by single aircraft – took place on Christmas

The aerial combats that took place not very high above our heads gave us considerable entertainment. If our fellow won he used to come down and do what was called a victory roll which must have been an awful strain on the old stringbags – for such was the name given to the early biplanes.

I remember one fellow who, obviously intended to combine business with pleasure, was flying very low over our heads waving to us when we suddenly noticed a German plane coming down out of the sun behind him. We waved and pointed, but the more we waved the more he did too. Eventually he tumbled to what we were trying to convey and in his excitement unloaded his cargo with the result that we got three small bombs and three nice plum puddings! I have no idea when the dropping of food to troops originated but, as far as I am concerned at any rate, it happened sometime in 1916 in the La Bassée sector of Northern France.

Soon after that war ended, on 15th June 1919, John Alcock

Day 1914, when seven seaplanes made an attack on German warships in the Schillig Roads off Cuxhaven. They were accompanied by the cruisers Arethusa and Undaunted, a destroyer flotilla, and submarines. Whilst waiting to pick up the planes (one of which failed to return) the ships were bombed by Zeppelins and seaplanes, as well as attacked by submarines. Little did we imagine that the events of this day were the prelude to a type of action which was destined to alter the whole aspect of naval warfare and the composition of fleets.

The first raid in which the word ton was used to define the weight of bombs dropped was carried out by the French on 13th October 1914, when forty planes dropped four tons on the Mauser small arms factory at Oberndorff, Wurtemburg. This was, too, the first mass raid on a particular target. Again, who would have thought that in thirty-one years' time bombs weighing ten tons each would be dropped by single aircraft, and that the scale of aerial warfare would become such that 364 enemy planes alone would be destroyed in one day.

The first discharge of poison gas from the air was made by the Italians on defenceless women and children in Abyssinian villages in 1936 – a blot on civilization so ghastly that not even time will eliminate it. The use of poison gas was considered so foul that nations fighting for their very existence shunned its use. It just shows how low an Empire can sink and to what depths of depravity these Latins can be dragged.

On the 2nd and 9th August 1945, atom bombs were dropped on Hiroshima and Nagasaki respectively – events which have shattered man's faith in man and heralded the arrival of a power of destruction so enormous that it defies speculation.

and Whitten Brown (who were both knighted for their performance) flew the Atlantic in a converted Vickers-Vimy bomber. In 1927 Lindberg flew the Atlantic solo; in 1928 Kingsford-Smith flew the Pacific, and so it goes on. New records in endurance and speed are continually being broken in the same way as this house is continually being shaken – or so it seems – by planes going through the sound barrier at over 700 mph.

One cannot conclude this brief story of flight without mention of flying boats which played such an important part in the winning of the Battle of the Atlantic during the dark days of the last war. They were used during the 1914–18 War but were not efficient enough to play a fraction of the important part they did in the 1942–44 period when, together with carrier-borne aircraft, they completed the vital air observation against U-boats. They have had their day as regards being a part of the equipment of warships as the ordinary plane can now be launched by catapult and thus avoid the necessity of the parent ship having to stop both to launch and pick them up. Whether they will be used again in a future war remains to be seen. Their speed, due to the fact that their floats are not retractable, makes them comparatively slow. Speed, and more speed, is the cry today and it would seem that anything that can only crawl along at about 300 mph is about as welcome in the skies as a brewer's dray is in Piccadilly.

It is not so much the rapid advance in aeroplanes that frightens us as that of the weapons that they carry. Have you ever stopped to think what this advance has been during the last fifty years, or has your attention been too centred on the planes themselves?

In 1914 and early 1915 planes were dropping pointed darts with no explosive in them at all – they were released from bundles rather like asparagus. Then came the small bombs of 10 to 20 lbs. If the first war had not ended when it did, it was the intention to drop some 500 lb bombs on Berlin. By 1940 500 lb bombs were nothing unusual, and shortly afterwards the same could be said for these weighing 1,000 lbs. By 1945 we had got to the atomic age when one bomb alone killed 80,000 people and permanently injured many more. Think of it, the potentiality of ONE bomb had increased 80,000 times in only thirty years and we are now told that that is quite a small bang compared to what is available if war should come again.

Perhaps the best way of realizing the increase of the destructiveness of bombs is to compare it with any other lethal weapon. I cannot think of a better example than that of the arrow to the most modern gun. The former, first used hundreds of years ago, killed one man; the shell from the most effective gun (I exclude atomic-firing weapons) might, unless it happened to demolish a building at the same time, kill, say, 100 people – make it 200 if you like. Compare these figures with the atomic bomb. It makes you think, doesn't it?

Finally, we come to rockets which are really outside the scope of the present chapter but, for more reasons than one, cannot be ignored.

The statistics regarding the VI (commonly referred to as the 'Doodle Bug' were that it flew at 400 mph, had a range of about 190 miles, and was fitted with 1,540 lbs of explosive in its warhead.

The V2 (or rocket) went up to a height of 60 miles, had a range of about 220 miles, flew at 3,600 miles an hour, and weighed 12 tons.

They were hit or miss in that the sender had no idea where his present would land. We can now radio-control them so the prospects don't look very cheerful for those who reside in the intended target area.

As I have related, I was criticized for saying that I had seen a man-made machine fly over a tree so I will not run the risk of trying to prophesy the future.

The subsequent history of the aeroplane is too recent, and too well-known for me to have to enlarge on it here.

Those who were in the first war will recall the numerous different types, both English and German, which used to stooge about over our heads dropping arrows or tiny little bombs with extreme inaccuracy and, perhaps, the grinning faces of the pilots as they came down to do their show-off victory rolls after having been lucky enough to hit one of the enemy. At first, I recall, the pilots armed themselves with revolvers and then the passengers who took up a rifle. Then came the Lewis gun which was precariously balanced on the side of the machine whilst the passenger (or observer) took pot shots at targets of his fancy. Then came the Buckingham (I think it was) syncronized gear which regulated the discharge of the bullet from the machine gun in such a way that it passed between the blades of the propellor. The Germans came out with the same sort of thing and from then onwards aerial combats became serious affairs.

Quite apart from their combative use, 'planes came into their own for observation purposes till it is now quite impossible – or should be – for opposing forces not to have ample warning of any intended attacks by large forces of the enemy.

Bombs gradually became bigger and better – or worse according to the way you consider them – till now the child of the Wrights has become the curse of the world. We are in, or fast approaching, the era when even a 'plane will not be necessary to blast whole cities to powder from ranges which will remain top secrets for years.

I shall long remember the remark made by an American which I heard a few years ago. I was standing on the balcony which surrounds the Corcovada, the enormous statue of Christ overlooking the beautiful bay at Rio de Janeiro, when I heard two Americans discussing their use of the atom bomb on Japan. Finally, one turned to the other and said, 'Here we are standing at the feet of Christ arguing as to whether it is right to kill his children a hundred thousand at a time.'

I will conclude this brief summary of aviation leaving my reader to think over that remark.

Miscellany

I have grouped together in this chapter many military and quasi-military items that I hope will be of interest which, in most cases, do not warrant more than a few paragraphs each.

It has been difficult to decide whether there is sufficient military connection to warrant the inclusion of certain items, or to say so much about them, but so many articles used in war are adaptations from those in civilian use that it seemed to me to be better, both for the continuity of the account and for the sake of interest, to be accused of including too much rather than too little.

It is often quite impossible – at any rate I have found it so – to pinpoint the actual origin. One can say that a certain item was mentioned in a book published in the fifth century, for instance, from which fact it is impossible to judge whether at that time it was something quite new or already old.

Accolade

The word is derived from the Latin ad, to, and collum, the neck, and normally signifies an embrace. It is generally supposed to signify part of the ancient ceremony of conferring a knighthood, the embrace, together with the kiss, given at the same time, was a token of friendship between the new knight and his fellows. There is also the opinion that the accolade was the dubbing, the blow on the cheek or shoulder, which the new knight received, and here I quote Gibbon, 'as an emblem of the last affront which it was lawful for him to endure'.

That prolific writer, Gregory of Tours, who died in 594, in his *Historia Francorum* describes the blow on the shoulder as being part of the ceremony with which the first kings of France conferred knighthood so that it would seem that the act was performed many years before the Norman conquest.

The accolade with a tap on the shoulder is still in use in England when the sovereign is conferring a knighthood; the embrace and kiss are used by the President of the French Republic when conferring the Legion of Honour on a recipient.

Adjutancy

This is an appointment, usually given to a subaltern or captain, but sometimes to a major. The office confers no additional rank. The duties of the adjutant consist of attending to correspondence, the issue of orders to and by his unit, the supervision of the drill, the keeping of duty rosters concerning regimental guards, etc. Orders signed by the adjutant are considered to be those of the commanding officer of whom he is really the scribe and mouthpiece. When on active service he is responsible for the ammunition supply throughout his unit.

Static units such as garrisons, depots and schools also have adjutants whose duties are to all intents and purposes the same.

The distinction was used by the Jesuits, founded by Ignatius Loyola in 1543, but I am unable to trace its earlier use except in conjunction with the word general.

Aide-de-Camp

This is a French term which originally denoted a military officer attached to a commander as a carrier of his orders to his subordinates. The military side of his work has been taken over by staff officers but he comes into his own in peace time at social functions at which he has to see that official garden parties and bun fights go off without any of the guests thinking that their social status has been ruined by being placed in the wrong position.

I feel sure that the title has some very direct connection with the word 'aids' which came from the French 'aides' which, though used in the plural, denoted our singular word 'tax'. The French probably derived the word from the Latin adiuda, or

Spanish ayuda, which signify assistance, succour or help. The aides were taxes levied by the lords upon their vassals as contributions towards their military undertakings and various other matters which are outside our scope. These aides were often very heavy, and seldom anything else but frequent, with the result that the vassals could not pay. The result was that they were called upon to do military service in lieu of their aides. Every lord had more than one such person serving for that reason who became known as aides – in other words the men so serving took their name from the reason for their service in the same way as we now refer to national servicemen.

Today, a field-marshal is entitled to four aides-de-camp who are usually of the rank of subaltern or captain. The Sovereign may appoint as many as she pleases. In the case of military officers appointed aides to the Sovereign the appointment confers the rank of colonel if, of course, the officer is not already senior to it.

Aiguilette, Aiglet, Aglet

According to the Oxford dictionary this is a 'tagged point hanging from shoulder upon breast of some uniforms', a definition which conveys little or nothing. In military context it refers to plaited cords worn over the shoulder and nowadays looped up to the breast, the ends, admittedly, ending in metal tags. The origin is supposed to have been a piece of cord used for tying up bundles of forage by cavalrymen, and which in course of time became increasingly decorative and decreasingly useful, until finally they were worn only as a mark of distinction by officers of the General Staff, ADCs and the Household Cavalry. The earliest I have seen is in a portrait of the time of Charles I c. 1640 (see the figure on page 67 George V and George VI).

Air-Gun

It will probably come as a surprise to many to know that such a weapon has ever been used in war.

Ctesibius, the Alexandrian physicist, who lived somewhere about 200 BC invented a tube which, by means of compressed air, discharged an arrow. An account of this extraordinary man's hydraulic organ and ingenious devices for employing the expansive force of air can be found in Montucla's *Histoire des Mathematiques*.

The first air-gun in anything like its modern form was the invention of Monsieur Marin who, in or about 1570, presented Henry IV of France with a specimen. In general exterior appearance it was very similar to a double-barrelled shot gun with, however, the barrels being one above the other instead of alongside. The top one acted as the compression chamber in which the air was compressed by means of a plunger which operated through the centre of the stock. The releasing of the trigger allowed air to enter the rear of the lower barrel immediately behind the missile.

The general principle seems to have been a long way ahead of its time for nothing further was done till P. Giffard produced a somewhat similar idea in 1870.

The first time that compressed air was used as a propellant to discharge explosive shells was in 1876. The weapon was the invention of Louis Zalinski, whose Polish parents had emigrated to the United States in 1853 when he was four years old. His invention, referred to as the dynamite-gun, was first used on active service in Cuba in 1898. I can find no records to show how effective it was, or statistics concerning its range, but it is reasonable to suppose that the time it must have taken to recharge the compressed air cylinder mitigated its chances of competing with the breech-loading weapons which by then had become firmly established. In any case it would seem doubtful whether it could compare in range with its contemporary explosives.

Armistice

The words armistice and truce mean the same thing – a temporary cessation of hostilities either for a certain purpose, such as the removal of the wounded, or for a stated period. Truce is much the older word as regards its use in a military sense and was probably derived from what was known as the Truce of God which the clergy declared in 1042. It was the custom, but not always the rule, that none should attack his enemy between Saturday evening and Monday morning at the hour of prime. This truce was generally adopted in England, France and Italy during the eleventh and twelfth centuries as regards private feuds and subsequently soldiers used it in a somewhat loose sense for the periods when they were too tired to fight any more, or whilst they were raising bigger and better forces to continue the struggle.

We are now so used to peace sooner or later, usually the latter, following an armistice that it is as well to recall that this has not always been the case. An armistice was agreed upon between the Danes and Prussians in 1864 whilst a conference was held in London to try and solve their differences. It was agreed that fighting should cease for a month as from 12th May. On the 9th June the armistice was prolonged for another fortnight but agreement was not reached and the war started again on the 26th and did not end till the following October when peace was signed in Vienna.

Armour

One is inclined to think that the use of armour died with the advent of gunpowder. This, however, is not the case and the most one can say is that it remained in disuse for a few hundreds of years as splinter-proof vests were worn by the allied troops in Korea, 1950–53 and some are currently worn in Vietnam.

As armour is again in use we cannot ignore mention of it, but this is no place for a treatise on the subject about which many large works have been written so that our account of its early use must be brief.

It is difficult to know where to start when dealing with such a vast subject, but there is one very early account of the wearing of armour with which most people are familiar. I refer to 1 Samuel XVII which gives the story of Goliath of Gath's challenge to the men of Israel. In verses 5 and 6, referring to Goliath, it says, 'And he had an helmet of brass upon his head, and he was armed with a coat of mail; and the weight of the coat was five thousand shekels of brass. And he had greaves of brass upon his legs, and a target of brass between his shoulders'.

It is recorded by Herodotus that armour was worn by the Libyan members of what was probably the greatest invasion army the world has ever known – that of Xerxes which crossed the Hellespont into Greece in 480 BC. In these days of over-populated countries an army of two or three million men is considered large so one is left in amazement as to how he collected one of what is recorded as being of 5,283,000 and even more so by the fact that it was defeated.

The earliest armour was made of iron and brass, the golden splendour of Glaucus mentioned by Homer being the exception proving the rule. With the early Egyptians we find that the nobles wore metal and the soldiers padded quilts, both of which must have been rather trying to the wearers during their hot seasons.

The full Roman armour was composed of helmet, shield, lorica (cuirass), and greaves. The lorica was originally of leather but Livy records that Servius Tullius's soldiers were equipped with brass armour. The many variations of ancient armour can be traced by a study of the early coins and pottery which so often depict a warrior.

The armour of the early Britons owes its origin to Roman influence, or so it would seem. The Anglo-Saxons wore leather loricas and helmets and carried oval shields with a projecting boss in the centre. The shields were, it would appear, of leather for in the time of Athelstane we find a decree imposing a fine of thirty shillings for the use of sheep's-skin in the making of a shield. Some of the four-cornered helmets are of metal and gilt which might infer that they denoted rank, as the more usual were nothing more than a sort of leather cap with upturned fur.

Loricas, or breast plates as they were sometimes called, were worn in Saxon times and were referred to as being of the rigid type or rough and shaggy. It is reasonable to suppose that the former were of some kind of metal, whilst the latter may have been a sheepskin or the hide of some fur animal.

We are indebted, as is so often the case with our early knowledge, to a member of the Church, in this instance to Saint Aldhelm, Bishop of Sherborne in 705, for a description of the early forms of body protection but even he is not very explicit. He mentions a warrior's vesture which feared not darts drawn from long quivers, but we are left to guess whether he refers to the rough scaled-armour worn by Hengist or of the Phrygian type made from a multitudinous number of flat rings. Illustrations of royalty of about this period depict them in armour of the ringed type, and in some the rings are edgewise which must have made them extremely heavy.

Armour, like women's clothes throughout the ages, has been subject to fashion for we find that in the ninth century metal gave way to leather for the corietum was then the fashion. This was a garment made from numerous pieces of leather which overlapped. It came into vogue as a result of Harold's experiences when chasing the Welsh mountaineers in 1063. An account of the various protective clothing – one can hardly call it armour – of this period is given by John of Salisbury, an ecclesiastic and scholar, who was born in Salisbury and later chased out of the country by Henry II, but later returned to be present at the murder of Beckett in Canterbury cathedral in 1170.

It is interesting to note that the Saxon artists invariably depicted the king wearing a helmet though his attire differs otherwise if he is on the field or attending court. Even the Great Seal of Edward the Confessor shows him wearing a helmet on which is placed the kingly diadem. The casque, or helmet, of the nobility was usually pointed and made of metal, generally brass. It remained the same for many years as regards shape though the idea of adding ornamentations – even to the addition of gold and precious stones – gradually crept in. A small piece was added to the front to protect the nose – called a nasal.

Another early institution brought to light by the Saxon artists is the wearing of leg guards. These were made of strips of cloth which had been twisted into the form of a rope and then wound round the legs in exactly the same way as puttees. I find it difficult to believe that they served much purpose in the way of protection, but favour the idea that they sort of finished off the ensemble as a fellow must have looked rather absurd well covered up top with a pair of bare legs protruding underneath!

The early soldiers carried shields most of which were oval though they varied in size from being large enough to protect the head and body to what were known as 'little shields' which were not more than about two feet in diameter. The word 'shield' has been so loosely used that we are inclined to think that any form of protection that was carried was a shield. This is not the place to go into the whole subject but I think that we should give the various shapes and sizes their correct names. The large round, or oval, shield was known as a clipeus if the Latin derivation was used; an aspis, or sacos, if the Greek. The small circular shields were parmas, and the small oval ones peltas. The large shields which were either oblong or square were known as scutums.

The earliest shields – and now I am using the word to cover all the shapes and sizes – were made from osiers plaited in the same way as natives the world over make baskets. The frames were then covered with one or more layers of skins so that when Homer referred to a seven-hided shield he meant one on which seven layers had been stretched.

The making of shields improved with experience and, strange as it may seem, they even became weapons of attack. The first improvement was to line the rims with metal edges which, one presumes, made them stronger to withstand the rough and tumble which all military equipment has to endure. The next was to place a central projection on the outside, known as an umbo, to deflect arrows. By making this umbo pointed, the shield could be used in close-quarter fighting in a similar way to a kind of knuckleduster.

Homer records that the shields of important people were adorned with metal plates, and sometimes with embossed figures. The shield of individuals were illustrated with the events at which the owner had distinguished himself. Later, this idea spread to his followers so that men of various divisions could be recognized by their motifs in precisely the same way as happened during the two World Wars by the divisional and corps flashes. These personal and decorated shields are generally considered to be the origins of what we now call armorial bearings.

I cannot leave the subject of shields without mentioning the old Anglo-Saxon word 'targe' which signified a buckler, or small shield, from which we get the word target. It was at the targets of the enemy at which the bowmen aimed and so, naturally, long after shields became obsolete the word 'target' remained as the thing to be aimed at.

Much of what is known of armour at the time of William I has been gained from the Bayeux tapestry which illustrates fully armed Normans and Saxons. This tapestry shows the leg coverings to be of different colours and Ordericus Vitalis, the Benedictine monk, writing in about 1100 describes this wear as heuse or hose. Here, then, we may have the origin of our hosier and hose.

Probably the best way to follow the changes in armour from the time of William the Conqueror to its disuse is to study the Great Seals and the many illustrations which are to be found in churches, on tombs, windows, etc. The Seals would be the most accurate as I should imagine that less 'artist's licence' – or whatever the correct term is – was allowed. The Seals were quite large enough to allow the details to be studied. They varied in size from reign to reign. Those from 1066–1327 range from three and a quarter inches diameter to just under four. Those from 1327–1461 were about four and a half inches diameter as were those from the latter date of 1585 except for that of William and Mary which was slightly over five and a half inches. From that of Elizabeth I to our present Queen they have varied from 5.4 inches to 6.25 inches which was that of Queen Victoria. I mention these diameters to show that they were large enough to enable the details to be closely studied.

William the Conqueror on his Seal is shown wearing a hauberk on which the rings are set edgewise as in the case of Anglo-Saxon armour. Incidentally, a hauberk is a sort of loose jacket like a sack with holes for the head and arms. On this the rings or mascles were sewn. It stretched from the shoulders to the knees and had a slit at the front and back for horsemen and at the sides for foot soldiers. The shields of this period were heater-shaped which is similar to the long kites which children are often seen dragging round their playing fields in an effort to get them to rise.

The reign of William Rufus saw the introduction of the chapel de fer which is rather like a Tartar cap surmounted by a cone.

Tegulated armour appears to have been in fashion during the reign of Stephen. This is best described as consisting of small pieses of armour attached to a hauberk in such a way that they

M

overlap as do tiles on a roof. It must have been exceedingly heavy but had the advantage that it gave double-thickness protection.

The second Seal of Richard I is interesting in that it depicts him wearing a cylindrical helmet surmounted by the planta-genista, or sprig of broom, from which his House took its name. This same Seal shows him wearing an aventaille, which is a form of visor to protect the face. He also wears chausses, or leg-guards.

The Seal of King John depicts, I believe for the first time in any illustration, the sovereign wearing a surcoat over his armour. Surcoats originated with the crusaders who wore them as a sort of uniform so that the members of the different nations taking part could be easily recognized. This I consider to be the obvious reason for their introduction but there is another which seems to me equally obvious though seldom mentioned – that is to protect the armour against the hot rays of the sun.

Uniform, together with the various accoutrements, was more than hot enough for me and my mind boggles at the very thought of what it must have been like for our ancestors encased in armour. They must have been real he-men! In a wardrobe account dated 1212 there is mention of the charge of twelve pence for stuffing the hauketon of the king with a pound of cotton. This was a padded garment rather on the same lines as a tea cosy as regards its quilting and stuffing. This, with all the other apparel, must have been just the thing for a really hot day in Palestine!

Mail, or chain-mail, went out of fashion soon after 1400 and complete plate armour adopted, and at about this period black armour was introduced to be worn by those in mourning. Probably one of the finest suits of armour still in existence is that which is said to have belonged to Henry VII which is in the Tower of London. With it can also be seen the manefaire and poitral worn by his horse. The armour in the time of Henvy VIII was, as befits this pompous monarch, the most ornate having, as it did, various devices engraved on it; some was most beautifully damascened with gold.

Armour from head to foot fell into disuse soon after the accession of James I though still worn by the officers of Charles I who was the first sovereign to try and bring about some uniformity as regards the amount and shape to be worn by his officers. The idea that anyone should wear anything similar to royalty met with growing disfavour owing to behaviour of the monarch. We find, therefore, that since the time of the Protectorate the only armour that has remained (that is armour in the old sense of the word) is the helmet. The cuirass is still worn by the Life Guards on show occasions and it may well be that, if the splinter-proof waistcoat tried in Korea is considered to have proved its worth, a modern version of the original hauberk will be part of a soldier's equipment.

So much for the armour but I expect that many, like myself, have wondered how on earth the knights got into all their paraphernalia so that the following brief notes on the subject may be of interest.

From the time he stood in his underclothes till he was fully dressed he had to put on, and hold, no less than sixteen things in the following order:

1   The sabatynes, which were the steel boots, or clogs.
2   The greaves, or shin-guards
3   The cuisses, which were the guards that covered the thighs and consisted of small plates of metal overlapping each other which were sometimes attached to a leather background
4   The breech of mail which covered that part of the body behind No. 3
5   The tuilletttes, or tassets, which were the overlapping pieces below the waist
6   The cuirass, or breast-plate
7   The vambraces which were armoured covers for the forearms
8   The rere-braces which covered the upper arms. They were also known as arrière-bras
9   The gauntlets
10   The dagger was positioned
11   Some knights carried a short sword, but I am inclined to think that this was in lieu of the dagger
12   The surcoat was put on over the armour. The reasons for this garment have already been mentioned
13   The bacinet, or helmet
14   The long sword

This completes the things which he actually wore but he also carried two more articles,
15   The pennocel, or small recognition pennant
16   Finally, the shield.

Having read what the man wore one is left in wonderment as to what happened if he was wounded and shudder at the very thought of the agonies he must have endured until someone came to his assistance.*

A word of praise is due to the horses that carried these men for it seems, to me at any rate, remarkable that they did not get the most awful saddle sores as I cannot see how the riders could assist in any way to ease the strain of what must have been a dead weight.

Batman

A batman (originally pronounced bawman) was a person, not necessarily a soldier, paid by the government, allowed to every company on foreign service to look after the cooking utensils. Every company was allowed a bathorse (pronounced bawhorse) to carry these utensils and the cost of its fodder was paid by the government.

When the army was stationed at home the men were billeted on the inns, beer-houses, and public houses so that the need for the bathorse disappeared but the batmen were often retained as personal servants.

I cannot trace the exact period when batmen became purely officers' servants but, as bathorses were discontinued sometime in the eighteenth century I should imagine that the period of evolution as regards batmen took place at the same period.

As a matter of interest, a batman is also a weight which used to be used in the Levant to weigh silk brought into Aleppo, Smyrna, Constantinople, and other large trading towns. In Constantinople a batman was somewhere about 150 lbs which would make about the load of a horse.

* Indeed Philip de Commines describes how some Italian knights were unhorsed in battle in the 16th century, and so finely fitted was their armour that no-one could penetrate it to give them the coup-de-grace, and they rolled about on the ground like giant lobsters until some woodmen were summoned with axes.

I have absolutely no data to go by, but it is not beyond the bounds of possibility that the term bathorse originated from there as it seems a strange word to have originated in this country.

Baton

The fact that the carrying of a club denoted authority is almost as old as history itself, but I have found nothing to lead me to associate the carrying of one to denote the highest military rank until comparatively recent history.

A baton-sinister is a well-known heraldic device to indicate illegitimacy which was laid in a diagonal manner across the shield in such a way that its ends did not reach the edges. It is a pity, to say the least, that the symbol which we normally associate with such an exalted office as that of field-marshal has a connection not quite so venerable!

The first actual presentation of a baton that I can trace took place in 1569 when Charles IX of France made his brother Henry (who later became Henry III of France) a generalissimo and gave him one to signify his high appointment.

The first award of a baton to an English field-marshal took place in 1813.

Bearskin

A bearskin in NOT a busby (see below) and, despite frequent reports in the press to this effect, the Foot Guards do *not* wear a busby. They wear a bearskin cap, which is made up on a wicker work frame. The origin is to be found in a simple type of fisherman's cap around which a strip of fur was added, and in this form it is to be seen in the figure on page 66 (Lawson I 29). This subsequently disappeared, and the point and tassel of the cap became fixed to the top of a stiffened mitre cap widely worn throughout Europe by Grenadiers, both Horse and Foot, during the eighteenth century. In the latter half of that century the embroidered front (see plate A Lawson II 28) was replaced by a metal plate and edged with fur, the cloth still showing at the back. In course of time the entire cap was covered with fur and all ornaments done away with except the plume. Originally worn by grenadier companies only they were adopted by all companies of Foot Guards just prior to the Crimean War of 1854.

Billeting

I have seen this word ingeniously, but quite incorrectly, described as being derived from a billet, which was a piece of wood with which those demanding lodging were supposed to have used to bang on front doors. The truth is that it comes from the French word 'billet' denoting a letter. The letter was really a demand issued by the king's High Harbinger, the officer originally responsible for quartering the troops, to the magistrate or lord-lieutenant directing him to provide accommodation and provisions in a certain area for a certain period.

Billeting, as we now call it, formed part of a prerogative formerly enjoyed by the sovereign under the title of purveyance. Under this the king sent out officers called purveyors who had the right to purchase provisions and other necessaries for the use of the royal household without any agreement on the part of the seller. Those whose property was taken in this manner were entitled to some payment, but had no say in the matter as to how much. The nobles, as the ordinary people did not dare to ask under whose authority these near-confiscations were made, also indulged in the practice which was general till 1363. In this year, during the reign of Edward III, a parliament, which claimed to have been held 'for the honour and pleasure of God and the amendment of the outrageous grievances and oppressions done to the people, and the relief of their estate', enacted five statutes on the subject of purveyance. In sum, they confined the exercise of it to the king and queen, and decreed that in future 'the heinous name of purveyor shall be changed to that of buyer' and forbade the use of force. It also decreed that, when the buyer and seller could not agree on a price, a tribunal should be set up to make a valuation. All this looked very smug on paper, but the appearance of a buyer did not generate a much more pleasant atmosphere than that of purveyor. Elizabeth I used this prerogative to victual her navy so that, if the wretched householder thought that the military horizon looked clear, he still had to worry about the naval one – especially if he lived near the coast. Two attempts were made to deprive her of this right but she told the Commons, in no uncertain manner, to mind their own business.

Bacon, during the first parliament in the reign of James I, delivered a speech against the whole practice of purveying, but nothing was done. It fell into disuse during the Commonwealth and was not formally abolished till after the Restoration when Charles II exchanged the prerogative and received in lieu a percentage of the duty payable on exciseable liquor, as I mention elsewhere when dealing with the Civil List.

So much for purveyance which, as the reader will have noted, included the right of the sovereign to take, or make use of, anything belonging to the individual. It was a collective term of which billeting formed part till 1660.

When William I landed, he housed his men in monasteries and made the monks responsible for feeding them. Being short of transport, he even went further and made them hand over their horses and carts. Richard II was the first king to make any payment to the civilian population for lodgings, food, and equipment supplied to the army. To him, too, goes the credit for introducing billeting officers. In 1387 he commanded the Mayor of London to furnish billeting officers to meet the Marshal when the army marched in. These officers were to have lists of all the houses wherein troops could be billeted. Payment was to be made and no man was to demand food without paying for it.

Charles I, in 1628, signed the famous Petition of Right under which, (1) No person could be made to make a benevolence without the consent of Parliament; (2) No person could be put in prison for not complying with an order which was not lawful; (3) No soldiers or sailors could be billeted on private individuals without the householder's consent. There were, of course, other clauses which do not concern us here.

The Petition was amplified in 1660 by another law to the effect that no officers, military or civil, nor any person whatsoever shall from henceforth presume to place, quarter or billet any soldier or soldiers upon any subject or inhabitant of this Realm, of any degree, quality or profession whatsoever without their consent. It goes on to say that owing to the war (with France) it would be necessary to move large bodies of troops so that constables would be allowed to obtain billets in ale houses, etc, but not in private houses.

It is interesting to note that the law went on to lay down the different scales of charges for the billeting of the lowest ranks of the different arms. The rates were 2s a day for a trooper, 1s 2d for a dragoon, and 6d for a foot soldier.

The general system of billeting in use today was instituted in 1714 whereby the Chief Magistrate, or Constable, is notified in advance of the number of men for whom billets are required and the probable duration of their stay. In the last two wars this system has had to be modified slightly and now, in the event of an emergency, the Chief Constable is responsible for taking a census of the number of regular occupants of every house in his area, and for a list of all the houses which have available accommodation suitable for officers and men. There are certain categories of householders who are exempt from having men billeted on them. These consist of old people, invalids, schools, etc.

The commanding officer is responsible for seeing that all billeting monies are paid before his unit leaves the area.

The usual procedure is for the billeting money to be paid weekly but any person on whom troops are billeted can legally demand payment every fourth day. I cannot remember the right ever having been used, but I suspect that in many cases it was only because it was not known.

Bounty Money

This money, sometimes referred to as Levy Money, was the sum paid to recruits in newly-raised regiments. Various practices were resorted to in order to raise men and it was not uncommon for towns to open subscription lists among its inhabitants. The monies so obtained were shared out among those who enlisted between certain specified dates.

In 1759 the City of London, in addition to having subscription lists, conferred its freedom on all who completed the requisite service!

Bounty Money is still in use as additional payment to territorials and, I believe, in other services as a cash payment to those who complete their engagement.

Brevet

The term originated in France where it signified a warrant from the sovereign to carry out the duty to which it referred.

In the British army the term is used to denote an appointment to a degree of rank immediately above the substantive rank of the holder. It is given as a reward of service which is not considered sufficiently meritorious to deserve full substantive promotion; it does, however, qualify the holder to obtain the next vacancy in that rank over the heads of those who may be senior to him in his substantive one. For instance, if Captain D was appointed a brevet-major whilst fourth senior captain of his regiment he would, on the first vacancy for a major, receive his substantive promotion over the heads of Captains A, B and C.

There are certain anomalies to the rank in that a brevetcy carries no seniority in the regiment so that our Captain D would be junior on parade to the other three. If he and, say, Captain A were serving together on some extra-regimental duty such as a court-martial, of course, where officers from other units were present, his brevetcy would make him the senior of the two. Brevet officers take seniority amongst themselves, when away from their parent unit, according to the dates of their appointments. Only three ranks can obtain brevetcies, captains, majors, and lieutenant-colonels.

During the time that France was a monarchy she enlisted a contingent of Swiss who served under an officer known as the colonel-general of Swiss troops. He had the authority to nominate subalterns to serve as captains by virtue of a certificate signed by himself. Such seniority was only operative whilst the officer was serving with his regiment. If such a captain transferred from one regiment to another he was placed at the bottom of his rank but, and this is the point I wish to make, he retained the seniority given him by his certificate when employed in a detachment composed of troops drawn from several regiments.

Swiss troops served in the French army from 1480–1860 that is for some time after Switzerland became a republic in 1798. My reader may recall the massacre of the Swiss Guards in August, 1792, immediatly prior to the setting up of the revolutionary tribunal and the declaration of a French Republic.

The introduction of the brevet rank into the English army took place soon after the arrival of William and Mary, say about 1689, according to one contemporary historian, but I cannot see any association between the two events. I suggest that he may mean 1685 during which year the King's forces met the wandering Duke of Monmouth at Sedgemoor, near Bridgwater, in Somersetshire. The next occasion when the introduction of the rank might have been necessary was during William's campaign in Ireland where he defeated the followers of James at the Battle of the Boyne.

Some of my readers may have seen mention of a general brevet which was an occasion and not a rank. The most notable was that which took place after the Battle of Barrossa (5th March 1811) during the Peninsular War, when the Duke of Wellington, on the authority of the Government, appointed all the majors who had commanded their battalions during that engagement brevet-lieutenant-colonels.

Having dealt with brevet ranks I think this might be the place to deal with those known as substantive, acting, and temporary as I have noted a slight confusion concerning them.

A substantive rank can best, and most briefly, be described as the one below which an officer cannot be reduced except by sentence of a court-martial.

An officer can be appointed to act in a capacity senior to his substantive rank and whilst holding such appointment is granted acting rank. After he has held his acting appointment for three months he is granted temporary rank, so that a temporary rank is an acting one which has been held for over three months.

An officer can, at one and the same time, hold three ranks. For instance, he can be a substantive captain, temporary major, and acting lieutenant-colonel.

Neither of the appointments need necessarily be consequentive in seniority by which I mean that a captain could be temporary lieutenant-colonel and acting brigadier; in this case there is an intermediate rank between each of them.

A brevetcy is held in addition to temporary and acting rank so an officer could be a captain with a brevet majority and hold an additional temporary and acting rank.

Busby

A Busby is a fur cap which is not worn by the Foot Guards. The Oxford Dictionary states a 'Tall fur cap of Hussars and RHA' but then loses its nerve and puts a question mark in brackets! It is quite correct as far as it goes, but nowadays full dress is confined to the King's Troop RHA (established by King George VI, in whose memory it retains its title) and to bandsmen on ceremonial. The origin of the busby was much the same as that of the bearskin. It was worn by Hungarian light horsemen and when this type of cavalry became popular and was adopted by other nations they adopted the fur cap also. After Waterloo, British Hussars adopted the shako, but by the time of the Crimean War had reverted to the fur cap which has been worn ever since (see plates 3 & D).

Cheval de Frize

This was a wooden beam, usually from six to nine feet long, through the centre of which holes, about six inches apart, were drilled at right angles. Sharp metal stakes were then threaded through extending to three or more feet on either side of the beam. A series of these frizes were chained together in a long line and, usually, stretched across ground over which cavalry were likely to make a charge. They were also put at the bottom of ditches as a protection against infantry attack.

The reader who has read an account of the attack on the fortress of Badajoz, in 1812, during the Peninsular War, will recall the clever use made by the defender, Baron Philippe, of these frizes in the strengthening of the south-eastern corner known as the Trinidad bastion.

That ubiquitous curse of the infantry, barbed wire, has replaced chevaux de frizes due, in great measure to its portability and the fact that artillery merely shifts it vertically, and perhaps laterally, but never really eliminates it as those of us who fought on the Somme in 1916 will readily testify.

Cipher

The word is of Arabic origin signifying emptiness, such as the

Arabic word 'sifr' which can best be described literally as having no meaning. This is, of course, exactly what cipher is until the unravelling code is used and the original has been deciphered. The word is used to denote the figure 0, and it is, I believe, from it that Arabic arithmetic was known as ciphering.

In recent years the use of ciphers became so complicated that special departments were set up to deal with it and the code books by means of which messages were deciphered became the most secret thing in charge of a commander. This is no place to elaborate on this vast and interesting subject as we are concerned with its origin and initial use.

The first mention that I have found of its military use was by Julius Caesar when sending despatches to his brother-in-law Emeporor Augustus. It is difficult to follow the exact method that was used but it was on the principal of the interchange of alphabetical letters. An example using our present alphabet was that T was taken as the first letter followed by 'U', 'V', 'W', and so on. In this way the letter 'S' took the place of our 'Z'. In this way the word 'bat' would have been spelt 'uta'. Instead of the length of the word giving any clue, the message as a whole was probably divided into blocks in such a way that each contained the same number of letters.

We know that some form of alphabetical cipher was used by Pope Sixtus IV (the Pope who built the famous Sistine Chapel in the Vatican) for there are accounts that Battista Alberti, in revenge for the Pope's nepotism, divulged the secret and a new cipher had to be made in, or about, 1480.

In 1868 Sir Charles Whetstone patented a machine for writing in cipher known as a cryptograph which, when set, typed the coded message.

There are two ways of making a written message secret. One is to make it visible but meaningless except to the recipient; the other is to make it invisible by means of sympathetic, better known as invisible, ink.

Invisible writing agents, such as lemon juice and spittle, nearly always figure in spy stories. Was it not Ovid in his *Ars Amatoria*, written about AD 2, who advised all maidens to write their love letters in fresh milk so as to avoid the curiosity of their friends? One can hardly say that writing in a substance that is not visible till heated is a modern idea! Probably the first person to make a study of the subject was Peter Borel who wrote about it in 1653, and was followed in 1669 by Le Mort.

A somewhat elaborate treatise on the subject was written by a Mr Henry Rochfort in 1836, and I note that he has done his best to hide the subject matter of his work by calling it arcanography – a word which is not to be found in any of my dictionaries.

Civil List

Though the name itself may not appear to warrant a place in a book dealing with military origins, it should be included as the monies from it pay many of those mentioned in these pages.

Originally all the expenses of the country, whether for military or civil purposes, were paid from the Royal Revenue. This was obtained from the rents of land and other royal prerogatives. All monies so received were under the personal control of the sovereign. There were many occasions when the royal revenue was not sufficient to meet the cost of wars so that the government voted extra sums which were paid to the king, but it was left entirely to him as to how they were to be spent.

This state of affairs was altered after the Restoration when the expenses of the country were divided into two categories known as extraordinary expenses and ordinary expenses. The former included those for wars; the latter those dealing with the every-day matters which would necessitate expenditure whether the country was at war or not.

Certain revenues were allotted to the latter which were called hereditary, or civil list, expenditures. The monies came from crown lands and certain taxes whose revenues were handed over to the sovereign. The principal sources of the monies received by William III were the Post Office and an excise of 2s 6d on every barrel of beer. The total that he received was in the region of £680,000 per annum from which he had to pay the salaries of the Lord Chancellor, the judges of the King's Bench, all the ambassadors to foreign courts, annual incomes to members of the Royal Family, and pensions to various people who had retired from his employment. The king was also responsible for the upkeep of the royal palaces and residencies together with the staff of servants maintained at each.

On the accession of George I it was considered inadvisable that the king's income should be dependent in most part on the thirst of his subjects so that Parliament voted a fixed income of £700,000 a year for the Civil List, plus the revenue from certain other sources. The same procedure was adopted on the accession of George II with an additional clause that if his income did not total the sum of £800,000 a year the difference would be made up by Parliament but that he should retain any surplus. At the accession of George III the sum of £800,000 a year was voted for the Civil List but the revenue from the taxes was withdrawn with the result that the department ran into debt and had to be kept on its feet by further government grants.

The total received by the Sovereign first exceeded a million pounds in 1804 but did not remain at this figure after 1830 when certain expenses were taken over by Parliament and the annual grant reduced to about £510,000.

The present law is that the amount of the Civil List must be voted within six months of the accession of a new sovereign and that the sum then fixed shall remain in force throughout the reign. This sum, the Privy Purse as it is called, is disbursed by the Keeper of the Privy Purse. The sovereign's expenditures are divided into four classes, (1) personal expenditures; (2) upkeep of castles and royal residences; (3) salaries of all members of the Royal Household from the highest to the lowest; and (4) food, furnishings, fuel, cars, cleaning, etc, etc.

The well-known Maundy Money, which derives its name from the maunds, or baskets, in which the gifts were made, is paid from the Privy Purse and so are, therefore, personal gifts from the sovereign.

Cocked Hat

The cocked hat is, or was, merely a wide brimmed hat. For convenience it was turned up at one side, as worn by Australian troops. Later it was turned up on two sides, with the point worn in front to form the tricorn of the eighteenth century. In course of time the front point was ironed out to give a bicorne which could be worn fore and aft as by Wellington, or athwart as patronized by Napoleon. It still survives on the heads of Quartermasters of the Foot Guards.

Commission

A commission, from a military point of view, is a document authorizing the holder to perform duties in the service of the State. Commissions are granted by, or on behalf of, the Sovereign and the recipient, if the commission concerns military service, is ranked as an officer. The word is so loosely used nowadays that it would be well to clarify the true meaning as opposed to the accepted one.

Let us suppose that Arthur and John Smith are brothers. Arthur has done his preliminary training and proved himself to have all the necessary qualifications to become an officer. His name is submitted to the Army Council who submit (in theory at any rate) it to the Sovereign. If acceptable he will in due course receive his commission signed by, or on behalf of, Her Majesty. This is a somewhat long-winded document which, among other things, orders all to obey Arthur's orders which will be backed by the whole might of Military Law.

Now let us deal with John Smith who hated the very sight of anything to do with the army and became, to use a modern term, all 'arty' and developed a flair for portrait painting till he became so famous that the Sovereign commissioned him to paint her portrait. Now, he will have a sovereign's commission but no authority whatever to order anyone about.

A commission is, therefore, in the sense that we shall use it, a document from the sovereign authorizing someone to do a specifically mentioned job – in our case to join the army as an officer. We speak of a person as holding a commission when we really mean possessing one.

Having said that one must hold a sovereign's commission before one can be an officer, it might be as well to go straight on to describing what is meant by a warrant officer and a non-commissioned officer as it will complete the story though mention of these ranks might be considered slightly out of place.

First, then, let us deal with the senior of the two – a warrant officer. (See *Warrant Officer.*)

A warrant is also a piece of paper which is signed by a person authorized to issue warrants. The sovereign delegates such authority to the Army Council who in turn re-delegates it to commanders-in-chief. A warrant officer, therefore, receives a paper signed by someone delegated to do so by the Army Council on their behalf, whereas the officer's is signed by, or on behalf of, the sovereign. In this connection I would say that commissions have not been signed by the sovereign in person since soon after the outbreak of the First World War and more is the pity that it has not been so as there is just that indefinable something about such commissions which the others haven't got.

It is outside the subject to mention it, but readers will be familiar with the terms 'warrant for arrest' and 'search warrant' which are written authorities signed by a chief constable giving the holder the particular right to arrest the individual named or enter and search certain specifically mentioned property.

The rank of non-commissioned officer is one that can be granted by a commanding officer at his own discretion without the giving of any paper to show for it. The fact that a private has been made a non-commissioned officer is published in the unit's orders which should be displayed in various places so that all members can see them. As soon as they are published they constitute the authority for the person named to wear the insignia of the rank and entitle him to the privileges as regards authority and social amenities that go with it. A commanding officer may grant a non-commissioned rank either with or without pay which is the reason for that much-maligned rank – unpaid (or acting unpaid) lance-corporal.

An officer cannot have his commission taken from him except by authority from the sovereign though a court martial may sentence him to be reduced in rank. Once commissioned he holds it for life which constitutes the reason for a retired officer retaining it. A warrant officer can only lose his by sentence of a court martial; a non-commissioned officer by sentence of a court martial or trial by his commanding officer. The last remark should be qualified by the statement that it rather depends on the nature of the crime which, if serious enough, will be tried by court martial in any case.

I have, in an endeavour to clarify the basic meanings of the three kinds of officers in the army, run ahead of purpose which is to give an account of the early meanings of the term com-mission.

We shall see that it was used in a somewhat looser sense than what I have just described though the fundamental are the same in that the authority for making officers originated with the king in person.

In olden days, when an army was required either to repel a threatened invasion or for the purpose of an overseas expedi-tion, it was the custom for the king to send his commission (which historians call his royal command) to his chief barons and heads of the clergy commanding them to meet him at a certain time and place together with their followers and the necessary (and usually specifically specified equipment. In order that the whole assemblage was a going concern by the time the king arrived the barons appointed their own officers because, though perhaps not stated in so many words, it was the king's intention that the army should be ready to move at once. The right to grant junior commissions was implied in much the same way that it would be absurd to have to include on a search warrant the authority to open a door.

A particularly interesting commission was that given, in 1442, by Henry VI to the governor of Nantes in which he was ordered to maintain 210 archers, 20 men-at-arms on foot, and 50 with which to defend the city. The commission was written on parchment and then torn in two, the king retaining one portion and the governor the other.

Here, at the risk of a further digression, I might interpose that the practice of doing this with important documents was probably copied from the traders of the time.

It was the custom, when giving credit, to give the purchaser a piece of what we would now call the invoice. When the bill was paid the merchant gave the buyer the piece retained by the seller as his receipt. This was, as can well be imagined, a very good protection against forgery. If one goes back even further to the days when accounting was done by cutting notches on sticks we find that notches to the number of the pounds or shillings involved were cut on the tallies, as the sticks were called. They were not cut an equal distance apart so that no two tallies for the same amount were the same. After the

N

notches were cut the sticks were split lengthwise and one half was kept by each party to the transaction. When the bill was paid the half retained by the seller was handed over to the buyer after, of course, care had been taken to see that the notches exactly corresponded as regards their distances apart and their depth.

Commissions of Array, as they were called, had been the means whereby the sovereign raised armies from the time of Alfred. Queen Elizabeth I, at the time of the threatened invasion by the Spaniards, in 1572, issued commissions to the justices of the peace in different counties commanding them to muster and train forces. They were empowered to commission officers to command bodies of 100 men and these in their turn were allowed to appoint their juniors. The privilege of granting commissions to officers in the national militia, subject to confirmation or annulment by the sovereign, was made law by Charles II and continued in force till recent times in the case of officers for the Territorial Army.

Condottieri

These are not the wives of the famous Italian sharpshooters known as bersaglieri though the word is from that country and signifies a chief, or leader, but was more usually employed to designate the soldiers of fortune who raised and maintained at their own expense corps of cavalry and infantry which they hired out for military service on different parts of the continent.

The reader must not make the obvious mistake of thinking that because they were continentals that they had nothing to do with our history and therefore a mention of them is out of place in this book.

The hiring of mercenaries commenced in the early part of the fourteenth century, in Italy, where the princes adopted much the same system as common in England in that they allowed their subjects to commute their personal service for cash payments with which bands of condottieri were hired.

The first English king to employ these cut-throats was Edward III during his wars with France. His fame and prowess were well-known and these roving hunters of loot were only too keen to ally themselves with anyone who seemed likely to give them a plentiful supply. One is tempted to say that whilst the war was on things were not too bad. The real trouble started after the Peace of Bretigny (1360). The French king had been taken prisoner at the battle of Poitiers (1356) and sent to England so the country was without a leader. Both sides had employed hired troops which now had nobody to fight. They were, one might say, all dressed up and nowhere to go. They, like the many discharged soldiers ever since could not adjust themselves to the hardships of peace which meant having to do some work after having worked hard to find some to do!

France must have been full of these desperate men who finally banded themselves together into what they called cotellis, or companies. They took the excommunication by the Pope in their stride and led by some of the most experienced leaders of the time they formed a body of some 40,000 strong that ruled – or at any rate overawed – France. They plundered farms and castles alike and then, like a swarm of locusts which had found better pastures, they left. The reason for their going was the outbreak of a real war in Spain.

I was rather amused at an account of the system of payment among these rogues. To start with, they demanded a month's pay in advance and a sort of overtime for the periods during which they were not actually fighting, and occasional bounties. They were utterly unscrupulous as is shown by an account of the battle of Anghiari – if one can call it a battle. It was here that Piccinino met Capponi (maybe an ancestor of Al Capone, the Chicago booze gangster). The engagement lasted four hours during which Piccinino was completely outbid and left the field. There are other occasions when the 'battle' was won by the highest bidder for the possible spoils.

They appear to have died out in the country of their origin as a result of the introduction of artillery which they were unable to maintain after capture. Old condottieri, like old soldiers, just fade away.

Perhaps the most famous condottieri was an Englishman, Sir John Hawkwood, who served with the Black Prince in France and then, after the peace of Bretigny, organized his well-known White Company which, with his own services, he hired out to various Italian princes. He eventually became the adviser and captain-general of the Florentine army. He died in Florence in 1394 and I think I am right in saying that there is a memorial to him in the church of Sible Hedingham, a village not far from Braintree, in Essex.

In more recent times we have heard much of mercenaries in Africa. (See *Mercenaries*.)

Conscription

When the French populace destroyed the castle known as the Bastille on the night of the 14th–15th July 1789, they started that orgy of fratricide known as the French Revolution. The old order – in fact any form of order – was swept away and any form of obedience became repugnant to those who were infected with the idea that anyone above themselves was a royalist, plutocrat, or some vile person who had to be humbled. The populace became so busy with their anarchy that they failed to realize that the country was in danger and lacked an army to protect it. Compulsory service was suggested to the National Assembly which rejected the idea as it would interfere with the liberty of the citizen but it did, however, issue a national appeal. Men flocked to serve and one must give them their due by recording that in some way or other they managed to save the country from invasion. By 1797 France seemed safe and, as always happens after wars, men lost interest in military service with the result that the army dwindled away to dangerously low proportions.

In 1798 General Jourdan submitted to the Council of Five Hundred a draft for a new mode of recruiting, under the name of conscription, which was approved and became law on the 5th September 1798.

This, then, is the origin of conscription which we now call National Service.

The law just mentioned decreed that all Frenchmen between the age of twenty and twenty-five were to be called up for service in the regular army whether the country was at war or not. The men were divided into five classes according to their age, the first being those between twenty and twenty-one; the second from twenty-one to twenty-two; and so on. The government decided how many men were required each year and this number was proportioned out among the various departments (which correspond to our counties) which were made responsible for doing the calling up.

The first levy by conscription was made in 1799 and raised 200,000 conscripts. They many campaigns indulged in by Napoleon took an awful toll of the manhood of France which could barely supply his requirements. There was no time limit of service; once a man was in the army he never got out till death, disease, or wounds made him of no further use.

When addressing the Council of State, in 1804, Napoleon made a remark concerning conscription which was as true then as if it had been applied to our National Service. He said, 'The law of conscription is the dread and desolation of families, but forms the security of the State.'

Convention

A convention is a truce arranged between two commanders for a temporary cessation of hostilities and is often, but not necessarily the forerunner of a peace treaty.

The most famous in our military history is probably the misnamed Convention of Cintra.

The Duke of Abrantes, after his heavy defeat at the Battle of Vimiera, feared a general rising of the populace in Lisbon so sent General Kellerman to the British commander-in-chief with a request that the fighting should stop and that the French troops should be allowed to retire unmolested from Portugal. The meeting took place at Cintra on the 22nd August 1808, but the truce was not ratified till the 30th, in Lisbon.

After the signing, Junot and his army together with the guns, horses, and what was politely called their private property, were conveyed to France and the Russian fleet, then in the Tagus, was ordered to sail to an English port till after the conclusion of peace.

I can recall no other occasion when the victors signed away their rights with such abandon as was done on this.

Cuirass

The word is derived from the French 'cuir', meaning hide or leather which shows that the original ones were of this substance, though afterwards chiefly of metal, both iron and brass.

The cuirass was a defensive piece of armour, made from well-hammered plate, extending from the neck to the waist, both at the front and back; the front piece was called the breast, the rear the back-plate. The two parts were connected by straps, leather thongs, or by some other means.

The idea of wearing a protection for the front and back is of very early origin for there is a breast and back-plate of Roman workmanship in the British Museum.

The wearing of a cuirass went out of fashion for many years and does not appear to have been revived till the early part of the fourteenth century. A contemporary defence was the corslet

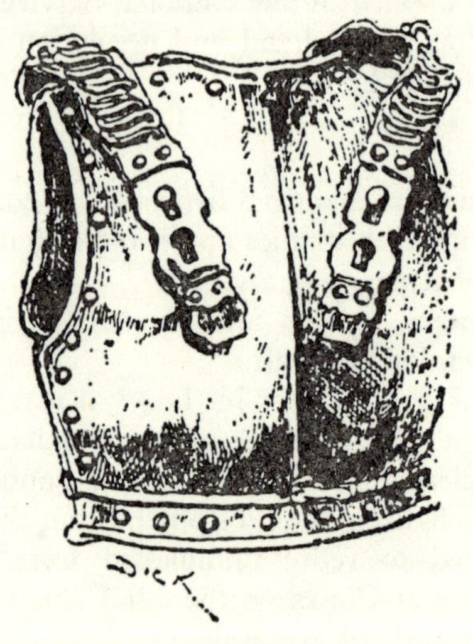

A cuirass

which was a breastplate on its own and not merely the front portion of a cuirass. In reading accounts of military events in the middle ages one may come upon the term 'pair of plates' which was another description of a cuirass.

An interesting thing about these early cuirasses is that they were not hung from the shoulder like the boards of the familiar sandwich men sometimes seen in London, but were made to fit in such a way that they rested on the hips and thus relieved the shoulders to exert full play in the use of sword or spear.

There is a very fine effigy of the Black Prince, who died in

1376, in Canterbury Cathedral which shows him wearing a cuirass and hauberk covered by his royal jupon, which is a sort of sleeveless jacket bearing his insignia.

The fifteenth century forms an interesting period as regards the wearing of armour for it would seem that the knights were experimenting with the different kinds to see which struck the happy medium between protection and cumbrousness. In about the middle of the century it was found that greater flexibility could be obtained by dividing the front portion of the cuirass crosswise in such a way that the lower part could be fitted to overlap the upper; the two being joined by straps similar to those at the sides.

In about 1460 another garment, known as a brigandine jacket was introduced. It was similar to a cuirass but was made of leather, or some heavy material, on to which were fixed small overlapping pieces of metal. A lighter version of this garment was worn by infantrymen up to the reign of Charles II; the last worn in action by cavalry were during the reign of George II.

The changing of the guard at Buckingham Palace and the Life Guards on duty in Whitehall are two of dollar-earning attractions of Britain. There is rather an amusing true story attached to the cuirasses worn by the Life Guard sentries.

They were first worn on these ornamental occasions in, or about, 1821, and during a meeting of a committee in the House of Commons to consider naval and military expenditures Colonel Lygon was asked the purchase price of the cuirasses worn by the Life Guards to which he replied, 'I apprehend they cost nothing; they have been lying in the Tower for years, and were worn at the battle of Dettingen.'

Dolman

A braided jacket or coat after the Hungarian Hussar fashion. (See Plate 8). It is still worn in full dress by the King's troop, R.H.A.

Drill

Drill, in anything like the form which we have today, originated in the French gendarmerie when commanded by Charles the

Bold who was killed at the battle of Nancy on the 5th January 1477.

The gendarmes were, as their name states, men-at-arms who were raised by Charles VII in 1439 to maintain order in France after the English had been driven out. They were organized in companies of about 450 strong whose main object was to replace the lawless mercenaries who, as described elsewhere, as soon as the fighting stopped roamed in large and small bands all over the country instituting a reign of terror.

Charles the Bold, Duke of Burgundy, introduced a code of drill in 1473, but I cannot trace which were the movements that he instituted.

I came upon an account of musketry drill in battle which seemed to refer to a period of about 1580–1600 but I may be wrong in this assumption. The account said that men were to be drawn up in squares of 25 men which in turn were to form a square of a hundred. The smaller formations were called escadrons, the larger companies. The idea was that the front rank should fire and then march to the rear and there reload. By the time the other nine ranks had done the same the first should be ready to fire again.

The foregoing is an account of some early type of what we would now call fire control and not drill in the sense which the modern recruit calls 'square bashing'.

The first drill book was edited by William Nead who gave it the title of *The Double-armed Man* because it contained particulars of the movements for men armed with both the pike and the bow. He presented a copy of it to Charles I in 1625 and the king was so impressed with its contents that he gave commissions to Nead and his son (also called William) to instruct the members of the trained bands.

The Earl of Essex, Captain-General of the parliamentary forces in the Civil War, issued a pamphlet, published on 29th September 1642, to his officers which exhorted them to exercise their men in the drilling with arms and it is interesting to recall that it was the steadiness of his infantry that won him the battle of Edgehill fought during the next month.

The Duke of York who became commander-in-chief in 1795 was the first to standardize the same drill throughout the army which was modified by the secretary of war (as he was then termed) Dundas who held that office between 1794–1801.

At the commencement of the Peninsular War, in 1808, the continental system of having three ranks for the infantry was used but in 1809 the two-rank formation was introduced which remained till after the first World War when it reverted to three.

Enlistment

Enlistment in its original sense was an engagement to serve as a soldier for an unlimited period or a specified number of years on receipt of enlistment money.

Enlistment is different from enrolment in that it is a voluntary act whereas the latter is compulsory. During the latter part of the eighteenth century it was the common practice to impress men and carry them away secretly to serve overseas. The ill-feeling that this occasioned brought about the introduction of what was termed voluntary engagement.

The pay and general conditions of service did not attract the right type of men so that it is not far wrong to say that it was not the glamour of the profession but the lure of the few shillings as enlistment money that acted as the chief bait. Recruiting sergeants were appointed to go round and find suitable men and were given a bonus for all such that they produced. The results were what could, or should, have been expected. The sergeants frequented the public houses with the sole intention of roping in those who were too drunk to know what they were doing. They were dragged along to the nearest barracks and thrown into a cell till they had sobered up enough to be coherent and then threatened with dire punishment by the sergeant if they did not profess to the recruiting officer that they had yearned for an army life ever since they were knee high to a grasshopper. Naturally, when they had sobered up sufficiently to really understand what had happened they were in the army and it was too late to make excuses and explanations. It is not very difficult to appreciate that the flower of the manhood of the country hardly resided in the barracks, or that garrison towns could not be confused with health resorts!

The quality of the new recruits degenerated to such an extent that some means had to be found whereby a better type of man was found and, above all, one who did not start to air his objections in no illusionary terms the moment he could remain vertical without any visible means of support.

In about 1820 the 34th clause of the Mutiny Act dealing with the subject of enlistment was altered to read so that those who had received their enlistment money were considered to have enlisted; but within forty-eight hours he was to be given a notice, or one was to be left at his home, notifying him what he had done. Furthermore, within four days from his receipt of the money he was to be brought before a magistrate who was to ask him whether he was a deserter or had previously served in the army or navy. The magistrate then read him the articles of war relating to mutiny and desertion and administered the oath of allegiance. If the recruit refused to take it he could be imprisoned without trial until such time as he canged his mind.

The recruiting sergeants had learnt off by heart a wonderful blarney which led the young recruits to believe that, whilst heaven might be their goal in after life, there was no existence to compare with that of a soldier whilst mortal. Should, therefore, the recruit become surprised – to use the original expression – at what he found he was allowed to go before a magistrate and declare his dissent and, on returning his enlistment money and a fine of a pound plus expenses, he was discharged.

There does not appear to have been any medical examination for the regulations stated that if the recruit was subsequently found to suffer from a disability which he had not declared he could be transferred for permanent garrison duty, or to one of the veteran or invalid battalions quite irrespective of the arm of the service in which he enlisted.

Epaulette

This was originally merely a strap on the shoulder to prevent the belt slipping off. In course of time it became more decorative and served to indicate the rank of the wearer. The epaulette was abolished in the British Army after the Crimea, but survived on the full dress of the Royal Navy until abolished after the last war (see figure opposite).

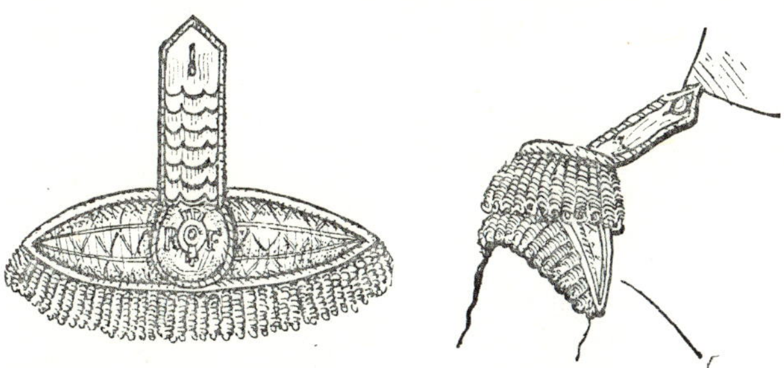

Left, Wing worn by officers of Grenadiers, Light Infantry and Fusiliers up to the Crimean War. Right, Epaulette worn over a wing by Field Officers of Light Infantry and Fusiliers from c 1816 to 1830.

Establishment

The word in a military sense is rather difficult to describe as it is so readily confused with 'strength'.

There are two kinds of establishments to every military formation known as Peace Establishment and War Establishment. They both give in great detail the maximum number of men and material which a unit is allowed to have during peace or wartime as the case may be.

For the sake of simplicity, let us deal with officers and men only whilst remembering that the establishment is equally detailed as regards vehicles and equipment.

As a matter of strict accuracy a peace establishment is a small pamphlet which gives the number of the various ranks of officers, warrant officer, non-commissioned officers and men that constitute the maximum that may be allowed to serve with the unit in peace time.

The strength of a unit is something quite different and signifies the number of men present. A unit may be allowed, say, five hundred privates but on a certain date there are no more, including those away on leave, etc, than four hundred. In this case the establishment is 500, but the strength only 400. The numbers of men on a parade is known as a state – statement – a parade state – and has nothing whatever to do with either establishment or strength or condition.

Every year Parliament passes an Army and Air Force Annual Act which, in addition to making military punishments legal, lays down the establishment of the army as regards numbers – in other words it authorizes the standing army to consist of a fixed number of men which cannot be exceeded without further legislation.

First Field Dressing

The first mention that I have found of soldiers being in possession of any specially issued medical equipment was in an account of the Prussian Army during the Franco-Prussian War, 1870. Field dressings were first issued to our troops for service in the Egyptian Campaign of 1884.

Fusiliers

The origins of Fusiliers was simply to have infantry armed with a lighter weapon or fusil which could be slung over the back and shoulder by a sling. This necessitated a cap as opposed to the broad brimmed hat then in use, and the first of our fusiliers, the Royal Fusiliers, who were raised to guard the artillery train, wore a fur trimmed cap (see figure on page 82).

Gazette

We are not concerned with the origin of newspapers, but the dividing line between some of the early publications and what we would now call gazettes is so difficult to define that perhaps a few words on the subject will not be too out of place.

The first newspaper, or news sheet was the Acta Diurna, published in Rome in 691 BC. It was not till the sixteenth century that anything approaching this existed in modern times, if the sixteenth century can be considered modern.

The earliest regular publication, known as the *Frankfurter Journal*, appeared weekly in that town in 1615. The first newspaper to appear regularly in Britain was the Weekly News which was produced in London by Nathaniel Butter. The first time that the word 'gazette' was used occurred in Paris, in 1631, when Renaudot produced his *Gazette de France*.

There are in existence today many papers which contain the word 'mercury' in their title which is derived from the 'mercuries' who ran about the streets of Paris selling the paper which I have just mentioned.

During the war between the Republic of Venice and the Turks in Dalmatia, in 1563, it was the custom in Venice to communicate military and commercial news by written sheets which were read out at stated times and places. Those who wished to stand and listen were charged a gazetta, a small coin worth about two-thirds of a penny. The name was gradually connected to the paper itself and found its way to France and England. The Venetian government took good care that these sheets were never printed with the result that only a few copies were written out so that the merchants and those who wished to hear the latest news had to go to the appointed places. Some of these papers are still to be seen in the library in Florence.

Before the introduction of printed newspapers in England, it was the custom of the great families to employ gazetteers in London who transmitted to them the news of the day in written letters for an annual fee of ten pounds. They were, I presume, the original news-hawks, or correspondents. I need hardly add that this is how we get the term correspondent though he's far more likely to use the telephone, or wireless, to send his red hot news to his paper than to sit down and write. News today which is more than an hour or two old is almost stale.

Lord Burghley, one of Queen Elizabeth I's ministers, is credited with being the first person to issue printed sheets of public intelligence. The earliest now preserved is No. 50 which records the arrival of the Spanish Armada. The title of the sheets was *The English Mercurie,* and were said to be published for the contradiction of false reports. The last number refers to the Queen's thanksgiving in St Paul's Cathedral after the Armada had been destroyed.

The first signs of what we would now call newspaper propaganda that I can trace took place during the Civil War when both sides produced their own papers extolling their cause.

The first papers to publish official government intelligence, as it was then called, were the *Mercurius Politicus* and the *Publique Intelligencer* which originated during the Commonwealth in 1655. Though almost from their first appearances they were used by the government as official mediums it was not until 1659 that an order of the council was published to that effect.

The restoration of the monarchy took place in 1660 and in 1644 the Great Plague of London broke out as a result of which Charles II and his court moved to Oxford.

It was here, on the 14th November 1665, that the first copy of the *Oxford Gazette* was published. Twenty-three numbers were published from Oxford and by the time the twenty-fourth was due the court had returned to London so that the twenty-fourth number of the *Oxford Gazette* became the first of the *London Gazette* by which name it has ever since been known.

The *London Gazette* is a government publication and the editorship is a government appointment with his salary paid from public monies. It is published twice a week, on Tuesday and Fridays.

When we say that someone has been 'gazetted' we mean that his name has appeared in the *London Gazette* and from that date his appointment becomes, as it were, official. The promotion and appointment, of officers may be what is called ante-dated which means that the appointment will be as from the date mentioned and not that on which the gazette was published. If, for example, the gazette was published on the 1st June it might contain the information that Captain Smith has been promoted to the rank of major with seniority as from 1st May so that he is ante-dated exactly one calendar month. The converse is also true in that an appointment, usually in the case of senior appointments, will take effect from some future date.

Though we are only concerned here with the military aspect of the *London Gazette* it contains many other details such as the proceedings in bankruptcy, dissolution of business partnerships and various other details which the law decrees should be published in it.

Geneva Convention

The Convention owes its origin to two Swiss, Monsieur Moynier and Docteur Henri Dunant the latter of whom wrote an account of the horrors which he saw on the battlefield of Solferino where the French defeated the Austrians on the 24th June 1859. They formed an association to agitate that all ambulances and places where the wounded were receiving attention should be inviolate. Their advocation met with such success that an international conference, at which the representatives of fourteen governments were present, was held in Geneva on the 26th October 1863.

The points raised were referred to the respective governments who agreed to a further meeting on the 22nd August 1864, at which twelve of the Powers signed what has since been known as the Geneva Convention. Supplementary conventions have since been held; the latest British ratification is dated 16th April 1907.

It is not necessary to mention all the clauses of the original convention but it worth mentioning the gist of some of them as they give us the origins of certain things which we now take for granted as having existed since war, or at any rate chivalry, existed. They were:

1 Hospitals and ambulances should be considered as neutral as long as they contained any sick or wounded;
2 All medical staff in hospitals should be considered as neutrals and should be allowed to leave with their private property and ambulances;
3 Any house that harbours a sick or wounded soldier shall be exempt from having soldiers billeted therein;
4 That all wounded soldiers, when they have recovered from their sickness or wounds, shall be repatriated on condition that they do not again carry arms during the rest of the war;
5 All hospitals and places harbouring wounded, as well as ambulances shall exhibit the flag of their nation and a distinctive and uniform one bearing a red cross on a white ground, and that their staff shall wear an arm-band of the same design.

One can read through all this a desire that the horrors of war be reduced as much as possible, especially as regards those who have already suffered.

How does all this compare with the sinking at sight of merchant ships carrying women and children, the unrestricted bombing of towns, napalm bombs which burn all in their range without discrimination, and finally the stark reality that the two halves of the world are exerting great efforts to produce bombs which, even in their original form, can blast a large town to smithereens and in doing so kill over 100,000 people and maim for life a further number nearly as large?

Gentleman of a Company

This rank has entirely disappeared and I cannot think of any that descends from it.

A Gentleman of a Company is mentioned in Sir James Turner's *Pallas Armata* as, 'something more than an ordinary soldier, hath a little more pay and doth not stand sentinel. They march and watch with arms, they go common rounds and patrouilles, and near the enemy they are to be forlorn centinels (sic) whom the French call perdus'.

This extract is very contradictory for in one place it says that they do not stand sentry and then goes on to say that they do.

Those who have read my *British Battles and Medals* will have seen my remarks concerning the term 'forlorn' when I dealt with the medals issued during the reign of Charles I. The word has obviously got something to do with leading, or being out in front so, in the same way as forlorn hope parties were those in the van, I imagine that forlorn sentinels were those posted furthest out in front.

The German word 'forloren' means lost, and as the sentries were also called 'perdus', or lost ones, by the French, we should not be far wrong in thinking that the forlorn sentries were those who operated so far out in front that their chances of survival were considered very small.

The word gentlemen is contained in such court officials as gentlemen-at-arms, gentlemen ushers, etc, and more particulars concerning them will be found in the chapter dealing with the Royal Household.

God Save the King (or Queen)

There seems to be some doubt as to the author of our National

A.   *Officer's Grenadier cap, Suffolk Militia, c 1750. Courtesy S. R. Butler, Esq, Wallis & Wallis, Lowes, Sussex*

B.   A General Officer of Hussars, c 1830.

Anthem. I have seen it stated that it was composed by the Somersetshire composer in 1606 to be played at a dinner held in the Merchant Taylors' Hall at which James I was present. The consensus of opinion is that Henry Carey, the illegitimate son of George Saville, Marquis of Halifax, wrote it in about 1740, in which year it was first played. It immediately became popular and was adopted in France in 1776, and subsequently became the Danish, Prussian, and German national anthems. The music was again used by Doctor Samuel Smith, in 1843, for the American hymn, 'My Country 'tis of Thee'.

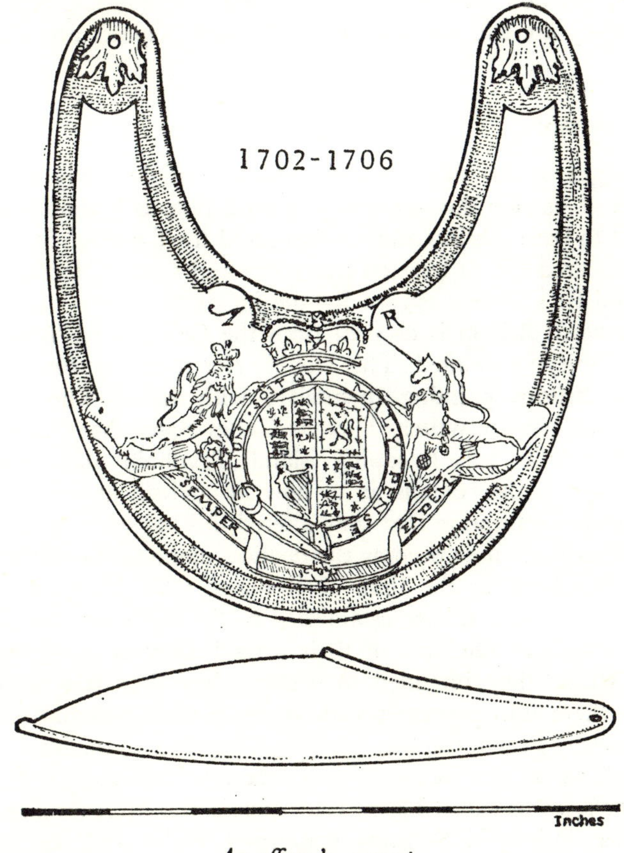

An officer's gorget.

O

Gorget

This was originally the piece of armour worn round the neck. When the wearing of armour fell into disuse the gorget continued to be worn as a badge of rank by officers when on duty. By the time of its abolition in the 1830s it had become merely a small decorative half-moon shaped plate, which was suspended from the collar by cords or ribbons attached to two buttons. In course of time the patch of cloth, button and small cord which had supported the gorget became in themselves a distinction, to be worn on the collar in a variety of colours to indicate the wearers position on the Staff, and were commonly called staff tabs. They are still worn in scarlet by full Colonels and higher ranks.

Great Britain

The origin of this title, and of Britannia, might justly be considered as outside the scope of this book but, as it should be of interest to both soldiers and civilians, and the figure of Britannia has appeared for so long on our coins and medals, I trust that that will be sufficient excuse for the inclusion.

The word Britain is derived from the Celtic word 'brith', or 'brit', signifying painted. This would refer to the custom of the ancient Britons painting themselves with woad. The middle eighteenth century writer, Thomas Carte states that this island was known as Inis (meaning island) Prydhain and, without going into further details as to how he arrived at this, it is a reasonable assumption that time altered this last word to Britain.

Britannia has now become the poetical name for Great Britain and dates back to the time of Romans, who disregarded the boundaries that had been established by the tribes who inhabited these islands at the time of their arrival. Having surveyed the areas which they intended to occupy they then proceeded to divide them into provinces with rivers as their boundaries.

Britannia Prima, the first province composed all the land south of the Thames, the Saxon Wessex; the area between the Severn and the sea was called Flavia Caesariensis, the Mercian kingdom of Offa; Britannia Secunda comprised Wales and the Welsh Marches; Maxima Caesariensis, between the Humber and the

Tyne, was the former Northumbrian province of Deira; the Lowlands of Scotland and Northumberland, with a northern boundary between the Firth of Forth and the Clyde, was called Valentia.

Great Britain has been the legal name of the island containing England and Scotland and Wales since the passing of the Act of Union on 1st May 1707.

The first article of the Treaty of Union states that the kingdoms of Scotland and England shall, from this date, and ever after, be united into one kingdom, by the name of Great Britain; in subsequent articles the kingdom is called the United Kingdom of Great Britain.

The expression had, however, been in general use from the time of the first parliament of James I who, on opening it, spoke at some length on the advisability of a legislative union of the two countries. In the debate which followed the speech the suggestion met with considerable opposition as it was not forgotten that Queen Mary of Scotland had been advised to style herself Queen of Great Britain. James overruled the objection and issued a proclamation on 20th October 1604, declaring his style to be, King of Great Britain, France and Ireland. He followed this up with another dated 16th November of the same year ordering that the coinage of both kingdoms should bear the inscription, 'Ja. D. G. Mag. Brit. F. & H. Rex', signifying that he was, James, by the Grace of God, of Great Britain, France, and Ireland, King.

Grenadiers

According to *Grose's Antiquities*, grenades were first used in 1594, and that the first regular troops to be armed as such were in the French Army in 1667, and appear to have been first raised in the British Army ten years later. One company was added to each regiment of Foot Guards and Troop of Household Cavalry. Grenadiers were universally considered élite troops, and in later times the title of Grenadiers would be given to a Regiment as a mark of honour, eg Bombay Grenadiers. In the British service the distinction of a grenadier was usually a special pattern headgear and a white plume.

A Horse Grenadier c 1750.

Heliograph

Heliography, the reflecting of the sun's rays, was used, so it is said, by Alexander the Great during his campaign in Egypt in BC 332 but, I should imagine, more as a means of showing location than a method of inter-communication.

The heliograph on the light tripod stand was the invention of Henry Mance, in 1875, and first taken on active service in India during the Jowaki campaign, in 1877–78.

Hussar

Light cavalry adopted in the British Army in 1807 from the Hungarian model. Hussar dress is a modification of Hungarian National costume.

Indent

I cannot trace the first use of the word as it stands, though there is mention of the word indenture in the rolls of Edward I 1307–27.

Identity Discs

The Boer War, 1899–1902, was the first in which British troops carried regulation methods of identity which consisted of strips of tape which were supposed to be carried in the pocket, but I should doubt whether the men remembered that they were there and in consequence they must have been lost as often as kept. Another disadvantage would have been that, as there was no regulation position in which they were to be carried, the seriously wounded and dead would require detailed searching to find whether the man had one on him or not.

The first discs, which were made of tin, expressly ordered to be worn round the neck were issued in 1906.

I cannot give the date when the policy of issuing two discs to each man was introduced. I still have those which I wore in the First War, one of which is circular and red; the other is a sort of octangonal shape of green. In their case my rank, initials, name, religion, and regiment is stamped on them; those for the Second War omit the regiment.

The idea of the two colours is that the red one should be removed from the dead at the time of burial. Burial parties were, as often as not, more in theory than practice, supplied with small bags in which to put the personal belongings of the dead. The red disc was then attached to the bag and served the dual purpose of naming the owner of the contents and a record of those who had been definitely traced as killed. The green disc being left on the body identified the corpse in case it had to be temporarily buried and then exhumed for reburial afterwards.

The two discs should have been attached to a cord worn round the neck in such a way that the red one could be cut off without having to remove the green. Most of the men used to consider them a morbid nuisance and, on the principle that it can't happen to me, hitched them on to their braces.

Air Raid Wardens and Members of the Civil Defence Services generally in the last war will agree with me that it was often less trouble to rescue people than it was to find out who they were, and it was not infrequent that the guesses were wrong and thus caused unnecessary grief to relatives.

I would say that one of the first laws that should be issued in the awful event of another war should compel every male to carry his name, address and blood group around his neck, and every female the same around her wrist.

Inspections

In this connection we must be careful to distinguish between mustering and inspecting. A body of men could be mustered, or what we would now call paraded, without being inspected, so we find that special officers were appointed for each purpose. The person responsible for summoning the men and getting them on parade was the Muster Master General; the person responsible for seeing that they were suitable and complete with all that they should have was the Commissary of Muster.

The first king to appoint the latter officer was Henry V, in, or about 1314.

Before stopping to think, one is inclined to wonder why both these officers were necessary and why the fellow who carried out the mustering could not do the inspecting.

If the reader would try to vizualize the period, he would, I think, agree with Henry V that this was the soundest way to ensure that when he wanted an army it arrived at the appointed place something better than a rabble.

The only means of intercommunication over long distances was on horseback so that people must have been extremely parochial in their outlook and customs. Without sending officers out to see how the barons in Devon were behaving as regards keeping their followers ready for war, it would have been impossible for the king to know what sort of support he was likely to get from that area when an emergency arose. In addition to seeing what was happening he also had to make sure that there was as much similarity as possible as regards the equipment and training of the men from Devon as those from, say, Essex.

We have much the same sort of thing today in the form of annual inspections when the cooks wash their hands and everything in sight is whitewashed in case, so it would seem, the inspecting officer has failing vision and might fall over kerb stones, dustbins, or the feet of the regimental police.

Invalids

The mention of this word conjures up visions of bath chairs and crutches so it may come as somewhat of a surprise to learn that they formed units of the army at one time.

Invalids were men who had been discharged on account of wounds, or age, and who were considered unfit for service abroad but quite capable to undertake that at home.

The 1st Battalion the Welch Regiment was originally known as the Regiment of Royal Invalids and was formed from veterans.

May I remind the reader that he must not always give old terms the same meaning as they now have else he might be inclined to think that the Royal Military Asylum at Chelsea had to be built owing to the number of lunatics in the army and wonder why more have not since been erected. That asylum was a school for the children of serving soldiers and had nothing whatever to do with lunacy – at any rate not primarily.

Khaki

Our word 'khaki' is derived from the Urdu 'khak' which signifies dusty, drab, or off-colour. I hardly think that the word 'invented' fits in with the way the use of the colour was introduced, first into the old Indian Army, then to our own. Its introduction was the result of observation and trial and error by that grand soldier, Sir Harry Lumsden, who raised the once famous Corps of Guides, whose march of 'one to a horse and two to a camel' from Kandahar to help in the relief of Delhi at the outbreak of the Indian Mutiny, always stands out in my mind as the finest forced march in history.

It was the custom, before the outbreak of the Mutiny, for troops to operate in the North West Frontier in much the same clothing as they wore to impress the generals on parade, whilst their opponents made themselves almost invisible in a nondescript outfit which could be smelt further than seen. These old scoundrels used to dye their clothing by boiling it in water to which the juice of the little mazari palm, which grows in the foothills of the Hindu Kush, had been added. The result of this treatment was that an artificially produced dirty colour was added to the clothing of these unwashed brethren who then lay in wait behind rocks to snipe at the unwary. One of the secrets of camouflage is to break up the outline of whatever it is one is trying to conceal. These tribesmen wore voluminous clothing over baggy trousers which helped them to 'melt' into their background. Lumsden noticed this and introduced somewhat similar clothing for his Corps of Guides and it was subsequently adopted by infantry of the Punjab Frontier Force in 1857.

As soon as the Mutiny was over the very idea that clothing that was purposely made to look dirty was anathematized so that khaki was, so to speak, hidden away for a bit (except for wear as rompers), but Lord Roberts saw the sound common sense in the idea of trying to hide the soldier from the enemy with the result that khaki uniform for service was worn for the Afghan War, 1878–80.

The first campaign during which the army from home wore other than their regimental uniform was that in Egypt, 1880–82, when a sort of field grey was adopted. The Germans used this colour in the 1914–18 War and the French a pale blue. We, on the other hand, stuck to khaki. I remember many arguments as to which was the most difficult colour to see at distance beyond a hundred yards. The general opinion was green. I think that we were right.

There is one question concerning this camouflage business to which I have never had a satisfactory answer.

Why are guns, vehicles, and other inanimate objects painted green whilst men wear khaki. If green is the best for hiding vehicles, etc., why is it not so good for small targets such as men? The general colour of a European landscape in summer is green, and darkish brown in autumn and winter. The most effective camouflage clothing for all-the-year-round wear is obviously a mixture of these two – a fact which it seems to have taken two world wars to disclose.

Lance Corporal

Originally called Lancespesate, the word is Italian and means 'broken lance'. Sir James Turner in his *Pallas Armata,* 1653 says thus: 'The lance corporal was originally a man at arms or trooper, who having broken his lance on the enemy, and lost his horse in fight, was entertained, as a volunteer assistant to a captain of foot, receiving his pay as a trooper, until he could remount himself; from being the companion of the captain, he was soon degraded to the assistant of the corporal, and at present does the duty of that officer, on the pay of a private soldier'.

Lancer

After some years of disfavour the lance came into its own once more during the Napoleonic Wars, and thereafter the nations of Europe formed regiments of lancers based upon the original Polish model, from which the distinctive square topped cap of Polish National dress was also adopted. Introduced in the British Army in 1816. See plate 7.

Land Mines

The first use of these devilish devices that I can trace was at the seige of Serezanella in 1487, when they were employed by the

Genoese in their war with the Florentines. They were also used during that extraordinary seige of Candia (now known as Crete), which lasted twenty-four years (1645–69), when the Venetians laid them against the attacking Turks.

Lanterns

In an order dated 1578 the Master of Ordnance was made responsible for supplying, among other articles mentioned, cressets.

Cressets were lanterns that had to be hung at the front and rear of transport in the same way as ordered during the last war for convoys travelling at night.

Ledgers

An order was issued in 1683 compelling all military store-keepers to, 'keep two counter or cheque (sic) books by way of Journal and Ledger'. This same order goes on to describe how receipts and vouchers are to be obtained and lays down that articles are to be classified as either serviceable, unserviceable, or repairable. In fact, if one ignores the old English, it is difficult to realize that it was written about two hundred and fifty years ago as so much of what it contains applies today, and will do so for many years to come.

In addition to the remarks about clothing it also mentions that monetary accounts were to be kept 'by way of debtor and creditor and balanced throughout'. It expressly stated that the left hand page 'exhibit and make him the store-keeper debtor, and on the other page to have credit'.

It concludes by saying that a Board must be formed to check all journals and ledgers every month.

The long-winded jargon so beloved by quartermasters can be traced back to this period for I found in an old ledger an entry to show that Colonel William Legg (sic) was, on 27th October 1688, issued with 'Harquebus Armour, Carbine proof, 1'.

Lord-Lieutenant

Prior to the Norman Conquest there were two officers responsible for each county known as the ealdorman and sheriff.

It is difficult to decide how far the functions of the latter were concurrent with those of the former. The confusion has been increased by the translation, in our ancient laws, of the word sheriff in Latin into vice comes, and in Norman French into visconte, or viscount, signifying deputy to the earl.

After the Battle of Hastings, William the Conqueror, as is well known, rewarded his nobles with grants of land confiscated from the descendants of the Saxon nobles killed in the battle. These earldoms, as they were called, were of three kinds. The senior was when a whole county was given in feud with jura regalia – the right to rule. In this case the county became a county palatine, or principality, and the person appointed to it was given royal jurisdiction and seigniory. Such a county was, therefore, a sort of feudal kingdom of its own, but held of a superior lord – the king. The counties of Lancaster, Chester, Pembroke, Hexham, and the Bishopric of Durham, have, at various times, been counties palatine; but there is no record that the title of earl palatine was given to the oldest of them, ie, Chester, before the reign of Henry II. The earls of Chester held their own parliaments and created barons, and had their own officers such as judiciaries, chancellors, and barons of their exchequer. This continued till the reign of Henry III when the county palatine was taken over by the crown.

The second kind of earls were those whom the king created earls of a county, with civil jurisdiction, and a third part of the profits derived from the county court, but they were not given actual possession, or seisin as it was called, of the county.

The third kind were those to whom the king gave a large piece of land which he designated a county over which he gave the earl civil and criminal jurisdiction to be held per servitum unius comitatus.

In the Anglo-Saxon period every man had to bear arms in defence of his country. The responsibility for seeing that men were available, and received a certain amount of training, rested with the county sheriffs. The thanes had to parade mounted to compose the cavalry, whilst the remainder of the male population, armed with a variety of hand weapons, formed the infantry.

The calling out of the populace was done by what were

called commissions of array, which required certain persons to muster and array (parade) the inhabitants of the counties to which the commissions were sent. All who were incapable of rendering military service had to furnish armour and other necessary equipment for their more agile countrymen. They were also detailed to collect firewood for beacons and to remain near them so as to light them when ordered. According to some accounts the arranging of all this was part of the duties of the sheriff. The powers granted these commissions were the cause of much complaint until they were clarified by statute in 1403 by Henry IV.

These commissions of array were replaced in the sixteenth century by what were known as commissions of lieutenancy by which nearly the same powers were delegated to certain persons as resident representatives of the crown for maintaining military preparedness and order in their counties.

Henry VIII, in 1545, issued a commission to the Duke of Norfolk appointing him the king's lieutenant and captain-general of all captains, vice-captains, men-at-arms, archers, and all others retained or to be retained against the French, in the counties of Essex, Suffolk, Norfolk, Hertford, Cambridge, Huntingdon, Lincoln, Rutland, Warwick, Northampton, Leicester, and Bedford. A similar commission was given to the Duke of Suffolk for the counties of Kent, Sussex, Surrey, Hants, Wilts, Berks, Oxford, Middlesex, Bucks, Worcester, Hereford, and London; and Lord Russell, Keeper of the Privy Seal, was given the same for the counties of Dorset, Somerset, Devon, Cornwall and Gloucester.

Camden, writing in the time of Elizabeth I, refers to them as extraordinary magistrates, constituted only in times of danger, as was the case with the commissioners of array.

The right of the sovereign to appoint commissions of lieutenancy continued till withdrawn by the Long Parliament during the Commonwealth. As a matter of fact the right to appoint these lieutenants formed one of the bones of contention between Charles I and his people.

After the Restoration, in 1674 to be exact, Parliament restored to the sovereign, then Charles II, the right to appoint lords-lieutenant. This meant that the control of the militia was given back to the sovereign, but this wretched monarch again blotted his already dirty copy book by ordering that all military offences were to be tried in the civil courts with the result that the militia lost prestige and suffered accordingly.

The subsequent choppings and changings that went on concerning the control of the militia till 1907 are outside our subject. In this year the Territorial and Reserve Forces Act was passed under which County Associations, of which the lords-lieutenant were appointed presidents of their respective countries, came into being for the purpose of administering the county Territorial Units.

The presidents of these associations – that means the lords-lieutenant (the present title is The Queen's Lieutenant for the County of . . .) – could recommend to the sovereign persons who he considered suitable to fill, as the rules quaintly describes it, 'first appointments to the lowest rank of officer'.

The old order has passed and now the Government, through the Army Council, controls both the Regular and the Territorial Armies with the result that lords-lieutenant, as far as military matters are concerned, are little more than another species of duck on the military pond which, however, when in full plumage, makes a magnificent spectacle on certain occasions.

Machine Guns

The modern machine gun has been referred to as the Queen of the Battlefield which I suppose it really is, though this titles does not sound like those which are more commonly used to describe one which happens to be firing at you!

If we are agreed that the bullet has replaced the arrow, then we are justified in going back along the long road of military history to see whether we can find any mention of a weapon which threw more than one arrow.

Our journey takes us back to 396 BC for, in an account of the war between the Syracusans and Catheginians mention is made of a weapon which threw many arrows. It is not described so that it would be unwise to visualize it as anything more than a sort of rack on which the arrows were placed so as to be discharged by either one or more bows on the release of a mechanism corresponding to our trigger.

The first weapons which fired (as opposed to discharged) more than one missile without reloading were referred to as organs because they consisted of several tubes either mounted side by side in racks, or tied together in a circular bundle.

The first person to use these fire organs was the Italian mercenary Bartolommeo Colleoni who employed them as a cavalry weapon in the war between Venice and Milan, in 1467. Whether he thought of the idea, or someone did for him I cannot say but, at the time mentioned, these guns were given what I can best describe as a machine gun effect by discharging the barrels with different lengths of fuses so that they went off one after the other. Incidentally, and nothing to do with our subject, Colleoni is the subject of what some consider to be the finest equestrian statue in the world, that by Verrochio and Leopardi in Venice.

The use of organ guns – later to have as many as eighty barrels continued with varying degrees of success till the arrival of the Gatling Gun, invented by Richard Jordan Gatling, in 1862. This had six barrels mounted in a circle which was revolved by a manually operated handle. As each barrel passed a tray it was loaded by the force of gravity, and one revolution of the set of barrels completed the process of loading a cartridge, firing one, extracting one, and ejecting one.

These guns, which were water cooled, were mounted on small two-wheeled carts and were the first mobile repeating weapons.

In 1851, two Belgians, Faschamps and Montigny, had been experimenting with something similar which they termed a grape shot shooter, or mitrailleuse, a name which is still in use in French-speaking armies to define what we call a machine gun. The general principle of their idea was somewhat similar to Gatling's as it was hand-operated but it had twenty-five, instead of six, barrels.

The Franco-Prussian War of 1870 proved the value of repeating weapons which soon became established in all European armies. The Gatling gun had become an international necessity so to speak.

In 1873 three Swedes, E. Unge, J. Winborg, and H. Palmcrantz, with financial assistance from the Swedish banker, Thorsten Nordenfeldt, produced an automatic weapon to which they gave the banker's name. Their weapon underwent various improvements and then, in 1879 another inventor, whose name has ever since been associated with weapons, the American B. Hotchkiss, produced his famous quick-firer.

So far, be it noted, all the weapons were fitted with barrels which were much larger than those of their contemporary rifles, they were really small pieces of artillery. It was the difficulty in deciding whether they should be counted as light artillery or infantry weapons that lead to their unpopularity for several years as their tremendous fire-power was not realized by the infantry and their lack of penetration, and the small size of the round that they fired, did not appeal to artillerymen. It was not for many years that it dawned on the military minds that here was a weapon whose employment should form a study on its own. It was as if a cabinet maker had decided that a certain hammer was too heavy and a blacksmith not heavy enough, so neither bothered about it.

The first automatic weapon to be taken on service by the British army was the Gatling gun, a few of which were taken to Ashantee during the war in 1874. They were not employed in action as they had to be left behind when the march to Coomassie started due to transport difficulties. The first mention that I have found of them being fired in action by our troops was during the relief march on Etchowe, by Lord Chelmsford's column, when a large body of Zulus was routed at Ginghilovo on 2nd April 1879.

We now come to the doyen of machine gun inventors, Hiram Steven Maxim, an American who became a naturalized British subject and was knighted in 1901.

Few would associate Hatton Garden, London, with anything else but diamonds but it was in a small workshop in this street that Maxim worked, and from which came his famous weapon in 1883. It was the first whose rate of fire could be referred to as so many rounds a second – not minutes. On its first official test it fired six bullets in less than a second and, from then on, revolutionized war for many years to come. It was, as those who remember the blood-baths on the Somme and elsewhere in

1915, the dreadful slaughter caused by automatics which compelled higher authority to sit down and have a good think. The result was the arrival of the tank which waddled on to the field in 1916 and, if not not employed in such penny-packet, fashion, might – I say might – have altered the whole course of our positions for the next winter and even, as many think, shortened the war.

The world is now well supplied with means of causing instant death, or the same result after periods of intense suffering, for we have machine guns, jaz, powerful explosives, pop and atom bombs.

Mention in Despatches

The question as to when the first 'Mention in Despatches' was made is one which I have yet to hear, or see, answered to my satisfaction. I do not wish to start an argument on the subject so will just give the date, place, and writer of the first despatch which mentions an officer under the rank of colonel for special commendation.

It is that of Lieutenant-General Sir C. Stewart who commanded the troops at the siege of Calvi, then a fortified port on the west coast of Corsica, which lasted from 12th June 1794, till it surrendered on 10th August of the same year. The place and date are given as 'Calvi, August 10th 1794'. An extract reads, 'It is with the utmost confidence that I presume to recommend to HM my ADC, Captain Duncan, of the Royal Artillery, whose activity, zeal, and ability in his own and the engineer's department, merit the highest commendation and advancement'.

As to who was the first non-commissioned officer or man to have been mentioned in despatches is far too controversial for me to raise. I know that a famous Lancashire regiment claims the honour for the Crimea, and that the Cheshire Regiment does the same for the battle of Meanee, which, incidentally, is spent Meeanee on the medal.

I remember hearing some officers of overwhelming seniority discussing this subject and they, as so often happens when the species start an argument, drifted further and further away

C.   *Full Dress and Undress Sabretaches, Royal Artillery, c 1890.*
Dress Sabretache, 2nd West Yorkshire Yeomanry Cavalry, c 1890.

D. *Hussar Busbies c 1900. The centre one is an officer's.*

from what they were trying to decide till they all got lost in that of decorations and orders.

I expect the mentioning of a subordinate by one in command of an operation goes back to the days of clubs and, even if we could trace the first occasion, we still haven't answered the question in its present meaning.

The significance today is that a person has been mentioned in the despatches of a commander-in-chief for meritorious service, and his name appears in the London Gazette so that he is entitled to wear an emblem on the medal subsequently awarded for the campaign in which the service was rendered.

The first medal on which such an emblem was authorized to be worn was the Victory Medal of the 1914–18 War but I cannot say who was the first person so honoured.

Mercenaries

A mercenary* soldier is one who fights for money, and the only real difference I can see between the soldiers of the middle ages and those of today is that the former fought for money and the latter for more money.

The Norman kings employed mercenaries – probably because they were so much better and cheaper, as fighting was their profession and they could be collected on the spot and thus save all the bother of two-way transportation.

It would be difficult to say which were the first to be employed by an English monarch and easy to state the last so I will take the line of least resistance.

The last body of mercenaries to be employed was the German Legion which fought for us in the Crimea. Before the troops were withdrawn, the men composing the legion were offered free passages to any of our Dominions. Many accepted the offer. The majority who did so chose South Africa; some went to Australia and Canada. See *Condottieri*.

Military Frontier

The north west boundary of India was so generally referred to

* In modern parlance, the word mercenary has an unpleasant connotation, but one should remember the Swiss Guards massacred defending the French Monarchy, and, within the meaning of the word, the Gurkhas – 150 years of loyal service of unparalleled excellence. *Editor.*

P

as 'The Frontier' that it seemed impossible that any other could exist, or ever had existed.

The first tract of land, to receive that nomenclature, known as the Military Frontier, extended from the Adriatic Sea to the Bukowina, a total length of about a thousand miles. It was distinguished from the rest of the Austrian Empire by having its own purely military government. All able-bodied peasants in this area of some 13,000 square miles were soldiers and held their lands under regulations very similar to our old Feudal System. This frontier was formed in the early part of the nineteenth century to form a barrier against the inroads of the Turks and was divided into four military commands in which the commander was responsible for the administration of civil affairs and justice. Frontier posts were established and nobody was allowed to cross the border either way without being examined.

The headquarters of the four commands were at Agram for the Croatian frontier; at Peterwarden for the Slavonian; at Temesvar for the Hungarian; and at Hermannstadt for the Transylvanian, the whole was under the supreme command of the Aulic Council of War in Vienna. This council, in spite of its rather ferocious title, corresponded to our Colonial Office if one substitutes the word state for colony.

I do not propose to go into more detail of this frontier whose early history can be found linked with that of the old Austrian-Hungarian Empire but, having mentioned it, I should say that the disintegration began in 1851 and finished in 1881 when the four commands that I mentioned were incorporated in the countries whose territories they were bordering.

A study of the way it was run makes most interesting reading as it has so many similarities with our North West Frontier of India, except that its inhabitants were more orderly and did not require twenty-three punitive expeditions in nineteen years as did our's between 1849–68.

Military Hospitals

The present Chelsea was originally a village reckoned as being two miles out of London. The old spellings were Cercehede and Chelched, though I note that the famous statesman-author Sir Thomas More (born 1478, executed 1535) called it Chelchith.

In the latter part of the sixteenth century the general spelling became Chelsey.

In 1609 the Dean of Exeter, Dr Sutcliffe, suggested that a college be formed to study the points in dispute between the churches of Rome and England. The foundation stone of what became 'King James's College at Chelsey' was laid on 8th May 1609. Though well endowed, and patronized by royalty, it never flourished and was ultimately seized by Parliament during the Civil War and used for various purposes. Charles II gave it to the then newly-established Royal Society, but it proved unsuitable and was sold back to the king for £1,300 in order that the site might be used for the projected Royal Hospital.

The college was dismantled and the foundation stone of the new hospital, designed by Sir Christopher Wren, was laid on 12th March 1682. The building was completed at a cost of £150,000 which sum, and more, was raised almost entirely by the army itself as a percentage of all pay was deducted to defray the cost. In addition to this percentage every officer and man had to give a complete day's pay. A further sum was obtained by deducting 5 per cent commission from both the seller and buyer of commissions.

So much for the actual building and now for its purpose.

At the time of its completion there were no arrangements in existence for the wounded and destitute soldiers who had left the army on account of wounds, age, or infirmity. They were the dross which was discarded to fend for itself.

In 1690, the year the building was completed, it was ascertained that there were five hundred and seventy-nine men who had served twenty years in the army and qualified for admission. Those admitted were called pensioners because, in addition to their keep and clothing, they received a small weekly sum which ranged from 3s 6d for a captain down to 8d for a private.

Soon after the hospital was completed the numbers of old soldiers who really qualified for admission far exceeded its capacity so that a system known as 'out-pensions' was introduced. These were, strange to say, much less than those paid to the inmates and ranged from 1s 6d for an officer to 5d for a private. One would have expected these meagre sums to have been paid the other way round.

The original members of the Board of Governors were all civilians but, after a few years, two military members were appointed. The establishment is now governed by Royal Warrant and the cost of the upkeep of the hospital comes from a non-effective vote, which is another way of saying that the sum allotted is not taken from that voted for the upkeep of the army.

Though Chelsea Hospital is the more famous, it is not the oldest military hospital as that distinction was held by the Hospital of Kilmainham, Dublin, to give it its correct title.

This hospital, like that at Chelsea, was built by Sir Christopher Wren. It was founded in 1675 by the Earl of Granard, who was then Marshal-General of the Army in Ireland. A Royal Warrant dated 27th October 1679, authorized the deduction of sixpence in the pound from all army pay towards its maintenance and for the care of aged soldiers and those, to use the current phrase, who became unserviceable. The property of the Knights Templar, in Phoenix Park, was appropriated in December 1681, and on 19th February 1686, a Royal Charter was granted to the governors of what was called, 'The Hospital of King Charles II, for ancient and maimed officers and soldiers of the Army of Ireland'.

I have given precedence to the better-known, and officially recognized, hospitals but it would be rank injustice not to mention, and by so doing give pride of place as regards institution, to one which was started and maintained entirely by private enterprise.

I refer to the efforts of Sir Thomas Coningsby who, in 1617, having built alms houses in the City of Hereford, presented them to the corporation on condition that not less than six of the inmates were old soldiers – or 'maimes' as he called them – with three or more years' service and natives of the county, or those of Shropshire or Worcestershire.

Many of us are familiar with the uniforms of the Chelsea Pensioners but, here again, it is only fair to Sir Thomas to say that he was the originator of uniforms for army pensioners.

The inmates of Sir Thomas's home were called servitors who, on admittance, were given a small annual pension and a set of clothing which included, and here I quote, 'A ginger-coloured suit of soldier-like appearance, a hat with a band of white, a jerkin with half sleeves, and a coat reaching down to the knees; a cloth coat lined in red to be worn on walks and journeys'.

When one remembers the attitude of almost contempt with which serving soldiers were treated, the kindly action of this gentleman makes pleasant reading.

The wording used in various old books and official documents when describing men who had served the best time of their lives in the army makes strange reading today.

They were referred to as invalid, maimed, decrepid, unserviceable, and even decayed!

I cannot say whether Major-General Sir Snifter Binder (Decayed) would have been the correct mode of address for a gallant warrior who had got a bit too long in the tooth for further service.

Military Law

This is a subject about which it is very difficult to trace the origin.

When we refer to Military Law today we really mean a collection of laws – a code in other words. For instance, if a man goes absent he is tried under a section, which forms part of the Military Law as a whole.

The early kings were, one might say, laws unto themselves both in peace and war. They were guided by no set rules as to how they treated their soldiers – or for that matter anybody.

It is worth noting that no form of military law existed in times of peace till the passing of the Mutiny Act in 1689. Prior to this the various articles and ordinances that were passed only applied during actual hostilities and lapsed immediately on the signing of peace.

When that warlike monarch Richard I ascended the throne, in 1189, he found a ready-made war going on in the form of the Third Crusade for which he promptly set off. Before embarking he issued written ordonnances (sic) to govern the troops while at sea and I think that we might be justified in considering them as the first written military laws.

As they have great historical interest, whether they can claim to be the first or not, I give them in full as given in *Grose's Military Antiquities*, Volume II.

To all his men going by sea to Jerusalem, greeting. Know ye, that by the common council of all good men, we have made the underwritten ordonnances.

He who kills a man on shipboard shall be bound to the dead man and thrown into the sea: if the man is killed on shore, the slayer shall be bound to the dead body and buried with it.

Any one convicted by lawful witnesses of having drawn his knife to strike another, or shall have drawn blood from him, to lose his hand. If he shall have only struck with the palm of his hand, without drawing blood, he shall be thrice ducked in the sea.

Any one who shall reproach, abuse, or curse his companion, shall, for every time he is convicted thereof, give so many ounces of silver.

Any one convicted of theft, shall be shorn like a champion, boiling pitch shall be poured on his head, and down of feathers shaken over it, that he may be known; and he shall be set on shore at the first land at which the ship touches.

The first complete set of statutes, ordonnances, and customs were probably those published by Richard II for the army that was raised to repel the threatened invasion in 1385; the next, those of Henry V which were issued in France prior to the battle of Agincourt in 1415. Then come those of Henry VII dated 1486.

The code now in use owes its origin to the Revolution of 1688, prior to which the crown, except during the Civil War and the short subsequent period of Cromwell's rule, had practically unlimited power over the military forces. The militia, which in those days signified the army, could be called out without the nation's consent as long as pay and quarters were available. The increasing demands of the people for their civil liberties compelled Parliament, after the new king was crowned, to bring in legislation to control the use of the armed forces. As luck would have it, a most opportune mutiny took place just at this time and so accentuated, and accelerated, their proposed action.

The Royal Scotch and Dumbarton's Regiment, under Marshal

Schomberg, on their way to the coast prior to embarkation for Holland, whilst quartered at Ipswich, refused to go any farther. They disarmed their officers, seized the military chest, and, with four cannons started to march back to Scotland. They were pursued by General Ginckel, with three regiments of Dutch dragoons, and forced to surrender.

With this event so fresh in their minds, the House of Commons and House of Lords passed the Mutiny Act on 28th March which received Royal Assent on 3rd April 1689.

The bill was mainly directed against the crimes of mutiny and desertion; but it actually began by saying that the raising and maintaining of a standing army in times of peace, except with the consent of Parliament, was illegal. It further decreed that no man was to suffer loss of life or limb, or to be punished in any way whatsoever except according to the laws of the realm.

It then stated that it was considered necessary to increase the number of men then serving for the defence of the Protestant Religion. Without acknowledging that any power existed to the crown for the appointment of courts-martial, it authorized it to grant commissions to general officers to assemble such courts for trying cases of mutiny and desertion. Provisions were made in the Act to ensure that no officer or man was placed outside the Common Law which meant that he was liable to be tried and punished for all civilian offences as well as military ones.

The Mutiny Act has, since its inception, varied in many particulars though remaining basically the same. I doubt whether there is any fairer law in the world than our Military Law – in fact it is impossible for there to be one. A soldier is tried entirely by members of his own profession who can bring experience to bear on every word spoken by the defence and prosecution. The members know just how much weight to give to excuses and, in my experience, a Court while deliberating the verdict will discuss every conceivable factor in favour of the accused which, in many cases, have not been mentioned by the defence.

The soldier knows that, unless his crime is extremely serious, he does not lose his job and neither he, nor his family, if he has one, will suffer weeks of poverty till a new employer has compassion on him.

We must now go back to the beginning to pick up another

thread of the story. You will recall that I mentioned ordonnances issued by Richard I. In course of time the royal ordinances became known as Articles of War, and were issued by the king after consultation with his Constable or Commander-in-Chief. They remained in force only for the duration of the particular campaign in which the men were engaged though the system of issuing such articles as and when required remained in vogue till 1803.

The year 1879 saw the introduction of a further Act, known as the Army Discipline and Regulations Act. This produced a rather complicated state of affairs for the army was controlled by two Acts. Two years later, however, this Act was repealed and the whole governing of the army came under the Army Act which, to give it legality, had to be passed by Parliament every year and thus became known as the Army (Annual) Act.

In 1917, when the Royal Air Force was constituted, the title was changed to the Army and Air Force (Annual) Act.

The Act is given in the Manual of Military Law, which is generally called, irreverently, the Soldier's Bible. It first appeared in 1884 and is the product of the Office of the Parliamentary Council, which is responsible for the drafting of the Army and Air Force (Annual) Act.

Parachute Flares

Parachute balls, or parachute lights, as they were then called, were invented by Colonel Boxer in 1865. A description of them which was published shortly after their introduction has a wonderfully accurate account of the uses to which they were put some fifty years later. It says, 'Being thrown by night in a burning state from mortars, or in some cases by hand, they serve to discover the working parties of the enemy'. From my experiences of them on wire-repair parties during the First World War, I could add further testimonials, not one of which would be printable!

Parole

This word has been adopted from the Norman-French to denote a verbal undertaking though, strictly speaking, every contract which is not under seal is a parole.

There are two meanings of the word in the military sense. The first is a verbal undertaking not to do a specified act – usually not to escape. No soldier can be made to give his parole though he may offer to give it. It is the duty of every prisoner (military prisoner I mean) to try and escape but there are occasions when it can be given with honour, such as visits for medical treatment.

The other meaning is synonymous with password, though I must confess that I cannot recall having heard it used in this way except as a charge under Section 6 of the Army Act under which a soldier can be tried for treacherously making it known to someone not entitled to know it.

Pelisse

A jacket or coat, usually braided after the Hungarian fashion, from which it was copied, carried, when not in use, slung over the left shoulder. (See Plates 8 & B).

Pensions

It was the unofficial custom, prior to the reign of George II, to carry two fictitious persons on the strength of every company so that the money supposedly drawn as their pay could be paid into a fund for those about to retire and those who had already done so.

Pensions in anything like the straightforward way in which we now know them were first paid in 1737.

Photography

Photography was first used for military purposes during the Crimean War, although I cannot say that I have ever seen any photographs taken during the campaign which could be said to have even the slightest military value. They generally consist of groups of very bewhiskered officers, seated in what is supposed to be a very informal group, in a variety of headgear.

The South African War, 1899–1902, was the first occasion during which an independent photographic section accompanied the army. This was composed of one officer and one non-commissioned officer who, mounted on bicycles, were employed with the 1st Cavalry Division on panoramic photography.

Pickers

These were small silver spikes, often shaped like an arrow, and attached to the shoulder belt of light cavalry officers. They were made of soft silver and could be thrust into the touchhole of muzzle-loading cannon and snapped off, thus rendering the piece useless. Hence the expression 'spike their guns'. They were worn in the British service from Napoleonic times to the present.

Point Blank Range

This term is a corrupted form of the French point blanc (white point) with which the centre of early continental targets were marked. The French soldier was instructed to aim at this point, and when he hit it he scored a 'point blanc' in the same way as we use the term bullseye. When almost every shot hit this central point the range was increased so that point blank range meant one at which the centre of the target was scarcely ever missed.

Railways

The first railway made by soldiers for soldiers was built during the Crimean War, 1854–56.

During the Egyptian Campaign, in 1885, a railway was built from Suakin, on the Red Sea, to Berber. After the necessity for it ceased it was taken up and brought home and relaid around Shoeburyness, though the carriages with 'Suakin-Berber Railway' on their sides were not repainted!

Light military railways, originally known as portable railways, were first suggested by an Austrian, Karl Leinwather, his idea being that the tracks should be made in short sections, like the pieces of a child's model railway. I have no idea when his suggestion was first used on service, but it certainly came into its own during the First World War.

Reconnaissance

Military reconnaissance used to be the duty of the officers of the quarter-master general for, at any rate so it would seem, there did not appear to be any real need to study the ground unless the intention was to form a camp.

There are many references in biblical history to people being sent to 'spy out the land' which the modern soldier would translate as being set off to make a reconnaissance.

Marechal Puysegur (1690) was probably the first commander in anything like modern warfare to appreciate the necessity for previously examining the country through which his army was to advance. He mentions in his *Art de la Guerre* that before his time it had been customary to rely on information obtained from the inhabitants. He goes on to say that disasters often occurred as a result of the lines of march being badly selected, and that sometimes, after long marches, and all the labours of making camp, the troops had to abandon the positions on account of their unsuitability.

The details which he gives concerning the information that should be obtained prior to a move, or military operation, are as accurate in these days of mechanized transport as they were in his time. There is mention of the particulars which the infantry, cavalry, artillery, and transport would require. The slopes, the strength of bridges, width and depth of rivers, houses and their billeting capacity, farms for the horses in fact everything except the requirements of an airforce!

Rockets

The origin of the very first rocket is probably lost in the mists of antiquity. I cannot go further back than to the writings of Marcus Graecus who, in 846 AD, in his *Liber Ignium ad Comburendos Hostes* gives the following prescription for launching fire against the enemy:

> *Take one pound of live sulphur, two of willow charcoal, six of saltpetre. Reduce each to a fine powder and mix together. A certain quantity of the final mixture is to be placed in a long narrow cover, and then discharged into the air.*

It is a pity that the exact amount is not stated and that it is not quite clear whether the narrow cover goes into the air as well. It is reasonable to assume that it was, so that here is the first mention that I have found of anything that might have been the forerunner of our rocket.

The inventor of the rocket used in the Napoleonic Wars was Sir William Congreve who produced military projectiles known as rockets in 1803.

Napoleon, it will be remembered, had gathered a large army in Boulogne with the intention of invading England. On 8th October 1806, rockets were launched from ships against the town and set it on fire.

They were used again during the bombardment of Copenhagen which lasted from 4th–7th September 1807, after which the city and the Danish fleet surrendered to Lord Cathcart and Admiral Gambier.

They were used during the unfortunate expedition to Walcheren, when 35 naval vessels and 200 transports, carrying 40,000 troops waited for the Earl of Chatham and Sir Richard Strachan to make up their minds what they intended to do. The island was captured on 15th August 1809, but further indecision and serious outbreaks of disease compelled the whole expedition to return with nothing accomplished.

An English rocket troop took part in the Battle of Leipsic which lasted from 16th–19th October, 1813, and sealed the fate of Napoleon as I doubt whether any historian would contend that the French ever recovered from this terrible defeat. It was the 2nd Rocket Troop, Royal Horse Artillery, which distinguished itself in this battle.

Rockets were employed in both the American and Peninsular Wars, and with devastating effect during the attack on Acre on 3rd November, 1840, when one penetrated a powder magazine which blew up and damaged a large part of the town.

They were also employed during the wars in Abyssinia (1868) and Ashantee (1873–74) and put the fear of Allah into the natives and I hardly blame them as they are most unpleasant things which have been known to create fear amongst those who would dislike being called natives.

Rolls

The word roll originally referred to the pieces of parchment, averaging from nine to fourteen inches wide and three feet long, on which all writings were made. When the names of men were written on them they were said to be in-rolled, or on the roll. When the names were being read out the ceremony was known as calling the roll.

Many of the earliest records were not written on what we would call rolls for they were written across the skins which were then fastened together at the sides like the pages of a book; others were fastened at the top like the pages of some calendars. In certain cases the bottom edges were perforated so that subsequent skins could be joined on so that the completed roll was often of considerable length. The piercing of the holes and joining the parchments together was known as filing.

Rolls were kept in leather bags, or cordwains, with a thong threaded through the top like a sponge bag, or in round pouches fitted with a lid and a cord handle so that they could be hung on a wall. These loops also enabled the bags to be taken down quickly and then, when two were tied together, they could be hung over the back of a pack animal for transportation. The bags were of different colours, or bore different devices, so that their contents was easily recognizable and those dealing with the same subject could be kept together.

I must now digress somewhat to describe the origin of what we now call an acquittance roll.

The earliest known method of accounting was by means of sticks, known as tallies. When two people wished to trade with each other on a credit basis two sticks were placed side by side with one of their ends level. Notches were then cut across both to signify the sum owing; the buyer kept one, the seller the other. When payment was made the two sticks were placed beside each other as before and a cancellation notch was cut across both. The cancelled tally returned to the buyer was known as his acquittance which signified that he was acquitted of owing any money.

When men were owed money for service their names were written on a roll, together with the sums due. When they were

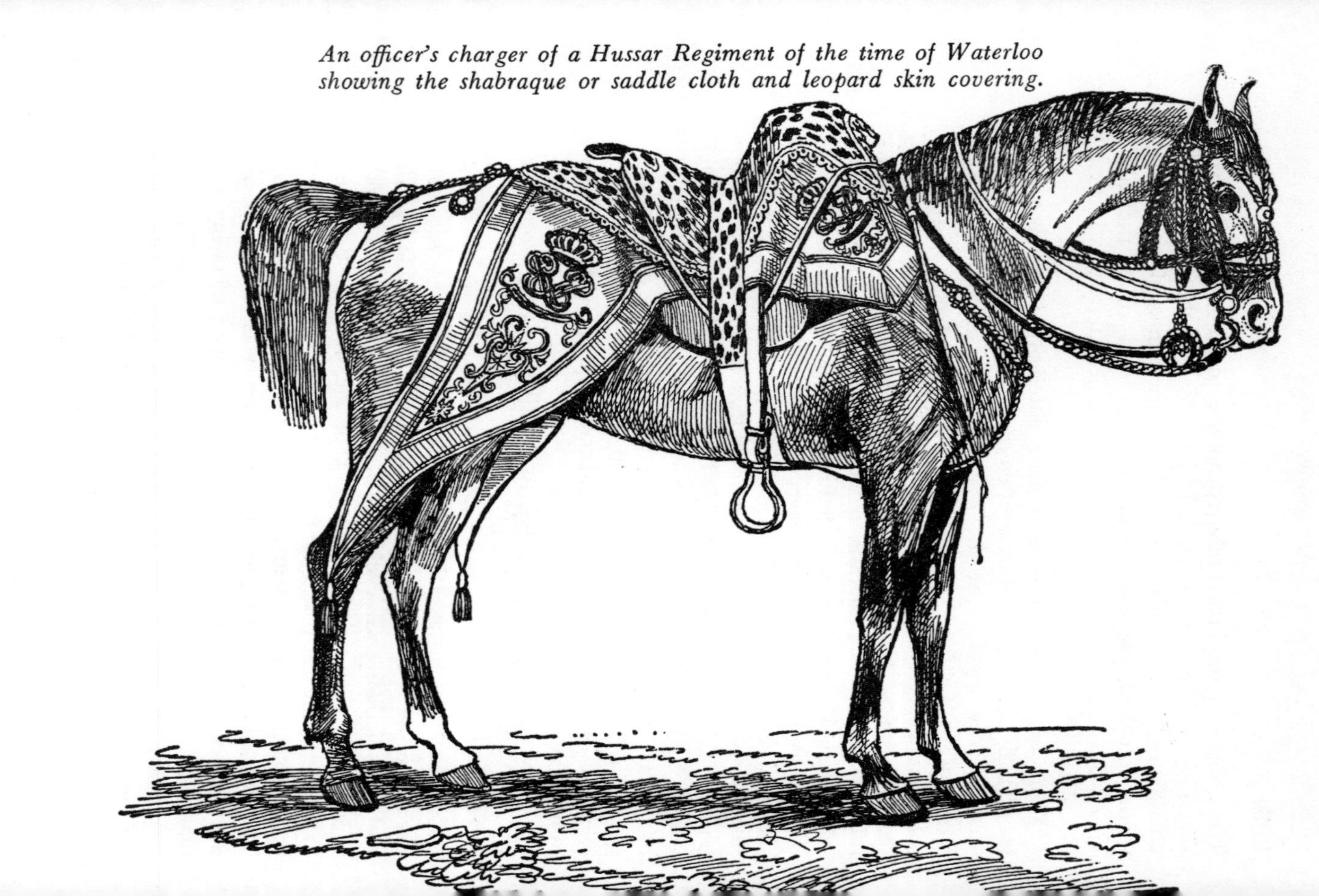

An officer's charger of a Hussar Regiment of the time of Waterloo showing the shabraque or saddle cloth and leopard skin covering.

paid the rolls were signed by witnesses and then referred to as acquittance rolls because the debt was said to have been acquitted.

Sabretache

This was originally a sort of haversack worn by Hungarian Hussars, and very convenient too. It was widely adopted by cavalry and mounted officers and served as map and writing case. Needless to say the military tailors and embroiderers got at them and they became eventually extremely decorative and useless items, although the weight did help to keep the sword from flying about at the gallop. Sabretaches are to be seen hanging beside the sword on plates 3, 6, 8 & C. They were abolished in 1900.

Scrounging

Among the original instructions issued to the cadets of the Royal Military Academy, Woolwich, are to be found those admonishing them against carving their names on the desks, or of trying to open them with the wrong keys, and of taking anything out of them under the name of 'smouching' which I cannot help but think had the same meaning as our 'scrounging'.

May the Lord have mercy on my soul for suggesting that the Royal Regiment of Artillery have the doubtful credit of being the first regiment to receive a special order prohibiting such disgraceful conduct!

Shabraque

This is a saddlecloth, and its origins are lost in antiquity. A fine example is to be seen in the figure on page 238 and plates 3, 4, 6, 7 & 8 show further types.

Shako

Shako, from the Hungarian shcako, means a hat with a peak. It became the most popular military headdress in Europe, and within the original meaning of the word still survives. It went through many modifications in the British army from the time of its adoption in 1801, as may be seen in our endpapers. When replaced by the spiked helmet, copied from the more elegant

German pickel-haube in, I think, 1880, it survived in the Highland Light Infantry and the Scottish Rifles.

Austro-Hungarian Army shakos, 1. Hussar, 1770, 2. Grenz-Infantry 1796, 3. Hussar, 1798–1806, 4. Regular Infantry, 1806.

Shrapnel

This type of shell was invented by Major Shrapnel in the same year that Congreve produced his rocket, 1803.

He was an artillery officer who served with the Duke of York's army in Flanders during which time he was struck by the uselessness of a cannon ball which had missed its target. He invented, soon after his return, a segmented casing filled with balls in the centre of which was a time fuse. The idea being that the fuse would ignite a small charge which would split the casing and thus release the balls.

They were first used at the storming of the fortress of St Sebastian, 1803, during the Peninsular War. The artillery first breached the walls and then fired shrapnel to keep the enemy's heads down while our infantry advanced.

Small Arms

I cannot trace the date of the introduction of this term but, by inference, I should imagine it to be during the reign of James I as documents of his time refer to small arms whereas those of Elizabeth I quote hand-arms.

The office of Keeper of Our Small Arms was instituted in 1683.

Soldier's Pocket Book

The first pocket-book was introduced by John Vernon in 1644. It contained details of drill and not those of the person owning it as is the case with the present AB64, which is the abbreviation for the well-known little brown Army Book 64.

Spies

The use of spies is as old as war itself. In the first verse of the second chapter of the Book of Joshua it says, 'And Joshua, the son of Nun, sent out of Shittim two men to spy secretly, go view the land, even Jericho. And they went, and came into an Harlot's house, named Rahab, and lodged there.'

Hugo Grotius, the Dutch theologian and founder of the science of international law (1583–1645) said in his *De Jure Belli et Pacis* (written in Latin) remarks, 'Spies, whom it is, without doubt, permitted by the law of nations to employ; Moses made use of such, and Joshua himself acted in that capacity.'

Q

There is the account, probably fictitious, of the attempted assassination of Lars Porsena of Clusium by Mucius Scaevola in 509 BC. Mucius, a Roman hero, is supposed to have concealed a dagger in his clothing and gone over to the king's camp with the intention of assassinating him. He, however, mistook a royal secretary for the king and murdered him instead. He was captured and threatened with being burned to death unless he revealed the whole plot. Showing complete contempt of this fate he thrust his arm into a sacrificial fire burning on an altar. His bearing so impressed Porsena that he set him free.

The present fate of spies, whether of the cloak and dagger species or information-hunting kind, is a long prison sentence. To me at any rate, this seems an unworthy fate for one who has to have more real guts, with a capital 'G', than the average soldier whose morale is bolstered by the presence of his fellows. I need hardly add, I hope, that I have no use for the traitor turned spy. My remarks refer to the soldier, or civilian, of an enemy state who pits his wits against his foes to gain information and who does not employ lethal weapons of any kind. Spydom – if there is such a word – has produced many despicable characters and some very brave men indeed whose bravery has even won recognition by those against whom they were spying.

Staff

The first formation of a permanent military staff was made in France in 1783. It was divided into two branches, one to study the ground over which the army was to operate; the other to gather all the reports that passed during an action so that a post mortem could be held to evolve better tactics for the future.

A school for instructing officers in the art of surveying ground suitable for positions, or routes over which large bodies of troops could be moved, was originated in England in 1800. The students were employed in the campaign in Egypt in 1801. After the army returned home the school was incorporated with the Royal Military College of which it became known as the Senior Department but was dispersed at the outbreak of the Peninsular War.

Steel Helmets

I should hate to get involved in a dispute as to when metal helmets were first worn. They have been unearthed on the site of the battle of Cannae, which was fought between Hannibal and the Romans in 216 BC. They have been dredged from the bed of the Euphrates and their date has proved too much for a panel of experts to guess at.

Helmets were found by Captain Cook in 1778, during one of his famous voyages; and, they are depicted on some of the oldest Greek remains.

There is no doubt whatever that the helmet, the original name for which was helm, is of very great antiquity as some form of head-covering was worn by soldiers of every country.

The Greek and Roman helmets did not usually protect the fact though, strange to say, the two found in 1752 on the site of Cannae did this and had projecting nasals.

Our earlier helmets were called different names according to their shapes. There were, for instance, chapelles de fer (hats of iron), bacinets, burgonets, castles, hufkens, morions, salades, skulls, etc, all of which were of metal. There was also what was known as a justing (or jousting) helmet, sometimes made of leather, which was used in tournaments.

In addition to the names given to various shapes there were the four parts which were introduced at various times. The nasal projected from the forehead for protecting the nose; the ventaile, or visor, was the front piece rivetted on either side so that it could be lifted to expose the face; some helmets were fitted with a bevor, a small movable apperture to enable the wearer to have a drink.

Those interested in heraldry will recall that helmets are still used over the shield or coat of arms. The full-faced helmet with six bars, all of gold, damasked, is for the sovereign and princes of royal blood; the full-faced helmet of steel for marquises and dukes; the profile, or side-facing helmet of steel ornamented with bars, for viscounts and barons, the full-faced steel helmet, with visor or bevor open, for baronets and knights; the profile steel helmet, with closed visor or bevor, for esquires.

The familiar 'battle bowler', or 'war bonnet' with which those who served in the last two Great Wars were issued originated from what were variously called bascinets, basinets, bacinets, or basnets, which were light helmets so called from their resemblance to basins. They were generally without visors, though the French writer Ducange refers to basinez à visière in his *Chronicles and Romances of the Thirteenth and Fourteenth Centuries*. Fauchet supposes them to have been a lighter sort of helmet that did not cover the face and relates how knights exchanged them for their helmets when tired yet could not 'with propriety go unarmed'.

Grose illustrates bascinets of the times of Edward II and III, and Richard II, as worn by the infantry; and, Sir Samuel Meyrick illustrates those of Richard II and Henry V in his *Engraved Illustrations of Antient Arms and Armour*.

Tactical Exercises without Troops

These, generally referred to by the abbreviation Tewts, were introduced by a German, Von Reisswitz, in 1780. They were first suggested as being of considerable value for training officers in our army by Prince Arthur of Connaught in 1872.

Telegraph

The word is derived from the Greek 'tele', distant, and 'grapho', I write, and signifies a method of communicating intelligence to a distance. The employment of electricity for the purpose is an invention of comparative recent date, though the use of signals for the quick transmission of brief messages by means of a pre-arranged code dates from remote antiquity. The use of beacons as a method of giving speedy warning of the approach of an enemy is mentioned by the prophet Jeremiah, who wrote something like six hundred years before the beginning of the Christian era, advising the Benjamites to 'set up a sign of fire in Beth-haccerem'.

An early description of telegraphic despatch is given by Aeschylus in his 'Agamemnon', of the use of a line of fire signals to communicate the news of the fall of Troy. There are, too, those lovely stanzas in the *Lay of the Last Minstrel* describing the rapid communication concerning the approach of the English forces from the border stations, along 'height, and hill, and cliff',

> *Till high Dunedin the blazes saw,*
> *From Soltra and Dumpender Law;*
> *And Lothian heard the Regent's order,*
> *That all should boune them for the border.*

The signals to be used had been laid down by an Act of the Scottish Parliament in 1455. The lighting of one faggot, or bale, was to be the signal to denote the approach of the English in any manner; two bales alight alongside each other were to denote the arrival of the enemy in great strength. These signals, though best for giving warning by night, were also usable in daytime by damping the bales and using the columns of smoke instead of the actual lights of the fires.

Torches moved in a certain manner, waved, say, vertically, horizontally, or in a circular fashion, were used by the ancients as signals which, however, were only of value providing there had been previous agreement as to their meanings.

It is obvious that some attempts were made to improve upon these simple signals for we find a description of a device said to have been the idea of Cornelius Tacitus (55–117 AD). His idea was that various messages should be written in a certain order and at pre-arranged distances up the sides of two identical tanks. The two people wishing to intercommunicate each had one of these tanks, both of which were kept full. On a given signal the plug was pulled out and kept out till the next signal when it was replaced. The message opposite the level of the water when the second signal was given was the one that it was intended to send. The idea seems unnecessarily cumbersome for a series of messages written on paper would have had the same effect if, instead of a start and stop signal, a number was transmitted to correspond with that of the intended message. Another system which Polybius says was the idea of Cleoxenus or Democlitus was very much more ingenious. The alphabet was written on five tablets which were numbered one to five. The sender of a message carried two torches, one in each hand. If he waved the one in his right hand once, it signified that the next letter would be on No. 1 tablet. The number of times he waved his left torch signified the number of the letter on the tablet. If, for instance, the sender wished to transmit the word 'bad' he would wave his right arm once to signify that the next letter, or letters, were on No. 1 tablet and then he would wave his left arm twice, then once, then four times. We would consider the idea crude and very slow, but it was a beginning. There were, so it would seem, variations of the same idea. One of these was for the sender to hold in his right hand the number of torches to correspond with the number of the tablet and to do the same with his left hand as regards the number of the letter on the tablet. The great thing to bear in mind here is that the sender was able to send any message he wanted and was not restricted to any pre-arranged code as we still are on certain occasions. I wonder whether the reader can, without cribbing the footnote* name the use that is still made of a system which may well be based on that used a thousand or more years ago.

The first military pamplet on the subject of signalling of which I have note was published in 1823, entitled 'Description of the Universal Telegraph for Day and Night Signals'. A system of semophore was introduced in 1808 under the rather fearsome name of anthropo-telegraphy. This was the idea of a Mr Knight Spencer which employed two circular wicker-work discs, painted white with black circles in the centre, with handles about six inches long. By holding these in various positions it was possible to send both letters and figures.

I read an amusing account of an idea which was said to have been, 'Invented by Lieutenant Spratt for telegraphing by means of a white handkerchief, held in various positions to express the numerical characters and a few other conventional signs. The inventor employed this mode of communication some time before the battle of Trafalgar, as a means of carrying on conversation with a distant vessel; and he had used it successfully to converse between Spithead and the green ramparts at Portsmouth. With a common telescope it may be used at a distance of four miles.' I have an idea that if sailors started to wave white handerchiefs (always presuming that they ever had such

---

* On rifle ranges a white disc is shown stationary under the bulls-eye to denote a hit of that name. Different movements of the reverse side of the disc, which is black, denote the three other kinds of hits on the target.

things) it must have been very difficult to distinguish between the important message being sent by an officer and the urgent enquiry from the handkerchief-waving matelot anxious to know how many kids he could expect to find at home after his long absence!

It would weary the reader to take him through the details of the many ideas of visual signalling, so let me conclude by saying that the first field telegraph laid on active service was completed on 7th March, 1855, when the Royal Engineers connected the commander-in-chief's (Lord Raglan's) headquarters with Kadikoi during the Crimean War. The original length was slightly under three miles, but this was later extended to five; and, later still, some seven or eight exchanges were installed on a total length of about twenty-one miles.

The first Telegraph Battalion, Royal Engineers, was formed in May, 1884, during the Egyptian Campaign.

The first wireless message to be sent any reasonable distance was transmitted by Sir W. H. Preece across the Sound of Mull in 1895. The first press report to cross the Channel was sent by Marconi's invention from Wimereux, near Boulogne, to the South Foreland, on 30th January, 1899.

Wireless telegraphy was invented, so it will be noted, prior to the Boer War though not used during it.

Tommy Atkins

This was the name given to the soldier in the account book which was introduced in 1829. It was used in the example given in every book to show what details the soldier had to fill in.

Uniform

What is uniform? I don't know. The Local Defence Volunteers, formed soon after the outbreak of the Second World War, were given arm bands which bore the initials 'LDV'; when wearing these they were supposed to be considered as soldiers under the Rules of War. Is, therefore, an arm band uniform? If the answer is in the affirmative then one must infer that the wearing of one gaiter, or, for instance, a pair of army boots also constitutes being in uniform.

In the time of the Feudal System what we now term uniform was called livery which had no particular significance as regards the kind of service rendered by the wearer.

The colours of the liveries varied with the different nobles each of whom vied with each other to outdo the other in the splendour of their retinue. As a matter of fact this rivalry as regards turnout had one great advantage in that all were able to distinguish to which nobleman a man belonged and thus, more by accident than design, the germ of the idea of regimental uniforms was born.

The earliest record that I can find which shows any attempt to clothe the army uniformly is dated 1337, in which Edward III gave instructions that sufficient cloth should be obtained to provide a thousand men with tunics and mantles. It does not say that all the cloth must be of the same colour. We must assume that and, perhaps, that there should be some uniformity as regard design.

Rymer gives an account of how Henry VIII gave instructions to the Earl of Shrewsbury to see that the army to be raised in 1512 wore, 'suche badges, tokyns, or lyveres, as shall by you be thought most convenient for the same'.

In a military sense the word uniform is a noun used to describe the costume worn by soldiers, which is usually of the same pattern and colour of all members of the same unit. In other words they are uniformly dressed. Uniformity of dress and equipment are of early origin, eg the Roman Legions. Where large scale bulk manufacture and replacement are involved the advantages of standardization are obvious. The necessity of having something distinctive about the costume so that friend might be told from foe is also obvious. In feudal times this might take the form of wearing the badge or livery colours, ie those of the coat of arms, of the leige lord. This practice was continued until recent times in footmen's liveries, and is still worn by postillions etc of the Royal Household, and the Drum Majors of the Foot Guards and the bands of the Household Cavalry.

Military costume was, until recent times, merely contemporary civilian costume, of uniform colour, more or less modified for service, although as time passed they tended to become increasingly elaborate and expensive. Any economy drive would be followed by a further attack of creeping expense.

The pattern of British ceremonial uniform as exemplified in the Foot Guards and the Household Cavalry became set just after the Crimean War, 1854–5, and has remained the same King's Troop, Royal Horse Artillery, except that their jacket is from a much earlier period and dates from the late eighteenth century.

War Correspondents

The first officially credited correspondents accompanied the army to the Crimea in 1854.

A correspondent, whilst holding an official permit to accompany troops, is subject to Military Law. He is, by the same token, whilst wearing the uniform of the country to which he is accredited, entitled to be treated as a military prisoner of war if he should be captured.

War Department Marking

In 1683 one of the duties of the Lieutenant-General of Ordnance was to ensure that all ordnance property was marked with 'Our Mark', which consisted of an arrow with a large 'B' for Barrack on the left, and a large 'O' (for Ordnance) on the right. These initials have now been altered to 'WD' which stand for War Department and signify that the article so marked is the property of the Crown.

When such property is sold by the Crown the mark is cancelled by placing another arrow upside down on the first so that their points are touching.

Strictly speaking, anyone found with an article bearing the War Department marking which has not been cancelled is liable to prosecution for theft but, owing to the enormous amount of work involved in the cancellation of the markings on all objects sold, the rule has been allowed to lapse.

Warrant Officer

The meaning of the term is really in its title – an officer who holds a warrant. Commissions were originally granted by the sovereign to officers who, in turn, could appoint juniors to help them carry out their commission.

The translation of the word commission in this sense is that it was an order to carry out a certain task. The senior officer to whom the task was given was allowed to submit to the sovereign the names of those whom he wished to appoint as officers. It is obvious that there must be some ranks between those of officers and ordinary soldiers so authority was given to grant warrants to certain selected personnel giving them authority whilst performing a particular duty. When it was finished the warrant expired so that we find that warrant appointments only lasted during the commissioning of the ship, or during the particular campaign. The sovereign delegated the authority to grant warrants to the Admiralty, or Commander-in-Chief, so that today a warrant-officer receives his warrant from the Army Council. As only the sovereign can grant commissions in the Regular Army, it is obvious that warrant-officers are really non-commissioned officers though, by courtesy, the proper address to a unit refers to, officers, warrant-officers, non-commissioned officers, and men.

Water Bottles

These were introduced in 1662 though I cannot trace any particular pattern as standard. At this time regimental commanders were responsible for supplying such articles, which they did with an eye on cost rather than efficiency. They were supplied by regimental chandlers so that it is quite possible that the same type of bottle was in use by more than one regiment. The flattish type now in use was introduced in wood in 1874. Metal bottles were first issued with the new type of leather equipment in 1903; this equipment was the kind with the two large pouches for ammunition which, when full, almost prevented breathing. The leather was, however, considered a great delicacy by the rats infesting the trenches in the northern sectors during the First World War.

Index

Accolade, 169
Accountant, 134
Acting Pay, 137
Adjutantcy, 170
Aeroplane, original, 164
Aide-de-Campe, 170
Aiguilette, 171
Air-Gun, 171
Ambulance Service, **first, 93,**
   94
Apothecary, general, 93
Armour, 173
Armistice, 172
Army Hospital Corps, 98
Army Nursing Service, 99
Arquebus, 102
Artillery, 69 et seq.
Assembly, call, 129
Aventaille, 178

Baker Rifle, 107, 117
Baldriske, Baldric, 92
Bagpipe, 130
Balloon, 151
Barber, 92
Bandmaster, 131
Bandoliers, 113
Banners, 32
Banniere Quarre, 37

Batman, 180
Baton, 181
Bearskin, 181
Beer Money, 137
Billetting, 182
Blindage, 79
Blood Money, 137
Blue Ensign, 39
Blunderbus, 39
Bolts, 69
Bomb, 78
Bombproof, 79
Boulogne, 1544, 15
Bounty Money, 184
Breach-loading weapons, 117
   et seq.
Brevet, 185
Brevet Pay, 138
Brown-Bess, 107
Brunswick rifle, 117
Bullet, 114
Busby, 187
Butt, 102

Caliver, 104
Cannon, 70 et seq.
Cannon Balls, 77
Captain of Gentlemen-at-Arms,
   16, 17

Captain-General of the Royal Company of Archers, 20, 21
Captain of the Yeomen of the Guard, 13
Carabs, Carabins, Carbines, 103
Chain Shot, 78
Chapel of St George, Windsor, 35
Chausses, 178
Cheval de Frize, 187
Cipher, 187
Civil List, 189
Clerk of the Cheque, 18
Close Rolls, 55
Coat of Arms, 23
Coat and Conduct Money, 138
Cocked Hat, 190
Collar, 31
College of Arms, 26, 27
College, or Free Chapel of St George, 35
Colonel-Drummer, 131
Colours, 38
Comptroller, 134
Command Pay, 139
Commission, 191
Condottieri, 194
Conscription, 196
Contingent Allowance, 139
Controller of the Accounts of the Army, 134
Convention, 197
Cordite, 77
Corps Pay, 140
Crest, 31
Cuirass, 197
Culverin, 74

Dangeld, 52

Dags, 104
Debentures, 145
Demi-Haque 103
Distinguished Unit Citation, 42
Dolman, 199
Dragon, 105
Dragoons, 65, 105
Drill, 199
Drum, original use of, 129
Drum Calls, 128, 129
Drum-Major, 131
Drum-Major-General, 131

Enlistment, 201
Ensign, 38
Equipment Allowance, 140
Esclopette, 103
Establishment, 203
Exons, 13

Falcon, 74
Fall In, call, 129
Fatique Pay, 140
Feudal System, 52, 53
Field Allowance, 140
Fife, first use of, 130
First Aid Nursing Yeomanry, 99
First Field Dressing, 204
Flint Lock, 111
Flute, origin of, 129
Fowling Piece, 107
Fuel Money, 148
Fusil, 105
Fusileers, 204

Garter, Most Noble Order of the, 35

Garter Principal King at Arms, 27
Gazette, 204
Geneva Convention, 206
Gentlemen Pensioners, 15
Gentlemen of a Company, 208
God Save the King, 208
Gold Stick, 20, 21, 65
Good Conduct Pay, 140
Gonfannon, 39
Gorget, 210
Grape Shot, 78
Great Britain, 210
Greek Fire, 71
Great Seal, 177, 178
Grenadier, 211
Guidons, 39
Guingate, 1513, 18
Guncotton, 77
Gunpowder, 70

Hagbush, 102
Hagbut, 102
Hakebut, 102
Haquebutters, 102
Hammer, 111
Hand-Cannon, 101
Hand-Gun, 102
Hand Mortar, 105
Haquebut, 102
Hauberk, 177
Haukerton, 178
Heliograph, 213
Herald, 27, 28
Herald Garter King at Arms, 27
Heralds College, 27
High Court of Admiralty, 144

High Treasurer of the Army, 133
Honourable Corps of Gentlemen-at-Arms, 14
Horn, original use of, 128
Hospital Conveyance Corps, 97
Household Cavalry, 63, 64
Hussar, 67, 213

Identity Discs, 213
Imprest accounts, 134, 141
Indent, 213
Inspections, 214
Invalids, 215
Ivory Stick, Gentleman-at-Arms, 18

Keeper of the Pells, 54
Keeper of the Rolls, 54
Khaki, 216
King's Royal Rifle Corps, 117

Lance-Corporal, 217
Lancer, 68, 217
Land Mines, 217
Lanterns, 218
Ledgers, 218
Length of Service Pay, 141
Lieutenant, Gentleman-at-Arms, 18
Life Guards, 64
Light Money, 148
Lodging and Furniture Allowance, 141, 148
Lord-Lieutenant, 55, 218
Lord Lyon King-of-Arms, 27
Lorica, 174

Lucifers, 110

Machine Arms, 221
Marching Allowance, 141
Master, or Master-General of
    Ordnance, 80
Match, 109, 110
Matross, 80
Medical Staff Corps, 97
Mention in Despatches, 224
Mercenaries, 225
Meritorious Unit Citation
    (Navy), 43
Meritorious Unit Commenda-
    tion, 43
Mess Allowance, 142
Military Bands, origin of, 121
    et seq.
Military Frontier, 225
Military Hospitals, 226
Military Law, 229
Minie Rifle, 117
Minstrel, 121 et seq.
Mortar, 75, 76
Mousquetoon, 107
Music-Major, 131
Musquet, 104
Musselburgh Silver Arrow,
    21
Mynion, 74

Navy Unit Commendation, 43
Nearest Guard, 17
Non-Effective Allowance, 142

Oboe, first use of, 130
Oriflame, 34

Palatines, 53

Parachute Flare, 78,
    232
Parole, 232
Partridge, 76
Passage Money, 142
Patronels, 104
Patrons, 113
Paymaster-General, 133
Pelisse, 233
Pencil, 39
Pendant, 39
Pennon, 39
Pennoncelle, 39
Pensions, 233
Percussion Cap, 112
Petard, 76
Photography, 233
Pickers, 234
Pistols, 104
Point Blank Range, 234
Posse, 55, 56
Powder Flask, 112
Powder Horn, 112
Presidential Unit Citation
    (Navy), 43
Pursuivant, 27
Prize Agent, 143
Prize Court of the Admiralty,
    144
Prize Money, 142

Queen Alexandra's Royal
    Army Nursing Corps, 99
Queen's Bodyguard of Scot-
    land, 19

Railways, 234
Reconnaissance, 235
Red Ensign, 39

Regimental Paymaster, or
Agent, 135, 136
Reiters, 105
Remount Allowance, 144
Riding Allowance, 144
Rifle Brigade, 117
Rifled Artillery, first use of, 73
Rifles, sequence of use in
British Army, 117 et seq.
Rifling, 115, 116
Right of the Line, 83
Rockets, 235
Rolls, 54, 237
Rose-Lock, 111
Royal Army Medical Corps,
98
Royal Company of Archers, 19
Royal Fusiliers, 81, 106
Royal Regiment of Artillery, 82
Rubin Rifle, 119

Sabretache, 239
Saker, 74
Scrounging, 239
Sergeant, 12
Sergeant-at-Arms, 11, 12
Sergeant-Bandmaster, 131
Sergeant-Minstrel, 124
Sergeant-Trumpeter, 124
Shabraque, 239
Sheriff, 55
Skako, 239–40
Shiremoot, 48
Shot, 114, 115
Shot Tower, 115
Shrapnel, 78, 240
Silver Arrow, 21
Silver Stick, 18, 21, 65
Small Arms, 241

Smoke Shell, 78
Soldier's Pocket Book, 241
Spies, 241
Staff, 242
Standard, 40
Standard, Gentlemen-at-Arms,
18, 19
Standard Bearer, Gentlemen-
at-Arms, 18
Stationary and Postage Allow-
ance, 145
Steel Helmets, 243
Stock Purse Fund, 145
Streamer, 42
Subsistence, 145
Surcoat, 178
Surgeon, 90, 91, 92
Sutler, 147

Table Money, 148
Tactical Exercise Without
Troops, 244
Tallies, 145
Tattoo, 129
Telegraph, 244
Tenure by Knight's Service,
53
Tommy Atkins, 247
Train of Artillery, 80, 81
Treasurer, 133
Trooping the Colour, 38
Trophy Money, 148
Trumpet, original use of, 121
Tunmoot, 48

Ulster King of Arms, 27
Uniform, 247

War Correspondent, 249

Warrant Officer, 249
Water Bottle, 250
White Ensign, 39
Wheel-Lock, 111
Witan, 48
Witanmoot, 48

Wright Brothers, 164

Yeomen of the Guard, 12

Zeppelin, 160